MORTAL CONSEQUENCES

MORTAL CONSEQUENCES

A HISTORY—

*From the Detective Story
to the Crime Novel*

JULIAN SYMONS

HARPER & ROW, PUBLISHERS

NEW YORK, EVANSTON,
SAN FRANCISCO, LONDON
1817

MORTAL CONSEQUENCES: *A History—From the Detective Story to the Crime
Novel. Copyright © 1972 by Julian Symons. All rights reserved. Printed in
the United States of America. No part of this book may be used or reproduced in any manner whatsoever without written permission except in the
case of brief quotations embodied in critical articles and reviews. For information address Harper & Row, Publishers, Inc., 49 East 33rd Street,
New York, N.Y. 10016.*

FIRST U.S. EDITION

STANDARD BOOK NUMBER: 06-014187-5

LIBRARY OF CONGRESS CATALOG CARD NUMBER: 72-138767

For Joan Kahn
with respect, gratitude,
affection

THE GUILTY PARTY

It is the author who creates the crime
And picks the victims, this blond dark girl sprawled
Across a bed, stabbed, strangled, poisoned, bashed
With a blunt instrument. Or the young middle-aged
Old scandalous and respected beardless greybeard
Destroyed most utterly by some unknown means
In a room with doors and windows "hermetically sealed."

So victims and means are found. As for the motive
It is often impersonal, a matter of money,
An estate to be gained, a will cheated on, a secret
Within the family, a discreditable
Business about the building contract for the new school.
It is simple for Hawkshaw, whose life has been
Logically given to the pursuit of logic.
He reads the signs, dustmarks, thumbprint, human and animal blood,
And arrests the solicitor.

                    The author
Puts down his pen. He has but poisoned in jest,
Stabbed and strangled in jest, destroyed in jest
By unknown means the smiling neuter victim.
What has he done that could deserve the tap
Upon the door of his butter-bright smiling room
Where crimes are kept in filing cabinets
Well out of sight and mind, what has he done
To bring this horde of victim villains in,
One paddling fingers in her own bright blood

And staining his face with it, another
Revealing the great wound gaping in his side,
The sliced-up tart carrying a juicy breast,
Inviting him to kiss it: and the villains all
Crowding him with their horrid instruments,
The rope that playfully tightens round his neck,
The blue revolver used to mutilate,
The dagger points to pierce out jelly eyes,
The saw and hammer at their nasty work,
The shapes of agony—and worst of all
The unnamed death that strips away the flesh
And melts the bone, a death unnamable
Yet clearly known.

                From all such visions,
Unreal, absurd, phantasmagorical,
We naturally wish to be preserved.
If for a moment this white neutral room
Is filled with smells of rotted or burning flesh
There is a specific by which a respectable
Writer may puff away such nastiness
And regiment like Hawkshaw the unruly
Shapes of life to an ideal order.
                   He picks up his pen.
                       J.S.

Contents

MORTAL CONSEQUENCES

I

What They Are and Why We Read Them

The first problem facing anybody writing about crime fiction is
to stake out the limits of his theme. Historians of the detective story
have been insistent that it is a unique literary form, distinct from
the crime or mystery story, not to be confused with the police novel,
and even more clearly separate from the many varieties of thriller.
Those who believe as I do that such classifications are more confusing than helpful, and that the most sensible sort of naming is
the general one of *crime novel* or *suspense novel* (and short story),
have to begin by countering a considerable weight of opinion. It is
worth looking at some of the views put forward by those who have
tried to formulate a critical canon.

For most critics, the detective story has been taken as the central
theme on which other crime stories and thrillers play variations.
They have tried to formulate strict rules, so that they can say of a
particular work: *yes,* this is a detective story; or *no,* this may be
excellent in its kind but it is not a detective story. Accepting their
classification, what is a detective story? The two qualifications
everybody has thought necessary are that it should present a problem, and that the problem should be solved by an amateur or pro-

1

fessional detective through processes of deduction. So Monsignor
Ronald Knox, laying down in 1928 his "Ten Commandments of
Detection," insisted that the criminal must be mentioned early on,
ruled out the supernatural, said that the detective must not himself
commit the crime, and added that "no accident must ever help the
detective, nor must he ever have an unaccountable intuition, which
proves to be right." So also the Detection Club in Britain, shortly
after its foundation in the same year, asked its members to swear an
oath promising that their detectives would "well and truly detect
the crimes presented to them" without reliance on "Divine Revelation, Feminine Intuition, Mumbo-Jumbo, Jiggery-Pokery, Coincidence or the Act of God." Since logical deduction was the heart
of the detective story, it followed that there was little room for any
depth of characterization or any flourish of style. R. Austin
Freeman, writing in 1924 about "The Art of the Detective Story,"
thought it a cardinal error to confuse it with "the mere crime story,"
and not to understand that it differed from all other types of fiction
in offering to the reader "primarily an intellectual satisfaction."
Allowing that it might be permitted humor, characterization, and a
picturesque setting, he insisted that these must be "secondary and
subordinate to the intellectual interest, to which they must be, if
necessary, sacrificed." S. S. Van Dine, writing in his real name of
Willard Huntington Wright, went further than this, asserting that
characters in a detective story should "merely fulfill the requirements of plausibility," because any deeper delineation would "act
only as a clog in the narrative machinery." Wright placed a ban on
love interest, and in this had the full agreement of Dorothy Sayers,
who severely reproved "the heroes who insist on fooling about after
young women when they ought to be putting their minds to the job
of detection," rapped Freeman over the knuckles for allowing his
secondary characters to "fall in love with distressing regularity,"
and concluded that, upon the whole, "the less love in a detective
story, the better." The beauty of the form, she thought, was that it
had "an Aristotelian perfection of beginning, middle and end." She
was writing, again, in the twenties, but her words were echoed in
1944 by Joseph Wood Krutch, who called the detective story "the
one clearly defined modern genre of prose fiction impeccably classi-

cal in form." And much more recently W. H. Auden succinctly defined the detective story's limits: "The basic formula is this: a
murder occurs; many are suspected; all but one suspect, who is the
murderer, are eliminated; the murderer is arrested or dies." The
point to which these ideas lead is made briefly by Howard Haycraft, in his *Murder for Pleasure:* "The crime in a detective story is
only the means to an end which is—detection."

The effects of such views on the work of the writers who held
them is discussed later on, but what must immediately be obvious
is that few books actually conform to them. Indeed, the lines so
carefully drawn are crossed by the critics themselves as soon as they
begin to make those lists of the "Hundred Best" which are such an
entertaining parlor game. Haycraft, for instance, is briskly dismis-
sive about Wilkie Collins's *The Woman in White,* which was, he
says, "a mystery rather than a detective novel," and so need not
concern him. But then what are Eric Ambler's *The Mask of
Dimitrios,* Dashiell Hammett's *The Maltese Falcon,* Francis Iles's
Before the Fact, and Mrs. Belloc Lowndes's *The Lodger* doing in
his list of "Detective Story Cornerstones"? Most people would call
the first two of these thrillers, the third a crime novel, and the fourth
a sensational murder story. Certainly none contains a detective
puzzle to be solved. Auden specifically excludes *Malice Aforethought* from the canon; another critic refused to consider *The
Lodger*. Ellery Queen's *Queen's Quorum,* which offers a choice of
the most important "Detective-Crime" short stories, contains such
books as *Get-Rich-Quick Wallingford* and O. Henry's *The Gentle
Grafter*. These are not even what most people think of as crime
stories, let alone having any association with detection.

This is not said to put Messrs. Haycraft and Queen into the
pillory, but to suggest that these rigid classifications simply don't
work in practice. They are also often inadequate to the books they
describe. In Hammett's *The Glass Key,* Ned Beaumont does not
solve the puzzle by any genuine reasoning process, and he is a near-
gangster who would hardly have been recognized as a detective by
Wright, with his desire that the detective should stand outside the
action like a Greek chorus, or by Knox, who thought that every
detail of his thought process should be conscientiously audited, or

by any of those who want crimes solved by a detective who rationally detects. And further than this, to call *The Glass Key* a detective story and leave it at that is to limit rather than to announce its merits.

When one looks at the attempts at definition more closely, they can be seen to apply only to the detective stories written in what is often called the Golden Age between the wars. Many of these books were written within a convention as strict and artificial as that of Restoration plays, but that does not make the detective story a unique literary form any more than the Restoration play is a unique dramatic form. Theorizing about detective stories began in the twenties, and would have seemed incomprehensible to Poe or Wilkie Collins or Sheridan Le Fanu. They would have been astonished, and perhaps indignant, to know that they were working in what Haycraft calls "a frankly non-serious, entertainment form of literature." The detective story pure and complex, the book that has no interest whatever except the solution of a puzzle, does not exist, and if it did exist it would be unreadable. The truth is that the detective story, along with the police story, the spy story, and the thriller, makes up part of the hybrid creature we call sensational literature. This hybrid has produced a few masterpieces, many good books, and an enormous mass of more or less entertaining rubbish.

Of course, this is not to say that there are no distinctions to be made between amateur detectives and private eyes, but however unlike Sherlock Holmes and Philo Vance may be to Sam Spade and Superintendent Maigret, and however little any of them have in common with James Bond and Len Deighton's unnamed hero, they all belong to the same kind of literature. When this has been accepted, there are distinctions to be made within the literature, too. Spy stories, and thrillers in general, *do* stand apart from books that pose a puzzle to the reader. The latter kind of book asks questions about Who or Why or How, sometimes about all three put together, where the thriller or spy story frequently just tells us How. But all deal with violent ends in a sensational way, and although spy stories and thrillers have been discussed separately, it would not have been right to ignore them. The tree is sensational literature, and these are among its fruits.

WHERE TO DRAW A LINE

The reason most often advanced for the division into categories is that once the floodgates are opened almost any book which has the faintest connection with crime will be let in, from *Little Red Riding-Hood* (an interesting case of disguise and attempted murder) to *Arden of Faversham* or almost any play by Shakespeare. In theory, this is true. In practice, readers will have no difficulty in drawing a line that separates books in which interest in the nature of, motives for, and results of a crime are at the heart of a story from those where the criminal interest is a subsidiary one.

It would be tedious to labor this point, but perhaps just one example should be given of a novelist often concerned with crime who is not a crime writer. Trollope's novels contain cases of fraud, assault, and murder, and in at least two of them a crime or an apparent crime is the hinge of the plot. *The Last Chronicle of Barset* is concerned with the accusation against Josiah Crawley, "the perpetual curate of Hogglestock," that he has stolen a check for twenty pounds. We know that Crawley is innocent, but the mystery of the way in which the check got into his hands is maintained almost to the end of the book. The theft of Lizzie Eustace's diamonds is the core of the novel with that title, and again a teasing mystery is offered which leaves us in doubt about exactly what has happened. Yet nobody could seriously consider that either of these books is a crime story. In other hands, this could be the material of crime fiction, but Trollope is using these apparent thefts to show the agonies of Mr. Crawley in one case and to illuminate the nature of Lizzie Eustace and her world in the other. The line, then, would be drawn by almost everybody to exclude Trollope, but this is not to say that it does not waver from person to person in relation to this or that book. That a line should be drawn is a matter of common sense, but its precise placing is a matter of individual taste.

WHY WE READ THEM: THE PSYCHOLOGICAL BASIS

Crime literature is almost certainly more widely read than any other class of fiction in the United States, the United Kingdom, and in many other countries not under Communist rule. In 1940,

Haycraft said that in the United States crime stories represented a quarter of all new fiction, and that most of the copies were sold to rental or public libraries. The proportion is probably not much changed today, although in the United Kingdom rental libraries have almost ceased to exist and the public library has become overwhelmingly the most important patron of crime fiction in hard covers. But the situation has been radically changed by the growth of paperback editions. No accurate figures are available, but any reasonably well-known crime writer can be assured of paperback sales, and popular books are reprinted over and over again. The readership of this literature cuts across definition by class or income group. Cozy detective stories and bloody thrillers are read by schoolchildren and working-class mothers, by stockbrokers and their clerks, doctors and their nurses, politicians and clergymen. Politicians and statesmen in particular have found it easy to relax (the compliment is a dubious one) while reading crime literature. Abraham Lincoln admired Poe's work in 1860, and Joseph Stalin enjoyed it more recently; Woodrow Wilson is said to have "discovered" the work of J. S. Fletcher; Lord Rosebery was proud to possess a first edition of *The Memoirs of Sherlock Holmes;* Stanley Baldwin greatly enjoyed *The Leavenworth Case;* and John F. Kennedy is supposed to have preferred Ian Fleming to any other writer of his kind. This list is not exhaustive, and it is not confined to Presidents and Prime Ministers. Although it is an exaggeration to say, as one writer has done, that crime literature is the "favourite of all that is most intellectual in the reading public," at least Freud liked the work of Dorothy Sayers. On a superficial level, what these and other readers looked for was pleasurable excitement removed from the reality of their own lives. But why did these mostly respectable people want detective stories concerned with a crime and its solution, or thrillers in which the heroes often did things that in real life the readers would strongly have disapproved?

Psychiatrists have strangely neglected the question of our motives for reading crime literature, and the historians of the genre have never shown much interest in it. Much the most suggestive psychoanalytical view of detective stories I have read is Dr. Charles Rycroft's article in the *Psychoanalytical Quarterly* in 1957. Rycroft begins by considering the hypothesis of another psychoanalyst, Geraldine Pederson-Krag, that the detective story has its origins in the "primal scene" of infancy. The murder represents parental intercourse, the victim is the parent, and the clues are symbolic representations of mysterious "nocturnal sounds, stains, incomprehensible adult jokes." The reader, according to Pederson-Krag, satisfies infantile curiosity by becoming the detective, thus "redressing completely the helpless inadequacy and anxious guilt unconsciously remembered from childhood."

Rycroft adds a very interesting gloss to this idea. If the victim is the parent, who is the criminal? He must personify "the reader's own unavowed hostility towards that parent." Thus, "the reader is not only the detective; he is also the criminal," and "in the ideal detective story the detective or hero would discover that he himself is the criminal for whom he has been seeking." Rycroft's exemplification of his own and Pederson-Krag's ideas in relation to *The Moonstone* is not always happy, although it is full of what might be called psychoanalytical Holmesian remarks. ("It is not necessary here to . . . point out the symbolism of the drawer in the Indian cabinet, of the decorative painting and the stain on the nightshirt, nor of the fact that Franklin gave up cigar smoking during his courtship of Rachel.") But the most important point of which Rycroft, perhaps through lack of familiarity with the form, seems unaware, is that the crime story has in fact followed the pattern he suggests. In early crime fiction the hero is often identified with the criminal, and in recent work ranging from that of Dashiell Hammett and Patricia Highsmith to that of James Hadley Chase and Mickey Spillane, the hero is a criminal, or pretends to be a criminal, or behaves like a criminal.

Apart from Rycroft, whose valuable piece should certainly be given wider readership, we are left with the stimulating but casual speculations of writers interested in crime stories and in psychology. Professor Roy Fuller has pointed out the similarities between the detective story and elements in the Oedipus myth, "the illustrious victim, the preliminary riddles, the incidental love interest, the gradual uncovering of the past, the unlikeliest criminal," and has suggested that it is "a harmless and purging surrogate for the Oedipus myth in every writer's and reader's life." W. H. Auden, in an essay which shoots off suggestions as a Catherine wheel sends out sparks, says that the detective story has a magical function and that its mirror image is the Quest for the Grail. According to Auden, the most satisfying detective stories are those set in idyllic and preferably rural conditions, so that the corpse appears "shockingly out of place, as when a dog makes a mess on a drawing room carpet." They contain the magical quality of easing our sense of guilt. ("The typical reader of detective stories is, like myself, a person who suffers from a sense of sin.") We live under, and in fact accept, the rule of law. What we are looking for in the detective-story ritual, through which the person whose guilt was presumed proves innocent and the person who appeared outside the circle of suspicion turns out to be guilty, is an escape from this reality and a return to an imagined primal innocence where we can "know love as love and not as the law."

Auden's valuable, wayward essay is written from a specifically Christian point of view, accepting the concept of sin as personal. I think one can amplify his suggestions, and those of Fuller, by relating the satisfaction gained from reading crime literature to the principle by which the primitive tribe is purified through the transference of its troubles to another person or animal. Murder is in many societies seen as the act which makes its perpetrator finally unacceptable. He may be expelled or destroyed, but never pardoned. Even in those societies where a temporary suspension of law is sometimes declared in relation to nonviolent offenses like theft, murderers are taken into custody until the law is invoked again. The murderer is therefore an appropriate villain, but he is also society's permanent scapegoat. Evil has been committed, suffering has ensued, a sacrifice is necessary. The murderer is seen as a devil personified, and his death insures the purification of the tribe. Nicholas Blake, writing in the forties, imagined a future Frazer calling the detective story "The Folk-Myth of the Twentieth Century" and examining it very much from this point of view.

In the beginning there was guilt: the basic motive for reading crime fiction is the religious one of exorcising the guilt of the individual or the group through ritual and symbolic sacrifice. The attempt is never wholly successful, for the true addict is a sort of Manichee, and his spirits of light and darkness, the detective and the criminal, are fighting each other forever. Human tribal sacrifices might be regarded as sacred, and often appeared in disguise before death, the human features being replaced by those of the devil who had to be expelled. The detective story shows this operation in reverse, the criminal appearing at first as an accepted and often respected figure. This mask is stripped away at the end of the book, when his real features as lawbreaker are seen. The detective is the equally sacred witch doctor who is able to smell out the evil that is corrupting society, and pursue it through what may be a variety of disguises to its source. The objection often made to stories in which the detective turns out to be the criminal is partly social (such an idea subverts the law) and partly religious, since it confuses the powers of darkness with the powers of light.

Much of what has been said above applies to the detective story, and not to the crime novel or the thriller. In a detective story, good people and bad people are clearly defined and do not change (except for the bad person who is pretending to be good). Policemen will not beat up suspects, nor will the criminal's state of mind be considered interesting, since the policemen are on the side of light and the criminal on the side of darkness. The psychological reason for the weakening of the detective story in recent years is a weakening in the sense of sin. Where an awareness of sin in religious terms does not exist, the detective as witch doctor has no function.

WHY WE READ THEM: THE SOCIAL REASONS

One of the most marked features of the Anglo-American detective story is that it is strongly on the side of law and order. This is not merely a statement of the obvious, for it was not always true and is not altogether true now. Dorothy Sayers puts it clearly when she says that some early crime stories showed admiration for the criminal's astuteness, and that detective stories could not flourish "until public sympathy had veered round to the side of law and order." This book examines in some detail the kind of stories written before "sympathy had veered round," stories in which not a detective but the rogue or criminal is quite often the hero. But the detective story, as developed through Collins and Gaboriau to Doyle and the twentieth-century writers, was certainly on the side of "law and order."

It is important to understand that what Sayers means by public sympathy is not a counting of heads, but the sympathy of the better-educated classes—or to put it in another way those above a certain income level, who have a stake in the permanence of the existing social system. The values put forward by the detective story from the time of Holmes to the beginning of World War II, and by the thriller and spy story up to the advent of Eric Ambler, are those of a class in society that felt it had everything to lose by social change. In this detective-story world, decent men played games and were not too highly intellectual, women slept only with their husbands and never drank too much, and servants knew their place—which was in the servants' hall. The thriller's code of conduct in the same period was similar but a good deal cruder, because, as Blake has said, detective stories were mostly read by "the upper and professional classes" and thrillers by those with less money and inferior social status. In the terms of early thriller writers, no Hun, and later no Red, was likely to be an honorable man, and this was particularly true of Reds, whose allegiance to some abstract impractical theory led them to behave in an unsporting and ungentlemanly way. They were quite the opposite of Bulldog Drummond, about whom Sapper said: "He lives clean, loves sport, and fights hard. I don't think he's ever done anything dirty; I can assure you he never will." Drummond sometimes seems to be a sporting tough parodying an English gentleman, but the rule about the wickedness of radicals was hardly ever broken. Raffles was only an acceptable character as gentleman burglar because he was good at cricket and died fighting for his country against the Boers. In France, Arsène Lupin atoned for his criminal career by joining the Foreign Legion.

On the social level, then, what crime literature offered to its readers for half a century from 1890 onward was a reassuring world in which those who tried to disturb the established order were always discovered and punished. Society's agent, the detective, was the single character allowed to have high intellectual attainments. He might be by ordinary standards (that is, those of his readers) eccentric, quaint, apparently a bit silly, but his knowledge was always great, and in practice he was omniscient. He was most often an amateur, because in this way the reader was able easily to put himself in the detective's position, and he alone was upon occasion allowed to be above the law, and to do things which for a character less privileged would be punishable. This lawlessness on the detective's part was only superficially a contradiction of sympathy for law and order. Behind the conscious Victorian and Edwardian adherence to a firmly fixed hierarchical society, there lay a deep vein of unease about the possible violent overturn of that society, especially by anarchists. The "propaganda by the deed" actions of those who called themselves anarchists in France and America, before and at the turn of the century, included the assassination of Presidents Carnot and McKinley, and many more or less successful bomb attempts to kill people and destroy property. Barbara Tuchman, in *The Proud Tower,* has suggested the thrill of horror which such actions caused to the respectable in every country. How could the machinery of justice operate successfully against somebody like the French anarchist Émile Henry, who said: "We inflict death; we will know how to endure it."

The aloof super-intellectual and slightly inhuman detective like Holmes, who occasionally acts outside the law, was particularly attractive when posed against such terrifying figures, because he was a kind of savior of society, somebody who did illegal things for the right reasons, who was really *one of us.* An intelligent French critic, Pierre Nordon, has pointed out that the whole Sherlock Holmes cycle is "addressed to the privileged majority; it plays on their fears of social disturbance and at the same time makes use of Sherlock Holmes and what he stands for to reassure them." These comments apply primarily to British society, which was powerful, prosperous, and marked by clear divisions between classes, but in America and also throughout Europe crime literature made its chief appeal to those who had a way of life and a position in society to preserve. So far from being, as some people have suggested, a surrogate satisfaction for murderous desires, typical detective stories of the period were remarkably free from the realities of violence.

Victim, murder, investigation—all have a hieratic and ritual quality. What the stories assert is the static nature of society, the inevitableness with which wrongdoing is punished.

The nature and appeal of crime literature did not change much in the years between the two World Wars, but its relationship to the world around was greatly altered. Before 1914, the exterior trappings of typical detective stories corresponded reasonably well to the world outside. The big country house still existed, with its lengthy visits by friends and relations, its mild local entertainments, its shooting and fishing, its small army of servants, and its multiplicity of rooms, including the corpse-filled library. This world was heavily eroded by the slump years, and had pretty well vanished by 1939, but detective-story writers pretended that it was still there. In a sense, obviously, all detective stories are games of let's pretend, but the imagination of the writers naturally grew feebler as it had less and less to feed on. There are still some readers, like Auden, who find it hard to read any detective stories except those set in a rural world belonging not to the present but to the past, but upon the whole these stories became steadily less successful in fulfilling their social function. Readers found it much more difficult to accept the pretenses upon which they were based. By the end of World War II, the reassurances offered by the classical kind of detective story had become very shaky indeed. The social and religious structure of society had changed so much that its assumptions seemed preposterous. The pretense that the world was static could no longer be maintained. The detective story with its closed circle of suspects and its rigid rules had always been a fairy tale, but the point and pleasure of fairy tales is that by exercising the imagination one can believe them to be true. In the postwar world, this sort of story changed from a fairy tale to an absurdity. In America, where social stratifications had never been so firm, the pattern was broken much earlier than in England, through Hammett and his successors. The process by which the detective story changed into the crime novel, which fulfills quite different emotional needs, is set down in this book.

Perhaps the reaction of Plain Man readers may be anticipated: "So *that's* why I read crime stories. And I thought they were just a bit of relaxation." It is a natural comment, but even Plain Men and Women should understand that there are social and emotional reasons for the kind of entertainment they enjoy. By understanding the reasons for the popularity of a certain kind of literature, and looking at the changes in it, we learn more about the literature and about ourselves.

PERSONAL FEELINGS AND THE DOUBLE STANDARD

If all this suggests an academic approach, that is an impression I should correct. Like the Plain Man and Woman, I am an addict, with a passion for crime literature that survives any rational explanation of it. This book is the result of the addiction, which started at the age of ten or eleven with Sherlock Holmes and Father Brown, and has survived the rigors of several years' reviewing of crime stories. My research has been that of an addict, rather than of an academic busy with his card indexes. It is based upon wide reading and rereading, but not upon an attempt to read the whole bulk of crime literature, which is now so vast that to try to cover the whole of it would have resulted in a mere catalogue. The most noticeable omissions are probably the result of my preferences, but there will be others caused by ignorance. I hope that proper severity about my mistakes of opinion and fact will be blended with an indulgence like that of Holmes's, in relation to the student who looked at the examination papers in advance, when he said that it is human to err.

So this is a book expressing personal preferences, as all such surveys do, although few admit it. My early enthusiasm for every sort of crime story has not remained unscathed. I can no longer read with any pleasure the work of those writers later labeled the Humdrums, although I did so once. I still enjoy enormously the best work of the Golden Age detective-story writers, but I admire much more the finest books of those authors I have called crime novelists. At the same time, I have done my best to be fair, and I have tried to produce a book which should offer for the first time some assessment of crime stories on literary grounds. For the first time? Well, certainly most of those who have written about crime novels and short stories have assessed them by extra-literary considerations. Auden, for instance, says flatly that for him "detective stories have nothing to do with works of art," but have rather the function of sympathetic magic. He remarks on *The Trial* as a work of art in which "it is the guilt that is certain and the crime that is uncertain," in distinction from the detective story which works the other way round. If one protests that such a comparison really tells us nothing, and that some books by Hammett and Chandler (among others) have at least some of the characteristics of art, Auden escapes by saying that such books are not detective stories by his definition and that Chandler's "powerful but extremely depressing books should be read and judged, not as escape literature, but as works of art." This does not seem to be right. Chandler's books are escape literature of a different kind, that is all. Chandler himself was evasive when asked who was the "best mystery writer," replying: "Can't answer, too many types. By sales Gardner and Christie. Can't read Christie, Gardner close personal friend. Carter Dickson I can't read but others love him. . . . Best plodding detail man, Freeman Wills Crofts. Best Latin and Greek quoter, Dorothy Sayers. . . . This is a lot of nonsense. You have to agree on definitions and standards."

You have to agree on definitions and standards: but that is impossible. How can one weigh the puzzle interest of the detective story against the interest in characterization that marks the crime novel, especially when the detective story often contains some characterization and the crime novel often contains a puzzle? These two kinds of book are very much like each other, but they are not the same thing. If detective stories are assessed by any recognizable literary standards, most of them seem at first sight of negligible interest. But, outside Dr. Leavis and his followers, nobody condemns Restoration comedy outright because it lacks the profundity of Jacobean drama. It is an inferior thing, but a thing with its own particular and unique merits. In the same way, the detective story is an inferior thing to the crime novel, but it has wholly individual merits for all except the most priggish. A double standard of judgment has to be used here, so that one can say first of all that the characteristic detective story has almost no literary merit, and second that it may still be an ingenious, cunningly deceptive, and finely constructed piece of work. The parallel with Restoration comedy still holds. And there are gradations within the detective story itself, so that just as it would be an erratic taste that preferred Vanbrugh to Congreve, so it would be a mistake to equate any other writer with John Dickson Carr as a master of the locked-room mystery. When Edmund Wilson says that "with so many fine books to be read . . . there is no need to bore ourselves with this rubbish," he is really denying the *convention* of the detective story any interest or attraction at all.

Most of the form's historians or critics err by applying a single standard of the opposite kind. They are so delighted by puzzles and problems that they confuse their undoubted interest with that of literature, claiming by implication that if *The Moonstone* was a work of literature, then the books of XYZ, which are just as cleverly plotted and even more baffling, must be literature, too. By mixing the names of writers of unquestioned talent who have been interested in writing crime stories, like Poe and Faulkner, with those of hacks who have clever ideas, all criminal coinage is debased. The assumption made here is that if we are to say what is good in crime fiction we should also say what is less good, commonplace, or poor; that the best crime stories are novels of quality; and that clever ideas and tricks are positive virtues, although they are often canceled by writing that is intolerably crude and slovenly.

SOURCES AND STYLE

The sources for most of what follows are the thousands of crime stories I have read. Most of my debts to the historians and chroniclers of the crime story are acknowledged in the text, but I may as well make them explicit here in lieu of a Bibliography.

Howard Haycraft's *Murder for Pleasure* (1941) is the book to which I have referred most often. It is much the best and most comprehensive survey of detective fiction up to the year of its publication, and if it shows a slight bias toward American writers, very likely this volume provides a corrective. The collection of essays edited by Haycraft called *The Art of the Mystery Story* (1946) contains much of the most important critical writing about crime stories, including pieces by Chandler, Sayers, Wright, and others which first appeared elsewhere. The English *Crime in Good Company* (1959), edited by Michael Gilbert, also contains a number of interesting essays of a later date. Ellery Queen's *Queen's Quorum* (1951) and *In the Queen's Parlor* (1957) have been informative. A. E. Murch's *The Development of the Detective Novel* (1958) contains a lot of detailed and valuable material about nineteenth-century crime fiction. Joan M. Mooney's thesis on *Best-Selling American Detective Fiction,* which has appeared in the magazine *Armchair Detective,* contains some interesting side glances at little-considered areas of crime fiction, like dime novels. The late Ordean A. Hagen's *Who Done It?* (1969) is a monumental but maddening guide list. It is full of valuable information, almost none of which can be taken on trust without checking. Errors seem particularly prevalent in the details about British writers.

These are the books about crime stories that have been especially useful. I have not consulted any colleagues, British or American, feeling that it would be better to stand by my own opinions rather than be drawn into friendly arguments which might have ended in tame modifications. Edmund Crispin, however, read the book in typescript, and I owe a particular debt of gratitude for his generous criticism, and for his correction of at least one howler. (I had forgotten that John Dickson Carr's Dr. Fell at one time had a wife.) He must also bear responsibility for the footnote on page 194 added at my English publisher's suggestion. Professor Roy Fuller has corrected some of my other errors. I have moved occasionally from third to first person when this seemed for some reason desirable or useful, and I have used similar freedom in dealing with names. After the first reference to a writer, the surname only is generally used, whether of man or woman. I have tried to give birth and death dates for writers, but in a few cases have been unable to find them. I have tried also to give the publication year of books.

II

The Two Strands: Godwin, Vidocq, Poe

Historians of the detective story are divided between those who say that there could be no detective stories until organized police and detective forces existed, and those who find examples of rational deduction in sources as various as the Bible and Voltaire, and suggest that these were early puzzles in detection. For the first group, the detective story begins with Edgar Allan Poe; for the second, its roots are in the beginnings of recorded history. Into the mud of this tiresome controversy, I propose to dip no more than one long paragraphic toe.

The decisive point is that we should be talking about crime literature, but that those who search for fragments of detection in the Bible and Herodotus are looking only for puzzles. The puzzle is vital to the detective story but is not a detective story in itself, and its place in crime literature generally is comparatively small. If we consider what Dorothy Sayers calls the first four detective stories, we find that they involve the use of natural cunning rather than detective skill. In the tale of Susanna and the elders, Daniel traps the elders by an adroit question, but he has no means of knowing that Susanna is innocent and they are guilty, and in the story of the priests of Bel the reason for supposing them to be lying is theological, the fact that Bel is a heathen idol. The tale of King Rhampsinitus's attempts to catch the thief who stole from his treasure house is no more than a battle of wits, with the rogue coming off best, and although the affair of Hercules and Cacus contains a deception about footprints, it bears no other relation to detection. The purposes of the histories and fairy tales in which these are fragments are quite different in nature from crime literature. The trick or puzzle element is present in several of the *Arabian Nights* stories, usually as an example of natural cunning used to escape a trap, on the level of the cock caught by a fox, in Chaucer's "The Nun's Priest's Tale" (mentioned by one historian), who persuades the fox to open his mouth and then flies away. The most interesting of these exercises is that in Voltaire's *Zadig* (1747). Without seeing the Queen's bitch or the King's horse, both of which have disappeared, Zadig is able to say that the bitch recently had puppies, limps in the left foreleg, and has long ears, and that the horse is five feet high, with very small hoofs and a tail three and a half feet long. He adds that the horse is shod with silver of eleven deniers proof, with bosses on its bit of twenty-three-carat gold. When he insists that he has never seen the animals, Zadig is sentenced to be flogged. His explanation, made after the animals are found, is a piece of true deduction. In the case of the bitch, hanging dugs and earmarks traced in the sand, with one paw more deeply impressed than the others, provided the clues. The horse had brushed off some leaves in an arcade at a height of five feet, and its tail had wiped away dust at a distance of three and a half feet. Marks left on stones showed the details about the bit and shoes. This brilliant fragment was borrowed by Voltaire from a romance by the Chevalier de Mailly published thirty years earlier, and at a further distance from the *Arabian Nights,* of which *Zadig* is an ironical imitation. And Voltaire's prime concern is not to show the power of reason, but its inadequacy in dealing with all the unreasonable people in the world. This ingenious piece of analytical deduction is a flirt of the imagination in a book that does not bear the slightest relationship to a crime story.

If we leave aside such puzzles and riddles, there is of course a great deal of fiction concerned with crime which goes back at least to the eighteenth century, including Fielding's *Jonathan Wild* and the tales of mystery and terror written by Mrs. Radcliffe, Maturin, and "Monk" Lewis. But Fielding's book belongs to the tradition of the picaresque novel about the adventures of a rogue rather than to the crime story, and although the Gothic novel bears a relationship to the detective story in the sense that it often poses a mystery to be solved, the solution is often banal and never in itself of much interest. The Gothic novelists wanted to arouse in their readers feelings of terror and delight at the horrific plight of the central character, and they used mysterious events to enhance these feelings. The solution of a puzzle was not for them the main object of a book. The characteristic note of crime literature is first struck in *Caleb Williams,* by William Godwin (1756–1836), which appeared in 1794.

"Psychological novel, detective, adventure or pursuit novel, and political novel—these are the labels most often attached to *Caleb Williams*," says Professor McCracken, introducing the most recent edition of the book. The novel points up sharply the weakness of any attempt to fit crime stories too closely into separate compartments. *Caleb Williams* is about a murder, its detection, and the unrelenting pursuit by the murderer of the person who has discovered his guilt. It was also for Godwin a means of expounding his anarchist beliefs, and because of this it is not usually considered as coming within the crime story's critical canon. Yet one has only to consider the account he gives of the book's conception to see how close he was in spirit to the modern crime story. He invented the last volume first, he says, as a volume of flight and pursuit with "the fugitive in perpetual apprehension of being overwhelmed with the worst calamities, and the pursuer, by his ingenuity and resources, keeping his victim in a state of the most fearful alarm." But how was he to account for this pursuit, why did it happen? He devised, as the material of the second volume, "a secret murder, to the investigation of which the innocent victim should be impelled by an unconquerable spirit of curiosity." And then, to make the implacable pursuit plausible, the first volume must show "the pursuer . . . invested with every advantage of fortune, with a resolution that nothing could defeat or baffle, and with extraordinary resources of intellect." This manner of working back from effect to cause, from solution to problem, is at the heart of crime literature, and no writer before Godwin had attempted it with his conscious deliberation.

Hazlitt thought that nobody who began *Caleb Williams* could fail to finish it, and that nobody who read it could possibly forget it, yet the book is so little known today that a summary of the plot may be useful. Falkland, a generous and charming country squire, is accused of stabbing to death his atrocious neighbor Tyrrell. He is tried and acquitted. A tenant of Tyrrell's named Hawkins is then arrested, together with his son, and they are both tried and hanged. One principal piece of evidence against them is a knife found in their lodgings, the broken blade of which precisely fits the piece left in the wound. Caleb Williams is the narrator of the story—or most of the story, for Godwin introduces another narrator in a way that slightly anticipates *The Moonstone*. He is a poor boy who enters Falkland's service as a secretary at a time when the murder lies in the past. He suspects that his master had something to do with the crime, and pursues his investigation with the unquenchable curiosity of the amateur detective. After Caleb has discovered the truth, that Falkland killed Tyrrell and then planted clues against Hawkins, he is dismissed, put in prison on a charge of theft (Falkland has secreted jewelry among his belongings), and then pursued and persecuted by Falkland and his agent Gines. The pursuit is relentless, frustrating his attempts at escape by disguising himself as an Irish beggar, a lower-class farmer, and a Jew. In the end, Caleb brings Falkland to trial, and the squire, now a dying man, admits his guilt and praises his accuser.

Caleb Williams is a remarkable rather than a great novel. The second and third volumes are absorbingly interesting, but the first, in which the nobility of Falkland's nature is contrasted with the brutishness of Tyrrell's, is heavy going for a modern reader. And Godwin's object in writing the book was political. In 1793, his *Enquiry Concerning the Principles of Political Justice* had appeared, and this outline of an ideal anarchism, the book by which he is now remembered, at once made him famous. In it Godwin attacked practically all the institutions of the state, including the legal system, opposing to them the vision of a world in which "there will be no war, no crimes, no administration of justice, as it is called, and no government." In the bright dawn of the French Revolution, this vision found many sympathizers, and Godwin became for a time the intellectual leader of the English Radical movement, as Tom Paine was its leader in action. *Political Justice* was an account of things as they might be, an expression of faith in the perfectibility of man. The original title of *Caleb Williams* was *Things as They Are,* and it is meant to show the corruption inherent in any legal system through which one man has power over another. Falkland is a good and generous man, and in Godwin's eyes his villainy springs from his trust in social institutions, which betray him until he commits and then has to conceal the ultimate crime of murder. Caleb's sufferings, in prison and throughout his wanderings, are forced on him directly by Falkland but indirectly through the authoritarian power exerted by evil institutions over the virtuous individual. And the climactic scene of Falkland's exposure is later seen by Caleb as his own terrible mistake. In desperation at the sufferings inflicted on him, he, too, has invoked the force of law, where he should have attempted "the just experiment" by confronting Falkland privately. "I despaired, while it was yet time to have made the just experiment; but my despair was criminal, was treason against the sovereignty of truth."

The particular importance of *Caleb Williams* is that it denies all the assertions to be made later through the detective story. In the detective story, the rule of law is justified as an absolute good; in Godwin's book, it is seen as wholly evil. The lesser but important strand in modern crime fiction which looks for corruption in officialdom and bureaucracy and often suggests a close alliance between police and gangsters finds its chief modern representatives in Dashiell Hammett and Raymond Chandler, but it was expressed here by the crime story's most significant ancestor. Godwin's attitude often gives extraordinary power to his assertion of the heroic nature of the outlaw. At times he might be speaking with the voice of Brecht, as in the credo of Raymond, leader of a gang of thieves joined by Caleb: "We, who are thieves without a licence, are at open war with another sort of men, who are thieves according to law." And the prototypical figure of the lawbreaker turned thief-taker appears here for the first time in the person of Falkland's agent Gines, who has been expelled from Raymond's band for his brutality, but becomes perfectly acceptable to society as an upholder of the law. There are some passages of biting sarcasm about the code of honor adhered to by such a figure as Gines.

It is a mark of Godwin's perceptiveness that he should have created such a character more than thirty years before the publication of the *Mémoires* of Eugène François Vidocq (1775–1857), the criminal who became in 1811 the first chief of the Sûreté, and later started the first modern detective agency, Le Bureau des Renseignements. We do not know many facts about Vidocq's criminal activities apart from those given in his own highly colored and ghosted autobiography. According to this, he began by stealing 2,000 francs from his mother while in his early teens, joined the Army, and fought fifteen duels in six months, and then at the age of twenty-two received an eight-year prison sentence. He received the sentence in connection with a forged order of release for another prisoner, with which by his own account he had nothing to do, and although he says that at the transit prison of Bicêtre he had a court of admirers, "this prison glory was hateful to me." He decided to become a police informer "for the interest of honest men" and wrote to "Papa" Henry, a divisional chief at the Paris Prefecture, to offer his services. Dates and details are confused in the *Mémoires,* but there is no reason to doubt the substantial truth in much of Vidocq's story. He says that he spent twenty-one months as a police spy in prison, first at Bicêtre and later at La Force. During this time, he proved his loyalty to the police. His "escape" was arranged, and he was appointed Chef de la Sûreté with a staff originally of four men, a number eventually increased to twenty-eight.

Almost all his agents were ex-convicts and there were persistent rumors that some of them, and perhaps Vidocq himself, engineered robberies that they later solved, instigated to do so by the arrangement through which they were paid no salary but received a fee and expenses for every arrest. These essentially probable offenses were never proved, but in 1827 Vidocq's resignation was forced by his superior in the Second Division, the Chevalier Duplessis. He was replaced by one of his most dubious ex-criminal agents, Coco Lacour, and although he returned to power in March, 1832, he was never really trusted. In November, he resigned again after a case in which one of his agents was accused of acting as *agent provo-*

cateur in a case involving the arrest of several thieves. After this the authorities pursued him intermittently, and eventually succeeded in wrecking his Bureau. He lived on for more than twenty years after its destruction, writing or at least producing books, doing some private detective work, even still acting occasionally as a police agent.

The influence of Vidocq on writers of crime fiction in his own lifetime and on detective-story writers after his death was immense. It did not rest on his skill in analytical detection, for he had none. He started a card-index system at the Sûreté, and his *Mémoires* mention at one point taking impressions of footmarks, but it cannot be said that he was in any way a forerunner of later police methods, his perceptiveness being confined to such general observations as that many criminals are bowlegged. Vidocq's importance rested in his nature as the archetypal ambiguous figure of the criminal who is also a hero. The interpenetration of police with criminals, and the doubt about whether a particular character is hero or villain, is an essential feature of the crime story, and Vidocq embodied it in his own person. A typical passage in the *Mémoires,* relating to his own early days as a police spy, runs:

> I frequented every house and street of ill fame, sometimes under one disguise and sometimes under another, assuming, indeed, all those rapid changes of dress and manner which indicated a person desirous of concealing himself from the observation of the police, till the rogues and thieves whom I daily met there firmly believed me to be one of themselves.

The capacity for physical disguise is of course a mark of ambiguity, and there is no doubt that Vidocq was very successful in disguising himself. His ability to do so fascinated several contemporary writers, including Balzac and Bulwer-Lytton. Balzac heard from Vidocq's own mouth, and Lytton read in the autobiography, stories about the false wrinkles, pigtail, snowy ruffles, and three-cornered hat that helped him to become a "very respectable gentleman" when necessary, of the time when he had his hair and beard dyed black, stained his face with walnut liquor, and garnished his upper lip with coffee grounds plastered on with gum arabic, and of the mock blisters and fetter marks made on his feet and legs when he impersonated a criminal named Germain. When, in old age, he paid a visit to London, the *Times* gave his height as five feet ten inches "when perfectly erect" (he was in fact five feet six inches tall), and added that "by some strange process connected with his physical formation he has the faculty of contracting his height several inches, and in this diminished state to walk about, jump, etc." The climactic emotional moment at which the man who has seemed to be bad is revealed as good and the true villain is exposed comes often in the *Mémoires,* when Vidocq abandons disguise and proclaims, "I am Vidocq," and of almost equal symbolic importance are such occasions as those when Vidocq in disguise is set to search for and destroy himself. Vidocq started a tradition of disguise in the French detective force which persisted at least until the end of the century. His English biographer, Philip John Stead, is not exaggerating when he says that it was Vidocq who "first struck the European imagination as the detective," although it should be added that he did so because he embodied in one person both the thieftaker and the thief.

It was the criminal rather than the maintainer of law who fascinated his contemporaries, and whom in some cases they admired. Balzac was a friend of Vidocq's, and based upon him the character of Vautrin, who appears in *Le Père Goriot* and other books. Vautrin, alias Jacques Collin, is, like Vidocq, a master of disguise, and like him also is a figure both genial and sinister. He gives up criminal activities and enters the police. Balzac's interest, however, was not in painting a portrait of Vidocq but in using him to create a major character whose philosophy transcends the conventions of legality. "In every million men there are ten who put themselves above everything, even the law, and I am one of them," Vautrin says, and on the occasion of his arrest he is allowed a splendidly forceful declaration: "Have you never seen a convict before? A convict such as I am is a man less cowardly than the rest, who protests against the hypocrisy of the social contract, as says Rousseau, whose disciple I am proud to call myself." As A. E. Murch has pointed out, Balzac sometimes gave a hero's role to the criminal, but never made a hero out of a detective.

His conception of the ethical relationship between crime, order, and society is nearer to Godwin than to Wilkie Collins.

Yet one shouldn't push this too far. Balzac often introduced criminals into his books and described their activities, but in the enormously detailed canvas of the *Comédie Humaine* they play a small part. One idea that continues throughout the series is the dependence of men on the society that nurtures them, a dependence that exists even when they defy it and try to exist outside its conventions. (It is suggested that Vautrin is homosexual.) Balzac's prime interest in crime is as a single element in the social fabric that orders human personality, and although his books often deal with crime they are not crime stories.

Much the same can be said of Eugène Sue (1804–1857) and Alexandre Dumas *père* (1802–1870). Sue's most famous work, *Les Mystères de Paris,* is a sensational novel owing a great deal to the Vidocq tradition, and indeed directly to the *Mémoires,* as well as something at a further distance to the horrors of Mrs. Radcliffe. An impossibly virtuous aristocratic hero living in the Paris slums becomes mixed up in the activities of a gang of thieves and murderers. The adventures are often absurd, and although there is a great deal of information about criminal habits, the "mysteries" hardly exist in a modern sense. There are several passages of deductive reasoning in Dumas's works, including one by D'Artagnan in *Le Vicomte de Bragelonne* which closely resembles Zadig's reasoning about the horse and the bitch. He was also the first writer to point out that an impression may be left on the second sheet of a pad of paper when the first has been torn off. The first appearance of this standby of the detective in fiction for discovering telephone numbers and messages (with its cousin, the mirror impression of writing on blotting paper) is worth putting down in detail. Fouquet, Louis XIV's Intendant of Finances, is told that his enemy Colbert has been making notes about his affairs, and says that he would be curious to see them. Then he learns that his former lover has got hold of them.

"How did she manage it?"

"Listen. I told you Colbert found paper on the table?"

"Yes."

"And took a pencil from his pocket."

"Yes."

"And wrote on the paper?"

"Yes."

"The pencil was a lead pencil; consequently it was hard; the marking on the first sheet was black; that on the other was white."

"And what happened?"

"He tore off the first sheet, and never thought of the second."

But for the most part Dumas recounts ingenious tricks, like those of the eighteenth-century picaresque novel, which are no more than deceptions practiced on gulls.

In one or two of James Fenimore Cooper's romances, there are similar incidents which anticipate the deductive method of the detective story, the best known of them relating to the tracking exploits of the scout Hawkeye as he points out the difference between one moccasin and another, but essentially these are repeating in a different time and country the feats of Zadig.

In England, Edward Bulwer-Lytton (1803–1873), later Lord Lytton, also stressed the romantic qualities of the criminal. Miss Murch in her study of early detection picks out for particular discussion his second novel, *Pelham* (1828), pointing out that Lord Pelham is confronted by a characteristic detectival problem when his friend Sir Reginald Glanville is to be committed for trial on a charge of murder unless Pelham can "by the day after to-morrow, ascertain any facts to elucidate this mysterious crime and point the inquiries of justice to another quarter." This subsidiary plot, however, is far from being at the heart of the book, as murder is the central fact of *Caleb Williams,* but is rather evidence of Lytton's absorption in the world of the criminal as opposed to the world of authority. In Lytton's four genuine crime novels, the hero is also a criminal. The first of them, *Paul Clifford* (1830), shocked many readers by having a gentleman highwayman for its hero, and annoyed them by suggesting similarities between "vulgar vice and fashionable vice—the slang of the one circle is but an easy paraphrase of the cant of the other." The best of his crime stories, *Night and Morning* (1841), points up frequently the distinction between Gawtrey, who commits crimes but is shown as essentially a good man led astray, and Lord Lilburne, who breaks no laws but ruins the lives of others in pursuit of his own pleasure. *Eugene Aram* (1832) was based upon an actual case in which the scholarly and virtuous Aram was convicted and executed for a murder committed fourteen years earlier. But again, although these books of Lytton's have a genuine connection with modern crime stories, one should not overstate the case. The books sprang from the conception of the criminal as a romantic outsider, a man condemned to the life he led by the cruelty of an unjust society and a corrupt or ignorant judiciary, which was prevalent during the first half of the nineteenth century. Lytton's early Radicalism and his unhappy marriage led him to create characters who were outcasts from the respectable world, and to show them as sympathetic, but the point for him (in the case of Eugene Aram, that a single act can be "at war with a whole life—blasting for ever the happiness") can hardly be the point for us.

The idea that detective fiction could not be written until organized detective police forces existed is logically persuasive but not literally true, for the first detective stories were written by Edgar Allan Poe (1809–1849) before a Detective Department had been established at Scotland Yard and at a time when few American cities had any kind of police system. The relationship between detective stories and the development of detective branches in police forces is discussed in the next chapter; it is a tribute to Poe's inventive genius that his stories had so little to do with actual police operations. He had read Vidocq, and it is right to say that if the *Mémoires* had never been published Poe would never have created his amateur detective, but one should immediately add that Poe owed to Vidocq only the inspiration that set light to his imagination. Almost every later variation of plot in the detective story can be found in the five short stories he wrote which, with a little stretching here and there, can be said to fit within the limits of the form. He is the undisputed father of the detective story, although he would have been disconcerted by many of his children and grandchildren.

It should be recognized also that Poe did not think of himself as writing detective stories (the word "detective" was unknown at the time the first of them, "The Murders in the Rue Morgue," appeared), or regard these particular stories as of much importance.

Poe's roots as a prose artist lay, like those of Lytton and others at the time, in the romantic tale of terror. As Edmund Wilson has said, he was, so far from being alien to the spirit of his age, one of its most typical figures, "a thorough romantic, clearly akin to his European contemporaries," and it was probably fortunate for him as an artist that he spent his adult life in the tame literary enclosure of the United States. His work looks longingly toward Europe, but it was the irritant influence of the philistines surrounding him that helped to mature the pearl in his oyster. When T. S. Eliot calls Poe provincial, and Henry James says that "to take him with more than a certain degree of seriousness is to lack seriousness oneself," they undoubtedly have in mind the endless endeavor he made to sound the artistic note of a civilization from which he was tangibly separated by the Atlantic. In prose, as in verse and science, he longed always to produce something new, and his curiosity was endless. To quote Eliot again:

The forms which his lively curiosity takes are those in which a pre-adolescent mentality delights: wonders of nature and of mechanics and of the supernatural, cryptograms and cyphers, puzzles and labyrinths, mechanical chess-players and wild flights of speculation. The variety and ardour of his curiosity delight and dazzle: yet in the end the eccentricity and lack of coherence of his interests tire.

Eliot's remarks are often taken as being in dispraise of Poe, but they should be regarded rather as outlining the limitations of his genius. The ingenuity and freshness of his mind were extraordinary, and throughout his writing life he was searching for new forms in which to express the ideas that crowded in on him, and in the horror stories to blend these with the neuroses by which he was increasingly obsessed. In these stories, Poe was always driving toward perverse sexual themes with which he could not deal directly because of the limitations imposed by his society. The result can often be grotesque, as in "Berenice," where the narrator is driven by some unspecified guilt first to murder his epileptic cousin and then, after she has been buried alive during a fit, to fulfill his obsession with her teeth by digging the living body out of the grave and extracting the thirty-two teeth with "some instruments of dental surgery." What he called the "tales of ratiocination," like his interest in cryptography and his discovery that the Lamentations of Jeremiah were written in acrostic verse, are the obverse of this horrific romanticism. If we ask, as some writers have done, why he did not exploit the ratiocinative vein further, the answer is simply that it did not interest him enough—or, to put it another way, that his obsessions eventually became so overwhelmingly important that they did not permit the production of purely rational work.

What he did should be summarized briefly. "The Murders in the Rue Morgue," which appeared in 1841, was the first in those hundreds of locked-room mysteries which proposed the puzzle of a dead body found in a room which seems to be effectively sealed. Sometimes the problem in such stories concerns the murder method (how was X stabbed, shot, poisoned, when nobody could have entered the room and there is no trace of a weapon or the poison), and sometimes the means of entry or exit. One common form of solution is that in which the murder was committed before the door was locked or after it had been reopened; another depends upon some mechanical device like a murder weapon which will operate at a particular time (in one of Melville Davisson Post's Uncle Abner stories, the sun, focusing through a bottle of raw liquor, explodes a percussion cap on a fowling piece); and another still is related to some possible means of entry which is not apparent. In Poe's story, the investigator Dupin deduces that the murderer must have come in through the apparently securely nailed windows, and finds that the nail at one window is broken, so that it only appears to be holding the window, which is also retained by a concealed spring. The police, thinking that the nail was completely driven through the window, did not trouble to look for the spring. By various other deductions, Dupin comes to the correct conclusion that the murders had been committed by an orang-outang which must have escaped from its owner.

"The Mystery of Marie Rogêt" was written and published in magazine form during the following year. It follows closely the murder of a girl named Mary Cecilia Rogers in New York. She was killed in July, 1841, and the case remained a mystery at the time

Poe wrote of it, changing the scene from New York to Paris and putting forward a solution through the comments of Dupin. The innovation here is that the story is told through newspaper cuttings which, although attributed to French papers, are almost word for word similar to those in the New York press. The cuttings are interspersed with the comments and conclusions of Dupin, who relies for his evidence wholly upon the sometimes contradictory press information, so that this story is the first piece of "armchair detection," the precursor of all those tales in which the detective solves a crime simply by analysis of and deduction from the material with which he is presented.

The third of the Dupin stories, "The Purloined Letter," first appeared in the American annual *The Gift*. It was dated 1845, but probably published in September, 1844. The story was the prototype of the detective novels and short stories which take as their theme the idea that the most apparently unlikely solution is the correct one, with the ingenious addition in Poe's story that what seems most unlikely is really perfectly obvious. A document "of the last importance" has been "purloined from the royal apartments." The identity of the person who took it is known, but he is a Minister, too important to be arrested without proof. The police search without success, every night for three months, the hotel in which the Minister lives. They probe cushions with needles, remove table tops, look for cavities in bed legs, examine the rungs of every chair and the moss between bricks, measure the thickness of book covers to see if the bindings have been tampered with. At the end of all this, Dupin pays a visit to the hotel and sees the letter at once. It is in full view, placed in "a trumpery filigree card-rack of pasteboard," soiled and crumpled and torn nearly in two across the middle. It has been put into a place so obvious that the police ignored it. Dupin goes to see the Minister again, and takes the letter when a diversion is created in the street with a musket by a man in his pay.

These three stories are directly associated with the detective story as we know it, but "The Gold-Bug" and " 'Thou Art the Man' " are so evidently the forerunners of much in later fiction that they should not be ignored. "The Gold-Bug" is a puzzle story, the interest of which is linked to the mystery of the apparently sane Legrand's insistence that the scarabaeus he has discovered is "a bug of real gold." We know from the beginning that Legrand will somehow be able to justify this statement, and he does so by deciphering a code on a scrap of paper left by the pirate Captain Kidd. Looked at in one way, the story is no more than a fictional exemplification of the principles laid down by Poe in his entertaining essay on cryptography, although the protagonist and the marshy island on which the bug is found have his characteristic imaginative strangeness; but many later writers are in debt to it. The directions for finding the pirates' treasure in *Treasure Island,* and the Sherlock Holmes code story "The Dancing Men" (in which the cipher is a simple one, like that of "The Gold-Bug," based on the predominance of the letter "e") are among the first of the many stories and passages in books that would not have been written but for the example of Poe. " 'Thou Art the Man' " blends Poe's interest in detection with the obsession about the narrow barrier between life and death shown in such a story as "The Facts in the Case of M. Valdemar," in which the body of a man who has been in a coma for seven months is roused to speech by mesmerism before disintegrating into "a nearly liquid mess of loathsome—of detestable putrescence." " 'Thou Art the Man' " is a murder mystery. The wealthy Barnabas Rattleborough has disappeared, and several clues indicating that he has been murdered are found by his friend Charley Goodfellow, all of them leading to the conclusion that Rattleborough has been murdered by his dissipated nephew Pennifeather. They include a bloodstained waistcoat and knife, both belonging to the nephew, and a bullet found in Rattleborough's dead horse, "exactly adapted to the bore of Mr. Pennifeather's rifle" and containing "a flaw or seam" which "corresponded precisely with an accidental ridge or elevation in a pair of moulds acknowledged by the accused himself to be his own property." At a party given by Goodfellow to celebrate the arrival of a case of Château Margaux, however, the case proves to contain not wine but the "bruised, bloody and nearly putrid" corpse of Rattleborough, who sits up, looks at Goodfellow, and says clearly, "Thou art the man." A confession follows, with the revelation that all the false clues have been planted by Goodfellow, and the further revelation by the narrator that he had found the body, obtained the jack-in-the-box effect by thrusting whalebone down the corpse's throat and then doubling it up in the case, and had used his ventriloquial ability to produce the few words of accusation. The originality of this improbable story from the detective point of view rests in the laying of false clues, in the fact that this is the first use of elementary ballistics, and in the commission of the crime by the most unlikely person. (Although actually the tone is one of such insistent levity about the absolute straightforwardness of "old Charley Goodfellow," and indeed of anybody named Charles, that Poe clearly did not intend to deceive his readers.)

Here, then, is the announcement of the themes which later writers are to use, expand, elaborate: but Poe's originality does not end with the provision of material for plots used by writers who may well not have read his stories. He also invented the first detective of fiction, the Chevalier C. Auguste Dupin, and established the convention by which the brilliant intelligence of the detective is made to shine even more brightly through the comparative obtuseness of his friend who tells the story. For nearly a century, this was to be a fixed pattern for most detective stories. The friend might be exceptionally thickheaded like Dr. Watson, Poirot's companion Captain Hastings, or Philo Vance's District Attorney John F.-X. Markham; he might be a more or less neutral receiver of the detective's bright ideas like Ellery Queen's father, the Inspector, or Thorndyke's friend Jervis; he might even be allowed his share of natural shrewdness like Hanaud's urbane dilettante Mr. Ricardo, but he had to be there as a recorder. Or at least that is one's first impression, although, like all categorical statements, this one has its exceptions. Father Brown, in particular, communicated only with God. But still the Dupin pattern of the omniscient amateur detective and his clumsy coadjutor was the one that nine out of ten writers were to follow.

Poe made Dupin in his own image, or rather in the image of what he desired to be. He was "of an excellent—indeed of an illustrious family," partly because Poe detested the leveling idea of democracy, and partly as compensation for his own upbringing in the care of a fairly unsympathetic foster father. He was poor but, like a romantic hero (and unlike Poe), regarded this very little, managing "by means of a rigorous economy, to produce the necessaries of life, without troubling himself about its superfluities." He believed as Poe did in the supreme importance of the intellect, yet he had a strain of wild romantic feeling that led him to close the shutters of the apartment in which he lived at dawn, and to go out into the streets only when "warned by the clock of the advent of the true Darkness." Like Sherlock Holmes later on (and Doyle fully acknowledged his debt), Dupin is able to interpret the thoughts of his companion by the way in which he reacts to exterior events, like being pushed aside by a fruiterer carrying a basket on his head. He solves the problems presented to him by pure analytic deduction. Aristocratic, arrogant, and apparently omniscient, Dupin is what Poe often wished he could have been himself, an emotionless reasoning machine.

A reasoning machine would not be interested in the motives and psychology of people, but only in making correct deductions about their actions. It should be repeated that Poe himself did not regard these stories very seriously. "These tales of ratiocination owe most of their popularity to being something in a new key," he wrote to a correspondent in 1846. "I do not mean to say that they are not ingenious—but people think them more ingenious than they are—on account of their method and *air* of method." The stories were exercises in analysis on matters that caught the interest of his brilliant mind, and he was right in mentioning their *air* of method, for all the Dupin stories reveal under examination mistakes that are damaging to them as pieces of rational deduction.

The most notable, and least known, of these are the criticisms made by Laura Riding of "The Murders in the Rue Morgue." They concern the way in which the ape got in and out of the window fastened by a secret spring undiscovered by the police. This is in itself a most unlikely arrangement, as she points out—why would such a mechanism be fitted in a fourth-story room of an old shabby house? In relation to the window, one cannot do better than quote Miss Riding:

The ape reached the window from the lightning-rod, which was five and a half feet away, by a shutter three and a half feet broad which could shut like a door to cover the whole window and was now lying flat against the wall. He grasped the "trellis-work" on the upper part of the shutter and swung himself into the room, landing unobserved directly on the head of the bed. [The head of the bed partly obstructed the window. J. S.] This is impossible. Poe at one point suggests that it was a double-sashed window: he speaks of the "lower sash." But he does not say whether only the lower sash moved, or both sashes, or whether the two sashes were really one single piece. If only the lower sash moved, then the ape, grasping the shutter and kicking himself backwards (frontways is impossible) into the room, would have been obstructed by the upper half of the window from landing directly on the head of the bed, which was pressed close against the window. If only the lower half moved, then it was only the lower half that was open. If, however, the upper sash moved too, the ape, on climbing out and shutting the window behind him, as he is said to have done, could not have fastened this upper sash by the secret "catch." . . . The window would have remained open.

I have never seen any answer made to this detailed criticism by writers about the detective story, who seem to be unaware of it.

"The Mystery of Marie Rogêt" takes its flavor from the fact that it followed so closely an actual murder case. "I have handled my design in a manner altogether *novel* in literature," Poe wrote on June 4, 1842. "I believe not only that I have demonstrated the fallacy of the general idea—that the girl was the victim of a gang of ruffians—but have *indicated the assassin* in a manner which will give renewed impetus to investigators." Three years after the story's appearance, he claimed in a footnote that "the confessions of *two* persons . . . confirmed, in full, not only the general conclusion, but absolutely *all* the chief hypothetical details by which that conclusion was attained." With one or two exceptions, critics have taken this statement as being correct, and have said that Poe "solved" the mystery. In fact it remained unsolved, with the balance of probability being that Mary Rogers died accidentally following an abortion. A year before his death, Poe, who had said in the story that "it was at once evident that murder had been committed," admitted this in a letter. "The 'naval officer' who committed the murder (rather the accidental death arising from an attempt at abortion) confessed it . . . but, for the sake of relatives, I must not speak further." The naval officer existed, although we have only Poe's word for his confession: but the point really is that the story was based upon the idea that Mary Rogers had been murdered, and if she died accidentally the logic of the argument is destroyed at its base.

Poe thought "The Purloined Letter" to be "perhaps the best of my tales of ratiocination," and he is probably right. The flaw here, noted by several writers, is not seriously damaging to the story. It lies in the fact that Dupin could have seen only the front or the back of the envelope containing the letter, and therefore could not possibly have observed at the same time the "large black seal" (on the back) and the address "in a diminutive female hand" (on the front).

Does such detailed criticism weigh too hard on Poe? It does in the sense that almost any "tale of ratiocination" would wilt if subjected to similar examination. Yet the criticism is important, because the prime merit claimed by Poe for his puzzle stories was that they were model exercises in accurate reasoning. If the reasoning is faulty, the merit of the stories is much reduced. For Poe these stories were above all an expression of his desire to oppose the forces in himself that were, as he said of Dupin, "enamored of the Night for her own sake." Against them is posed that longing for the morbid and perverse expressed in stories about a burden of unnamable personal guilt, like "William Wilson," in which the central character feels himself responsible for "unspeakable misery and unpardonable crime" and commits moral suicide when he stabs his black-masked double. In the pursuit by this figure of unmistakable genius of some completely original form, the detective and puzzle stories played a small part. Poe's paternity of the detective story is not in dispute, but his fatherhood was unintended. He thought that his mistress was Art, but really she was Sensation.

III

Dickens, Collins, Gaboriau: The Pattern Forms

THE "UNKNOWN PUBLIC"

Poe was the founding father whose genius suggested the themes to be followed by other writers: but the pattern of the detective story as it formed in the eighteen-fifties and sixties was closely related to the rise in Britain and America of a middle class with increasing leisure, to the spread of reading, and to the development of detective forces in several countries. Given these social factors, detective stories must inevitably have been written. The form they took was derived from Poe, but a look at their development in Britain shows how well the detective story was suited to the emotional needs of the growing middle class.

In 1858, Wilkie Collins wrote an essay on "The Unknown Public" which was, he said, "in a literary sense, hardly beginning as yet to read," and suggested that "the future of English fiction may rest with this Unknown Public which is now waiting to be taught the difference between a good book and a bad." The Unknown Public had been born with the Industrial Revolution, which brought with it a certain amount of education, strongly opposed by many who felt that to teach farm workers and domestic servants to read was no service either to them or to the country in which they lived. In the Sunday schools set up at the end of the eighteenth century, only works tending to the improvement of religious education were read, but the creation of a semi-literate class of skilled workers, small shopkeepers, clerks, and domestics had results not intended either by Hannah More, who wanted everybody to be able to read religious books, or by the Utilitarians, who thought that "the diffusion of useful knowledge" must be conducive to "the future welfare of mankind."

In the early part of the nineteenth century, the high price of novels limited their circulation (the price was often a guinea and a half for a new work, and the sale usually not much more than a thousand copies) and kept them out of the hands of the new readers, but, as always, demand created supply. In the eighteen-thirties, publishers began to issue reprints of "standard works" at six shillings, but even this kept them out of the reach of most readers at a time when a carpenter in Glasgow earned fourteen shillings a week and a handloom weaver less than half of that. A sub-literature sprang up to satisfy the needs of those who would in any case have found Scott, the best-selling novelist of the time, beyond their scope. It took the form of broadsheets and pamphlets, some of them political (the second part of Paine's *Rights of Man* is said to have sold a million and a half copies), but more concerned with crime. James Catnach published broadsheets and ballads about murder and executions, many of which sold up to a million copies, and other publishers and printers issued what were called blue books, abridgments or imitations of Gothic novels in thirty-six or, less often, seventy-two pages, which sold at sixpence. In 1841, Edward Lloyd, later the founder of *Lloyd's Weekly Newspaper,* put out books in weekly parts sold at a penny, which were called penny dreadfuls. The dreadful thing about them was supposed to be their subject matter, although the stories were no more than amalgams of excitement and romance, often belying the promise of such titles as *Vice and Its Victim: or, Phoebe, the Peasants' Daughter.* Some stories had a more directly violent or sexual content. G. W. M. Reynolds, who founded first of all *Reynolds' Miscellany* and later like Lloyd his own newspaper, wrote a series of enormously long "Mysteries" which were issued in penny numbers, with titles like *Mysteries*

of the Inquisition and *Mysteries of the Court of London*. They were
no more mysterious than Sue's work on which they were based,
but Reynolds's early serials in particular are much concerned with
torture and violence, up to the point of what Victorians considered
possible in open publication. In an obituary notice of Reynolds,
who died in 1879, the *Bookseller* called him "the most popular
writer of his time."

By the eighteen-fifties, penny dreadfuls were being aimed more
particularly at a juvenile market. Their readership changed largely
because of the spread of subscription and public libraries, which in
its turn reflected the rise of the new class created by the pressures
of an increasingly industrial and urban civilization. Circulating
libraries had existed in England for a long time, but they were given
wide popularity by Charles Edward Mudie. His library began in
the eighteen-forties, but really came into its own when in 1852 he
moved from a small shop in Bloomsbury to New Oxford Street.
Mudie offered a yearly subscription for one guinea instead of his
competitors' two, and arranged for an efficient delivery service in
town and country. He found that the greatest demand was for
novels, and although of course many of his country subscribers
were the clergymen and gentry who had formerly bought books,
in towns they were often the families of the highly respectable
tradesmen and small businessmen who were anxious to move away
from their origins and to assert their recently won privileges.
All these subscribers were able to feel assured that no work of a
morally doubtful kind would be offered to them by Mudie, who
was a Dissenter, and had no hesitation in refusing to stock any
book of which he disapproved.

So Mudie's and other subscription libraries helped to diffuse
reading matter, if not always useful knowledge. They were supplemented by the free—that is, rate-supported—libraries which, after
a good deal of opposition in the House of Commons on such
grounds as that if the working classes read more they would dam-
age agricultural interests by drinking less, were approved in 1850.
Between Parliamentary approval and local readiness to establish
libraries at the expense of ratepayers there was a considerable gap,
and as late as 1887 only two parishes in London had rate-sup-

ported libraries. Their opponents felt that they were a sure road to ruin, and in the early eighteen-nineties a correspondent of the *Evening Standard* wrote of a young man at Brighton who spent all his time at the public library "perusing light literature" and did no work. Another visitor to Brighton library said that "no greater curse existed than these libraries," and he "had rather see a young man hanging about a public-house then spending his time in these places." The free libraries were not used by the gentry. A breakdown of borrowers by occupation at Manchester in the eighteen-fifties showed that "artisans and mechanics" was by far the largest group of borrowers. Many of them wanted useful or improving books, but the demand for fiction was immediate, and grew by what it fed on. As early as the mid-fifties, about half the books lent or read at Sheffield Public Library were novels, and as the decades passed it was accepted that the purpose of libraries was to provide entertainment as well as education.

Circulating and free libraries presented a threat to ordinary publishing which was countered by the issue of novels in monthly parts, and by the publication of still cheaper editions. The immense success of *Pickwick Papers* in monthly parts was the signal for much popular fiction to appear first in this form, sometimes simultaneously with publication in the new magazines that appeared at the end of the fifties. The first issue of the *Cornhill,* which included an installment of Trollope's *Framley Parsonage* and Thackeray's *Roundabout Papers,* sold 120,000 copies. Cheap editions flourished, too, encouraged greatly by the spread of rail travel, and the length of the journeys. Every station of any size had its bookstall, and "railway novels," most of them yellowbacks with a picture on the front and advertisements at the back, were immensely successful. They sold at a shilling or one and sixpence, which may not seem cheap in comparison with modern paperbacks, but was within the price range of those who traveled by rail and ignored the free library.

This, then, was what Collins called the Unknown Public: a new generation of readers possessing some literacy and some leisure, and with a vague but pressing need to read books for amusement which would in some degree confirm the permanence of their own newly won position in society. There were plenty of books in the railway library or the free libraries that were written from a social attitude with which they agreed, but not many that expressed the concern they felt about the importance of law and order, their interest in the prevention and punishment of crime.

THE DEVELOPMENT OF THE POLICE AND DETECTIVES

There is a common impression that the Victorian age in Britain was one of settled calm, but that is not the way the early part of it looked to those who lived through it. It was not merely that they felt themselves threatened politically by the Chartist movement, but that the country was in fact a lawless place. It is said that 11,000 murders were committed in Britain every year during the early part of the century, and although this figure is conjectural it remains appallingly high even if it is halved. Certain areas of London, as of New York and other big cities, were practically immune from visits by the police, and the detection of crime was in the hands of the Bow Street Runners, who were in effect private detectives operating partly for private reward, and widely thought to be susceptible to bribery. Even when a professional paid police force came into existence after the Metropolitan Police Act of 1829, the Bow Street Runners survived for another ten years. They were replaced in 1842 by the Detective Department, which consisted of two Inspectors and six sergeants. The first head of the Department had distinguished himself two years before its foundation by what was then an unusual piece of detective work, when he noticed that apparent marks of forcible entry into a house had been faked, and that what appeared to be an "outside" crime was really an "inside" one.

It is impossible to understand the romantic aura which spread around detective departments and bureaus without realizing the thankfulness felt by the middle class at their existence. As they grew, the second strand in crime writing, represented by Godwin, Lytton, and Balzac, in which the criminal was often considered romantic and the policeman stupid or corrupt, almost disappeared, although it could still be found in the penny dreadful. The detective, as the protector of established society, gradually replaced the criminal-hero.

In this capacity, he was celebrated by Charles Dickens (1812–1870), whose articles about various figures of the Detective Department in *Household Words* were often expressed in terms of hero worship. Dickens's ambivalent fascination with crime led him to go on occasional expeditions with the police, not only in London but in Liverpool and New York. The articles that he wrote himself, and others that he sponsored, in *Household Words* played a considerable part in forming the public view of detectives and changing the hostile or critical working-class attitude toward the police. The hostility was based on two grounds: first that the police might be used as the state's arm to suppress reform movements, and second that they were inefficient. When a policeman was stabbed to death while helping to disperse a crowd at a political meeting in the eighteen-thirties, the jury brought in a verdict of "justifiable homicide." The efficiency in the early days of this collection of out-of-work tradesmen and unskilled laborers may be judged from the fact that in the first eight years of the Metropolitan Police Force's existence 5,000 men were dismissed and another 6,000 resigned. But by Dickens's time these growing pains were almost over, and he praised the imperturbability of the men in blue, although his greatest admiration was reserved for detectives. They were, he found, men of good deportment and unusual intelligence, never lounging or slinking about, showing signs of "strong mental excitement," and (a common, although unreliable, test of honesty) "they all can, and they all do, look full at whomsoever they speak to." Dickens's particular hero was Inspector Field. When he entered a thieves' den, "every thief here comes before him, like a schoolboy before his schoolmaster." His eye was keen and roving; he saw everything; he appeared to know everybody and to have access everywhere in criminal society. In the keenness and sagacity of Field (or Wield, as he appeared in other articles), and in his tricks of behavior like "the corpulent forefinger, which is constantly in juxtaposition with his eyes or nose," we can see the outline of the professional detective of fiction, the bloodhound counterpart to Poe's aristocratic amateur. It is fitting that Dickens should have created the first English fictional detective, natural that he should have been made in Field's image.

"Inspector Bucket of the Detective," as he calls himself, makes his appearance about a third of the way through *Bleak House* (1853), in a manner appropriately unobtrusive, and indeed almost magical. Snagsby the stationer is talking to the lawyer Mr. Tulkinghorn when he is aware of a third person in the room, who

was not there when he himself came in, and has not since entered by the door or by either of the windows. There is a press in the room, but its hinges have not creaked, nor has a step been audible upon the floor.

Bucket has several physical resemblances to Field, including his use of a fat forefinger for making points. Like Field, he is on familiar terms with lawbreakers, has an encyclopedic knowledge of their habits, and is greatly respected by them. He is able to disguise himself when necessary, an attribute probably derived from Vidocq. He is not at home among the upper classes, as is shown by his invariably addressing Sir Leicester Dedlock as "Sir Leicester Dedlock, Baronet," but his plodding assurance is untouched by Sir Leicester's supercilious attitude. He is sympathetic to the poor, and capable of genially offering to fit a second pair of handcuffs onto an arrested man's wrists in case the first pair is uncomfortable. Bucket engages in no spectacular feats of detection, but he is shown as a shrewd and sympathetic man. In a general way, he serves as a model for many later professional detectives.

Dickens's unfinished last novel, *The Mystery of Edwin Drood,* is sometimes classed as a mystery or detective story. It was left unfinished at a peculiarly tantalizing point, when Drood has disappeared, and the movements of the sinister John Jasper are being watched by several people, among them the obviously disguised Datchery. Had the book been finished, these puzzles would of course have been resolved, and fascinating though they are in themselves they do not mean that the novel was intended to be, or would have appeared when completed as, a mystery story. An immense amount of ingenuity has been expended in solving these fortuitous puzzles, and the clues left by Dickens (who did not, one should perhaps stress, intend them as clues) and his illustrators can be interpreted in several ways. On the balance of probabilities, Mr. J. Cuming Walters is reasonable in suggesting that Datchery was Helena Landless in disguise and that Jasper had killed Edwin, or at least believed that he had killed him, although I would have a small saving bet on the possibility suggested by Mr. Michael Innes that Datchery may have been somebody who had not previously entered the story, but was closely connected with one of the leading characters. But these are mysteries related to Dickens's intentions, and probably the completed book would have been a mysterious thriller rather than a detective story, resembling *The Woman in White* rather than *The Moonstone*.

It is by these two books that Dickens's close friend Wilkie Collins (1824–1889) is remembered today. Collins is generally regarded, as he was in his lifetime, as a writer whose merits lie purely in the field of melodrama. "Mr. Collins is in the habit of prefixing prefaces to his stories which might almost lead one to think he looks on himself as an artist," the *Pall Mall Gazette* said contemptuously in reviewing *The Moonstone*. "A conjurer at a county fair has as much right to prate about his art. . . . Is this, then, what fiction has come to? We scarcely see how anything could be meaner." Yet, as T. S. Eliot has pointed out, in Collins's time "the best novels *were* thrilling," and neither Collins himself nor his readers thought of him as writing down to them. In the preface to his second novel, *Basil,* Collins stated a creed from which he never wavered when he said that "the business of fiction is to exhibit human life" and that it was permissible to depict "misery and crime" if they were turned to "a plainly and purely moral purpose." In several of his novels, the moral purpose is only too evident, like the story of a prostitute's reformation in *The New Magdalen* or the attack on the laws of legitimacy that runs through *No Name.* But the intentions of Collins were no less serious than those of Dickens. Both of them pursued, and indeed captured, the Unknown Public, and although Collins was not a genius like his friend, he was a melodramatic writer of the highest class, and was perhaps the most skillful plot constructor of the century.

His first novel which shows any detective element is *Hide and Seek* (1854), in which, as one critic has said, he borrowed Fenimore Cooper's Leatherstocking, had him scalped by Indians, and set him down in London. The element of detection in the story, which relates to the unraveling of the history of an orphan and her mother, is real but slight. Some of the stories in the two collections *After Dark* (1856) and *The Queen of Hearts* (1859) also have a small claim to consideration. "A Stolen Letter," in the first collection, follows Poe's device in "The Purloined Letter" so closely that it can almost be called a crib, and in the second, "Anne Rodway" is a murder story with an unusually convincing low-life background and "The Biter Bit" a comic detective story about a lawyer's clerk who has been accepted as a recruit for the "Detective Police" and makes an appalling mess of his first and only case. Collins was particularly good at depicting bumptiously self-important characters, and this is one of the few successful comic detective short stories.

The Woman in White (1860) is the liveliest of Collins's crime stories, and the one most full of memorable characters. Upon the basis of an eighteenth-century French case, in which a woman was drugged and imprisoned so that she should be presumed dead and her estate pass to her brother, was built the idea of the substitution of one person for another, effected with the aid of a private asylum. In the interesting article Collins wrote a couple of years before his death about the book's construction, he discussed in detail the development from this original germ, the invention of the Italian Fosco because the crime was too ingenious for an English villain, the obesity which Fosco was given after the story had been begun because this was "in opposition to the recognised type of villain" (in Victorian days, fat men were jolly though sometimes unctuous; for us, to be overweight is in itself sinister), the various false starts and the ingenious shifts of viewpoint by which interest is maintained. But analysis of this kind does not fully account for the quality of the book. Marian Halcombe, almost the only mustached heroine in English fiction, and Fosco come through more clearly than any other Collins characters, and they do so because something about Marian's indomitable determination and about Fosco's fat charm struck a chord of romantic feeling in their author. This mild, genial little man, whose feet were so tiny that they were too small for women's shoes, had an obsession with physical deformity that is often ludicrous or disagreeable but is urbanely comic in the picture of Fosco's monstrous fatness. The feeling was accompanied by a penchant for dominating ladies seen at its most pleasant in Marian. Beyond this, the book has a high-spirited inventiveness that was uncommon even in Victorian fiction. The turns of the plot are always ingenious and often unexpected, and it is not surprising that Collins chose as a summary of his career on his tombstone: "Author of *The Woman in White* and other works of fiction."

From the beginning, the book was a great success. In England Dickens's *All the Year Round* and in America *Harper's Magazine* began to carry it on the same date, November 29, 1859. On publication day, the London crowds queued outside the magazine offices for it. Cloaks, bonnets and perfumes, waltzes and quadrilles were called by its name. Gladstone canceled a theatre engagement to go on reading it, and Prince Albert sent a copy to Baron Stockmar. The book established Collins, in the minds of some readers, as a rival to Dickens. It is possible that some feeling of this kind was in Dickens's own mind, for although he published the book as a serial, he animadverted on it with unusual sharpness in a letter, saying that "the construction is wearisome beyond endurance, and there is a vein of obstinate conceit in it that makes enemies of readers." In spite of a cool critical reception, the first edition of 1,500 copies (in the expensive three-volume form, it should be remembered) was quickly sold.

Judged purely as a novel of event and character, *The Moonstone* (1868) is not as good a book as *The Woman in White*. There are no characters in it equal to Fosco or Marian, and although Drusilla Clack, the spinster with her religious tracts, is a distinct comic figure, many readers have felt that they have had enough of her after a few pages. If we look at the originality of the conception, however, and at the skill shown in ordering the plot, *The Moonstone* is a masterly performance, a feat all the more memorable

because shortly after beginning the book Collins was distressed
by the illness and death of his mother, and during much of the
later writing he was tortured by rheumatic gout so intense that
several young men employed to take down from his dictation
found his cries of pain unendurable and had to leave. Nothing of
this comes through in a narrative told with an assurance, and a
skill in varying style and tempo, equal to anything in Victorian
literature.

But of course *The Moonstone* is not judged now primarily by
these lights, but as the first detective novel written in English.
Originality of this kind is something that doesn't last. As Dorothy
Sayers has said in writing about the book, "When we have grown
familiar with its successors and imitators the original classic no
longer appears to us to have anything original about it." This
is not, however, quite true of *The Moonstone*. Collins's mind was so
ingenious, and his skill in maintaining the deception about the
jewel so great, that a reader who has been brought up on modern
detective stories and then comes to the book is not likely to feel
that here is a period piece that was no doubt very good in its
day, but rather that he is reading one of the few crime stories that
combine great ingenuity in devising a puzzle with the ability to
tell an absorbingly interesting story. The solution to the puzzle
is perfectly fair, although its laudanum inspiration may now seem
a little unsophisticated, and as Sayers has said, the foundation
for everything that happens later is laid in the first few chapters.
The shifting of suspicion from one character to another is done
with great adroitness, and the theft of an immensely valuable
diamond, with its implied contrast between the mysterious East
and the humdrum reality of Victorian life, gives full play to
Collins's subdued romanticism. And as a corrective to this, bringing what Collins sometimes called a breath of the Actual, there is
Sergeant Cuff.

Cuff was founded upon Inspector Jonathan Whicher of the Detective Department, who appears in his days as a sergeant as
"Witchem" in a *Household Words* article. Whicher's career at the
time Collins wrote had been a checkered one. In 1860, he had
arrested Constance Kent on a charge of murdering her small

brother Francis, and had suffered a blot on his reputation at her acquittal which was not quite wiped away when she confessed five years later. In 1861, he had been responsible in another murder case for the arrest of a man who was undoubtedly innocent. It is likely that the skills of Whicher, who was known before these calamities as "the Prince of Detectives," were, like those of Field, much exaggerated, but Collins may have had in mind his rehabilitation. He used several details from the Constance Kent case, and some of Cuff's deductions resemble those of Whicher, although there was no physical resemblance. Whicher was short, thickset, pockmarked. Collins's portrait of Cuff, as described by the house steward Gabriel Betteredge, shows what a splendid eye he had for externals:

A fly from the railway drove up as I reached the lodge; and out got a grizzled elderly man so lean that he looked as if he had not got an ounce of flesh on his bones in any part of him. He was dressed all in decent black, with a white cravat round his neck. His face was as sharp as a hatchet, and the skin of it was as yellow and dry and withered as an autumn leaf. His eyes, of a steely light grey, had a very disconcerting trick, when they encountered your eyes, of looking as if they expected something more from you than you were aware of yourself. His walk was soft; his voice was melancholy; his long lanky fingers were hooked like claws. He might have been a parson, or an undertaker—or anything else you like, except what he really was.

Cuff is, like many later detectives, a master of the apparently irrelevant remark, the unexpected observation. Faced with a problem and asked what is to be done, he trims his nails with a penknife and suggests a turn in the garden and a look at the roses; asked who has stolen the moonstone, he says blandly that nobody has stolen it. The fascination of such remarks is that their meaning just eludes us. By making the proper deductions, we feel, rightly, that we should be able to grasp it.

"The first, the longest and the best of modern English detective novels": that was Eliot's description of *The Moonstone,* but its description as "the first" should certainly be corrected. There is no doubt that the first detective novel, preceding Collins and Gaboriau, was *The Notting Hill Mystery*. This was published in book form in 1865, three years before *The Moonstone,* but it first appeared in the magazine *Once a Week,* where publication began in November, 1862, and continued well into the following year. Its primacy is thus unquestionable. So far as I know, the book remains unmentioned by any historian, although it was reprinted just after World War II in a collection of Victorian detective stories made by Maurice Richardson. The original magazine publication was anonymous, but authorship of the book is credited to Charles Felix. The name sounds like a pseudonym, but I have been able to discover nothing more about him than the fact that he wrote at least one other book, *Velvet Lawns,* which is not a detective story.

The Notting Hill Mystery is in several ways an original work. It includes a map, a practice which was not to become common for a good many years, as well as facsimiles of a marriage certificate and of a fragment torn from a letter. The plot is in some ways strikingly modern in tone. The story is told in letters and reports sent to his employers by Ralph Henderson, investigator for a life-assurance company. Their suspicions have been aroused after the death of Madame R, by the fact that her husband, the Baron R, has taken out not one but five policies on her life, each in the sum of £5,000. Antimony is suspected as the cause of her death, but the Baron is able to prove that he never himself gave her food or drink. Henderson discovers that the "Baron" is really a German named Carl Schwartz, and that he possesses mesmeric powers. His conclusion is that the Baron employed these powers to induce his wife to take the antimony herself, but this is something that he is unable to prove. The book ends with the problem unresolved, and Henderson asking his employers what, if anything, can be done about a murder committed in this way. The story is interesting in itself, and the level of the writing is far above current hack work, although equally far below that of Collins. But the essential point is that *The Notting Hill Mystery* is a true detective novel, and the first of its kind.

This bow to the ghost of Charles Felix should not reduce appreciation of Collins. The combination of his particular gifts is rare. Perhaps if Somerset Maugham had written a detective story, instead of a spy story, and if he had been at the top of his form, the result might have been something like *The Moonstone*. Collins himself, in the two decades left to him, never wrote anything approaching in merit his two finest books, although historians of the detective story have surprisingly neglected *The Law and the Lady* (1875). The plot here owes something to the Scottish trial of Madeleine Smith, with its "Not Proven" verdict. Eustace Macallan, like Madeleine, is tried for poisoning by arsenic, and set free by a similar unsatisfactory verdict, and the story is concerned with the efforts of his second wife, Valeria, one of Collins's determined heroines, to prove him innocent. There is a genuine puzzle to be solved, and some parts of the book are excellent, particularly the long account of Eustace's trial. The quality of the writing, however, is very uneven, and the book is marred by one of his more unsuccessful grotesques, the self-styled poet Miserimus Dexter, a sort of legless Quilp.

Collins admired and kept upon his shelves the crime stories of Emile Gaboriau (1833–1873), and *The Moonstone* may have been influenced by the French writer's first three crime stories, *L'Affaire Lerouge* (1863), *Le Crime d'Orcival,* and *Le Dossier No. 113* (1867)—the dates given are those of the original serial publications in which Collins may have seen them, although *L'Affaire Lerouge* first appeared in book form in 1866. Gaboriau was a hack writer of historical and sensational serials whose work was transformed by his discovery of the possibilities of the detective story. This son of a country notary made a sidelong entry into literature when he became secretary to Paul Féval, who was himself a writer of many criminal romances which used occasionally the apparatus of detection, often borrowed from other writers like Dumas or Fenimore Cooper. In France, dislike of the police was stronger than it was in Britain, partly because they were unquestionably a repressive force used in the service of the state, and partly because of the corruption associated with the rule of Vidocq. Féval did not think of making a policeman his hero; and even in *Les Misérables* the ex-convict Jean Valjean is the hero and the policeman Javert is important, as Murch has pointed out, only as "the pursuing Nemesis that threatens to overtake him."

Gaboriau, like Dickens and Collins, was fascinated by police work and knew a great deal not only about the operations of the Sûreté but about the functions of the interrogating judge and the local policeman. A passage in his finest work, the posthumously published long short story, *Le Petit Vieux de Batignolles,* shows that he was aware of the difficulty involved in making his hero a policeman. The narrator, an amateur detective on his first case, accompanies a professional named Méchinet into the Prefecture:

This was the first time in my life that I crossed the threshold of the Prefecture of Police, against which I had hitherto been quite as prejudiced as any other Parisian. Those who study social questions may well ask how it happens that the French police are so generally hated and despised. Even the ordinary street policeman is the object of aversion; and the detective is loathed as intensely as if he were some monstrous horror, in lieu of generally being a most useful servant of society.

It was, then, a daring stroke to create a policeman hero, and Gaboriau sugared the pill by providing an amateur detective who often keeps him company. In *L'Affaire Lerouge,* Gévrol, chief of the Sûreté, is quickly replaced as the chief investigator by an elderly retired pawnbroker named Père Tabaret, known as "Tir-au-clair." It is Tabaret who makes the brilliant deductions by which the crime is solved, explaining them as he goes along to a young policeman named Lecoq, first introduced as a minor character, "an old offender reconciled with the law." But although Père Tabaret does not disappear completely—at the end of *Monsieur Lecoq* (1869) he points out to the professional detective the clues he has missed—he moves into the background and Lecoq becomes the central figure, with Gévrol as his butt and sometimes with a companion of inferior intelligence as his assistant. Gaboriau makes it clear that his hero was nothing like the hated detective of reality. "The most obtuse shopkeeper is sure that he can scent a detective at twenty paces; a big man with moustaches, and a shining felt hat, dressed in a black, threadbare surtout, carefully buttoned up on account of the absence of linen. Such is the type." Lecoq is nothing like that. His face is so mobile that he is able to "mould his features according to his will, as the sculptor moulds clay for modelling." He is a master of disguise, who on one occasion bitterly reproaches an agent for the inadequacy of his attempt to change his appearance. Unlike Cuff, Bucket, or Dupin, he has a distinct eye on the main chance. When as a young detective he writes a report which by implication criticizes the inefficiency of Gévrol and does not sign his name to it, Gaboriau explains that the reason is not modesty but calculation, because "by hiding one's self on well-chosen occasions, one gains greater notoriety when one emerges from the shadow."

Lecoq is self-seeking and vain, but he is also honest—it is explained in a later story that the original mention of him as "an old offender" was the result of a misunderstanding. He has reason to be vain, for his deductive feats are notable. He is the first detective of fiction to make a plaster cast of footprints, improvising for the purpose some old boxes, an earthen dish, plaster which he knocks off a wall, and water. He is the first also to observe that a striking clock may be used to tell the time a crime was committed, when he pushes the long hand of a clock round to half past three and it strikes eleven. He realizes in *Le Crime d'Orcival* that the criminal has deliberately planted the material clues, so that "I had only, to reach the truth, to take the contrary of that which appearance had indicated." Since five glasses were on the table, the number of people present was "more or less than five, but they were not five," and since the remains of supper lay on the table, they neither ate nor drank. He is able to tell his assistant that a man they are following is "of middle age and tall, wore a shaggy brown overcoat, and was probably married, as he had a wedding ring on the little finger of his right hand." The points are explained: his "heavy and dragging step" shown in convenient snow marked middle age, his height was marked by a block of granite on which he had leaned, the ring appeared through the imprint of his hand in snow, the color of his coat was indicated by a few flakes of brown wool torn off by a wood splinter. Dupin might at this point have sat back and solved the case, but Lecoq is not an armchair detective. "We hold the clue; we will follow it to the end. Onward, then," he cries.

Gaboriau's highly sensational themes often contrast oddly with the sobriety of his detection. The murder has usually been committed to prevent the revelation of a scandal, and passages of detection are interspersed with long explanatory flashbacks about family history. Sometimes the villain turns out to be an aristocrat. In *Monsieur Lecoq,* the detective in disguise pursues the murderer on an immense tour of Paris. He conducts a search of a grand mansion but goes away baffled, unable to believe that the nobleman who receives him with weary courtesy is the man he wants. Much of this is tiresome today, but there are compensations other than the passages of detection, in the accurate and interesting accounts of aspects of the French legal system, and the battles of wits in the dialogues between examining magistrate and accused, from which Simenon probably learned something. And in *Monsieur Lecoq,* the best of the novels, Lecoq plays a fascinating game of cat-and-mouse with the prisoner, which ends with his realization that somehow he has been betrayed and that the mouse knows exactly what the cat is doing. This is the best of the novels: but *Le Petit Vieux de Batignolles* is undoubtedly his finest piece of work, a story full of tricks and turns, in which the murderer overreaches himself by thinking that the police are certain to discover that his victim is left-handed. They fail to do so, and arrest the right man on a completely false basis of argument. Gaboriau lacked humor, and skill in characterization, but it is going much too far to talk as one critic has done of his tawdry puppetry, dull and irrelevant digressions, and dreary and artificial verbiage. He remains an interesting and still underrated writer, whose crime stories are rooted in sound knowledge of police procedure and marked by a keen analytical intelligence.

Collins and Gaboriau: after Poe, they set the pattern in which detectives were made. Poe created the aristocratic amateur who was to endure, and upon the whole to be supreme, until the Second World War. Collins and Gaboriau gave us the honest professional, often disdained by the amateur, who, as Auden says in relation to Freeman Wills Crofts's Inspector French, "detects for the sake of the innocent members of society" and succeeds because he has "the help of all the innocent people in the world who are doing their duty." After Collins and Gaboriau, the professional detective, whether uniformed or in plain clothes, no longer appears in fiction as the corrupt oppressor, but as the protector of the innocent. The detective's changed character in fiction reflected a change in the nature of society, and his standing as a watchdog against evil was not to be seriously questioned for sixty years, in the work of Dashiell Hammett and Raymond Chandler.

IV

Interregnum

The decade in which Wilkie Collins was producing his two best books, and in which Gaboriau was creating what was later called the *roman policier,* although his crime stories were first collected together under the title *romans judiciaires,* contained some notable crime novels by a writer of still unacknowledged talent, and one of the world's greatest novels, which had its origins in a crime. The notable stories were the work of Joseph Sheridan Le Fanu (1814–1873) and the great novel was Fyodor Dostoevsky's *Crime and Punishment.*

A few years ago, I included *Crime and Punishment* in one of those "Hundred Best" compilations already mentioned, claiming that a crime and its effects were at the heart of the story. The phrase is accurate, and so is the further comment that Dostoevsky (1821–1881) saw more deeply than any other novelist has done into the springs of violence, but I now feel less sure that the book should have been included. Dostoevsky moved naturally toward mystery and sensation, both here, in *The Possessed,* and even in *The Brothers Karamazov,* but they were for him only the means through which he expressed concerns far outside the interest of the crime novelist. At his best, the crime writer can illuminate the condition of society and interpret psychotic states of mind, but he never moves like Dostoevsky in mystical regions where spiritual truths are being considered. There are no spiritual implications to be found in Fosco's villainy, but for Dostoevsky the murder committed by Raskolnikov and the wonderful interrogation he suffers at the hands of Porfiry are no more than steps on the road to redemption through guilt. So, just as Kafka will not be considered here at all, Dostoevsky will not be considered in detail. Is this in itself a denial of what has already been asserted, that, contrary to Auden, the crime story may have the character of art? No: but it does imply that even the best crime story is still a work of art of a peculiar flawed kind, since an appetite for violence and a pleasure in employing a conjurer's sleight of hand seem somehow always to be adulterating the finer skills of a novelist. In a way, Dostoevsky *was* a crime novelist, with the true taste for sensational material, but in his single case the results far transcend those that the crime novelist achieves or even aims at.

Obviously, such considerations do not apply to Le Fanu. This Irish novelist and short-story writer has never been popular, either in his own day or in ours, although some of his stories appear occasionally in magazines and his best-known novel, *Uncle Silas,* has been reprinted more than once. He has had no discernible influence on other writers. Yet in the last decade of his life he produced a dozen novels mostly concerned with crime, of which four are worth remembering and at least one is a brilliant mystery puzzle.

First one should make some qualifications. In one aspect, Le Fanu was a romantic writer in the Gothic mode, writing half a century after the Gothic novel had faded. His books are full of old houses and castles falling into ruin; his heroines are often at the mercy of implacable and horrifying villains; he took great pleasure in ghost stories and was fascinated by hints of the supernatural. He was also the most notable Victorian example of a writer who seems not to have revised his original manuscripts, and certainly did not read his proofs, so that a character in his novels may appear with varying Christian names, and there are casual unexplained shifts between first- and third-person narrative. Le Fanu's merits are not so great that one forgets these things, but he was a writer of remarkable power in creating suspense, at his best a master of plot, and the creator of some of the most satisfying villains in Victorian literature. *Uncle Silas* (1864) is a thriller comparable to *The Woman in White,* but where Collins's literary manner was as genial as his personality, Le Fanu's is effectively chilly. His titular villain is memorable, with his marble face, black eyebrows, and silver hair as fine as silk, "like an apparition in black and white, bloodless, fiery-eyed, with [a] singular look of power, and an expression so bewildering—was it derision, or anguish, or cruelty, or patience?" And Madame de la Rougierre, who calls herself "Madame la Morgue—Mrs. Deadhouse," is an equally expressive figure. C. P. Snow has written that her discovery "with her feet in a mustard bath is the most terrifying reappearance of any heroine at any time," although it is stretching things to call her a heroine. *The House by the Churchyard* (1863) is in part a rambling Irish historical chronicle, full of thumping humor, but the parts about Dangerfield and his determination to dispose of anybody who knows about his criminal past are on another and higher level. The trepanning through which one of his victims dies is, as Sayers had said, one of the most horrific scenes in this kind of literature. But the book referred to as a brilliant mystery puzzle, *Wylder's Hand* (1864), is Le Fanu's chief contribution in the field of detection. It cannot compete with *The Notting Hill Mystery* for the title of the first detective novel in English, since there is no detective and no analysis of clues, but it poses a puzzle entirely in the manner of the detective story, and the solution of this puzzle is expertly disguised. The puzzle relates to the disappearance of the vulgar, tough, dissipated Mark Wylder, who goes first to London and then abroad. From various European cities, he sends home characteristically rude and aggressive letters, and we have been prepared for his departure by a threat from the villainous Captain Stanley Lake that if necessary he will force Wylder to go abroad. At some point in the course of the story, however, the reader is bound to suspect that Wylder is dead, although the evidence of the letters is so elaborate and convincing that he cannot be sure. (Had Hammett read *Wylder's Hand?* He certainly made use of a similar device in a similar way

in *The Thin Man.*) Le Fanu's supreme stroke is to show the reappearance of Wylder just at the moment when we have decided
that he must be dead. The book contains two impressive and well-
contrasted villains, the yellow-eyed sleepy menacing Lake and
the snake-like servile solicitor Larkin. It is too long, but it remains
a crime story markedly original for its period, and astonishingly
ignored. *Checkmate* (1871) is a much weaker story, although it
gives us another good villain in Walter Longcluse, and introduces
the theme of plastic surgery, used as a device to escape the law.
The operation is described in detail, with Le Fanu's characteristic
cold gusto in dealing with such matters.

All this should have been enough to establish Le Fanu as one
of the most important originators of the crime novel, but in this
respect he has never received acknowledgment. His short stories
are from the point of this study less interesting, since they are
mostly supernatural shockers. One or two, however, like "Mr.
Justice Harbottle" and "Green Tea" explore the possibilities of psychotic disorder in an interesting way. Is the monkey that perse-
cutes the pious clergyman Jennings in "Green Tea" of supernatural
origin, or is it a mental delusion? The question is left open.

With these exceptions, there was an interregnum between the
time when the detective novel proper appeared and the publication
in 1887 of *A Study in Scarlet*. The explanation is simple. The
history of the crime story up to the end of the nineteenth century
is linked chiefly with the few writers of talent who were interested
in police work, and the form itself was not yet sufficiently attractive to the public or sufficiently well-defined to receive much
attention from hacks. There was a division still between those
who in England read penny dreadfuls and in America the dime
novels, and the readers of novels that were expected to offer something a little more serious.

A few names should be recorded. Major Arthur Griffiths, an
Inspector of Prisons and the author of a standard three-volume
work on *Mysteries of Police and Crime,* wrote a good many crime
stories and historical romances, but although a few like *Fast and
Loose* (1885) and *Locked Up* (1887) include detectives of
sorts, the books are fifth-rate thrillers redeemed only by the

writer's knowledge of criminal habits. Fergus Hume's *Mystery of a Hansom Cab* (1886) is a curiosity because of the enormous sale it inexplicably achieved. Writing in 1896, Hume (1859–1932) claimed that the book had sold 375,000 copies in Britain alone, apart from "some few editions in the United States of America." When it was published, Hume was a New Zealand barrister in his middle twenties, and there is no reason to doubt the essential truth of his story that the book was rejected by publishers in Australia, on the ground that "no Colonial could write anything worth reading," that he then published it in that country at his own expense with some success, and that he sold the copyright for £50 to a group of speculators calling themselves the Hansom Cab Publishing Company, who reaped the benefit of his work. At least this account has never been seriously contradicted. His description of the way in which the idea for the book was generated is interesting, because it shows how widespread was the influence of Gaboriau:

> I enquired of a leading Melbourne bookseller what style of book he sold most of. He replied that the detective stories of Gaboriau had a large sale; and as, at this time, I had never even heard of this author, I bought all his works and . . . determined to write a book of the same class; containing a mystery, a murder, and a description of low life in Melbourne. This was the origin of the "Cab."

It is customary to say that the book is without any kind of merit, but in fact *The Mystery of a Hansom Cab* is a reasonably good imitation of Gaboriau, containing some fairly convincing scenes of low life. Was its success attributable to the fact that the murder took place in a hansom cab? Perhaps the setting had something to do with it. Hume wrote more than a hundred other detective stories and thrillers, none of which had any comparable success, although they earned him a comfortable enough living.

Gaboriau remained consistently popular for a long time after his death, and his chief French disciple Fortuné du Boisgobey (1824–1891) paid the dead master the dubious compliment of taking over his most famous character. *La Vieillesse de Monsieur Lecoq* (1875) finds the detective calling himself in old age Lecoq de Gentilly, adding a "de" to his name "in view of pushing his son, whom he wished to take rank among a class of people who do not disdain the appearance of nobility." The son, Louis, is accused of murder and about to be guillotined when Lecoq runs down the real murderer. The detective work is shaky, as might be expected from a man in his old age. Although du Boisgobey's name was coupled with that of Gaboriau, and although the London *Times* praised his facility in creating incidents and unraveling plots, he is almost purely a sensational writer, lacking the analytical skill and the interest in police procedure that distinguished his master.

In America, Anna Katharine Green (1846–1935) became the first woman to write a detective novel. *The Leavenworth Case* (1878) was immensely successful, perhaps partly because of her sex, partly because of the familiarity she showed with legal and criminal matters (her father was a criminal lawyer), and partly—one is bound to think—because there were so few detective novels being written. The drearily sentimental story shifts suspicion from one lovely Leavenworth sister to another after Mr. Leavenworth has been murdered, and there are passages of pious moralizing which are pulled through only with the most dogged persistence. (The book was the favorite detective story of Prime Minister Stanley Baldwin, a fact tending to confirm one's gloomy view of politicians' literary taste.) Some compensation is offered by a lively detective named Ebenezer Gryce, in the Bucket and Cuff workingman style. He is a city detective who could never, it is frankly said, pass for a gentleman. "It is not for me to suspect but to detect," Gryce says on an early page, and he does quite a bit of detection, although his deduction when he sees a line of smut on the cylinder of a gun after the barrel had been cleaned seems rather dubious. Gryce knew then, he says, that no woman had committed the murder. "Did you ever know a woman who cleaned a pistol, or who knew the object or use of doing so? No. They can fire them and do; but after firing them they do not clean them." There are one or two other interesting things in the book, like the use of mirror writing, and the detailed medical evidence, but as a story it is extremely feeble.

Green wrote many other detective stories, including some in which Gryce is a prominent character, but those I have read are on the level of *The Leavenworth Case*.

Samuel Langhorne Clemens (1835–1910), better known as Mark Twain, had less relationship to the detective story than some of his American admirers have claimed. Twain did, however, show considerable interest in the mechanics of detection. As Ellery Queen has pointed out, *Life on the Mississippi* (1883) contains a chapter about fingerprints as a means of identification, and in *Pudd'nhead Wilson* (1894) fingerprint identification is the turning point of the plot. Pudd'nhead explains in court the unique nature of the patterns, "such as arches, circles, long curves, whorls." Twain was unique among writers in appreciating the importance of fingerprints at a time when Galton's *Fingerprints* had only recently been published, and long before they were used by the police in America. *A Double-Barrelled Detective Story* (1902), Twain's last essay in detection, is a feebly humorous slap at the omniscience of Sherlock Holmes.

It seems surprising in retrospect that Robert Louis Stevenson (1850–1894) made no serious attempt to write a detective story. Stevenson preferred an episodic tale to one with a tightly constructed plot, and he had no taste for the details of police work, but the creation of a mysterious atmosphere came naturally to him, and he was interested in the borderland where adventure turned into crime. But although Stevenson hovered on the brink in some books that he wrote with his stepson Lloyd Osbourne, he never took the plunge. *The Wrong Box* (1888), with its dead body turning up in all sorts of places, is in part a lively parody of some absurdities in French detection, and one of the characters has written a detective story with the excellent title *Who Put Back the Clock?*, but it is basically a farce. The loosely linked tales in the *New Arabian Nights* (1882)—in particular the Suicide Club, with its patterns of suicide and murder decided by the choice of a card, and the story opening with the scene praised by Henry James of the young man who enters "an Oyster Bar in the immediate neighbourhood of Leicester Square" accompanied by two commissionaires, each carrying a dish of cream tarts which

he presses upon the company—certainly qualify the book in the
category of thriller. *The Wrecker* is a blend of thriller and adventure story, and there are elements of mystery in stories as dis-
parate as *Treasure Island* and *The Dynamiters.* But Stevenson was
attracted by the romance of mystery, not the science of detection.
He put his feelings clearly in a note on *The Wrecker* rejecting the
"police novel or mystery story" because of that "appearance of
insincerity and shallowness of tone, which seems its inevitable
drawback," so that the result was "enthralling but insignificant,
like a game of chess, not a work of human art." This is a telling
comment on many detective stories, not merely those of Stevenson's time.

One has a sense, in these twenty years of mostly indifferent
work, of a literary form awaiting its proper medium. The form was
there, the tale of detection with its apparatus of clues. The central
character had arrived, too, the aristocratic or workaday detective who operated by the naphtha glare of pure reason or the
candlelight of common sense. In the last twenty years of the
nineteenth century, through the development of printing techniques and the rise in the level of education, the perfect medium
appeared: the popular periodical, selling at a low price and publishing plenty of fiction and non-fiction which, although always
light and mostly trivial, was conceived on a level above that of
the penny dreadful and the dime novel.

"I am the average man. I know what he wants," said George
Newnes, who in 1880 founded the weekly *Tit-Bits,* a penny paper
which offered more or less informative and lively fragments
gathered from other periodicals, books, and newspapers, together
with contributions from readers. The formula flourished, and
was copied or improved on in Alfred Harmsworth's *Answers* and
Cyril Pearson's *Pearson's Weekly.* In 1891, Newnes used some of
the *Tit-Bits* profits for a more ambitious publication, the *Strand
Magazine.* He modeled the periodical on the successful American
magazines *Harper's* and *Scribner's,* asking for a picture on every
page, and a supply of good exciting stories. The first issue appeared in January, 1891, and sold 300,000 copies. In July, the

first short story about Sherlock Holmes was published in the Strand. It was one in a series of six for which the editor, Greenhalgh Smith, paid Dr. A. C. Doyle of 2 Devonshire Place, London, W, thirty guineas each. Asked for a second series, Doyle raised his fee to fifty guineas. He was surprised when this figure was unquestioningly accepted.

As soon as the Holmes stories began to appear, editors, readers, and writers half-consciously realized that the detective story had found its natural place in popular literature. There was to be a crime or an attempted crime, a problem, a solution reached through the skill of the detective, and all this was to be compassed within some five thousand words. Public response was immediate. The Strand soon reached a circulation of 500,000, which was maintained for many years. In America, two of the leading periodicals of the time were Ladies' Home Journal, which had a circulation of nearly a million by the end of the century, and Munsey's Magazine with a circulation of 700,000. Neither of these greatly resembled the Strand, but both used Doyle stories, and so did McClure's (circulation of 370,000 in 1900), in which the author invested $5,000 made from an American lecture tour. After the immense success of the Holmes stories, other editors asked for something similar, and it was quickly supplied. In this first flowering of the detective story, it was seen as being essentially a short story, one which neither permitted nor demanded much in the way of characterization but allowed almost unbounded scope to ingenuity. Often an original talent like that shown by Doyle in the Holmes short stories may be submerged by the subtle grace notes of his successors, but this has not happened in the case of Sherlock Holmes. For nearly three decades, the short story remained the dominant form in crime fiction, and hundreds of complicated and clever short stories were written, but looking back on the ingenious twists and turns of Chesterton and Futrelle, Freeman and Orczy and Post, it is plain that in most of the important things the best stories about Sherlock Holmes excelled them all.

V

The Case of Sherlock Holmes

THE CHARACTER

In 1886, Arthur Conan Doyle, an unsuccessful doctor in his middle twenties living at Southsea in Hampshire, made some notes concerning an idea for a character rather than a story, even though the notes were headed "A Study in Scarlet." They began "Ormond Sacker—from Afghanistan" ("from Soudan" had been crossed out). "Lived at 221B Upper Baker Street with Sherrinford Holmes." A brief outline of Holmes's characteristics followed, and a couple of fragments of dialogue. With Ormond Sacker turned into Dr. John H. Watson and Sherrinford changed to Sherlock, the characters came into being. *A Study in Scarlet* was written, and rejected by several publishers before, in October, 1886, Ward, Lock offered Doyle £25 for the copyright, although they said that they "could not publish it this year as the market is flooded at present with cheap fiction." Doyle's financial position compelled him to accept this wretched offer. The story appeared in *Beeton's Christmas Annual* for 1887, and attracted little attention although it was reprinted in each of the succeeding years. In America, the editor of *Lippincott's Magazine* found it interesting, and Doyle was asked to meet a Lippincott representative paying a visit to London. As the result of a dinner at which Oscar Wilde was also present, both

Wilde and Doyle wrote books for the magazine. Wilde's book was *The Picture of Dorian Gray* and Doyle's was *The Sign of the Four* which appeared in *Lippincott's* in February, 1890. Later in the year, it was published in London as *The Sign of Four,* which has been since then the accepted title.

It cannot be said that either of Doyle's first two Holmes books is a very original or well-devised novel. It has been suggested that he took the basic plot of *A Study in Scarlet* from an episode in *The Dynamiter,* and in *The Sign of Four* the Indian subplot with its theme of a treasure which is cursed owes an obvious debt to *The Moonstone*. The use of these themes is an embarrassment to Doyle because they involve passages in which detection is suspended and Holmes does not appear. After the arrest of Jefferson Hope, not much more than halfway through *A Study in Scarlet,* we are concerned with a historical adventure story in Utah. *The Sign of Four* is better organized, but the tale of the treasure plays a disproportionately large part in what is after all a short novel. The prime defect of both books, indeed, is that they could have been condensed to short stories. Doyle did not think of these books in terms of novels—as Collins, for example, conceived *The Moonstone*—but as problems, each of which could have been worked out in the form of a short story.

But if the two novels, and indeed the two other long Holmes stories that Doyle wrote, cannot be counted as successes, Sherlock Holmes triumphs as a character from the moment we meet him. In appearance, in manner, and in the style of his deductions, he was based on the consulting surgeon at the Edinburgh Infirmary, Dr. Joseph Bell, but although Bell was the model, Holmes was the product of Doyle's own invention. In a sense, Doyle was Sherlock Holmes (he showed his own skill in the analysis of more than one real-life murder case), as one need only look at a photograph to see that he contained elements of Watson.

In his emotional reactions, Doyle was a super-typical Victorian, a bluff Imperialist extrovert who congratulated himself on having "the strongest influence over young men, especially young athletic sporting men, of any one in England (bar Kipling)," and therefore felt it a duty to volunteer for the South African War. Twenty years later, he condemned the "liquid putrescence" of the Russian Revolution and said that Post-Impressionism and Futurism were part of "a wave of artistic and intellectual insanity" sweeping across Europe. Yet Doyle was also a man of generous impulses, even when they ran counter to his own beliefs. He drew up the petition for Roger Casement's reprieve, and did not flinch when he was shown the *Black Diaries,* remarking with his characteristic common sense that "as no possible sexual offence could be as bad as suborning soldiers from their duty, I was not diverted from my purpose" by the apparent revelation of Casement's homosexuality. It seems at first sight astonishing that this Victorian philistine should have created an egocentric drug-taking hero so alien from his own beliefs. The answer to this puzzle has already been suggested. The passion for absolutes of belief and behavior, the desire to wipe the slate clean of error and impurity through some saving supernatural grace, shows constantly in Victorian life below the surface of stolid adherence to established order. The influence of Nietzsche and Wagner was widespread, and affected even those who thought, like Doyle, that Nietzsche's philosophy was "openly founded in lunacy," affected indeed those who had never heard of Nietzsche. Part of Holmes's attraction was that, far more than any of his later rivals, he was so evidently a Nietzschean superior man. It was comforting to have such a man on one's side.

So much for the background. The character of the greatest of Great Detectives—the man who, although not infallible, is never seen to fail—was in accordance with it. At first he outrages several of the period's conventions. When introduced to us, he takes drugs—at the beginning of *The Sign of Four* he has been on three cocaine injections a day for months—and has fits of depression, when he lies upon a sofa "for days on end . . . hardly uttering a word or moving a muscle from morning to night." He plays the violin extremely well, but when left to himself will merely "scrape carelessly at the fiddle thrown across his knee." In an age that admired above all things the acquisition of knowledge, he is egotistically proud of the vast fields of his ignorance. When Watson jots down Holmes's abilities and limitations, he puts "nil" against his knowledge of literature, philosophy, and astronomy, although he acknowledges the detective's "profound" knowledge of chemistry and his limited skills in botany, geology, and anatomy.

This summary comes in *A Study in Scarlet,* and later the portrait is modified. It is explained that he really only turned to cocaine "as a protest against the monotony of existence," and the man who did not know the name of Carlyle and expressed total lack of interest in the solar system is able on other occasions to talk about Waterloo and Marengo, to quote Goethe and compare Richter to—Carlyle. A good many similar anomalies can be found in the whole saga. They reflect in part the small value attached to the stories by Doyle, and in part the need to make Holmes a more sympathetic figure which became increasingly urgent with each new series of stories. The very first short story, "A Scandal in Bohemia," makes it clear that there will be no love interest. "As a lover, he would have placed himself in a false position. He never spoke of the softer passions, save with a gibe and a sneer." Doyle was not in the least misanthropic or misogynistic but he recognized in his readers (and no doubt felt himself) the need for Holmes to be a man immune from ordinary human weaknesses and passions. It remains part of his attraction that he "loathed every form of society with his whole Bohemian soul," and upon occasions disregards the law. So in "The Abbey Grange," Holmes and Watson jointly decide that they will not reveal to the police the identity of the man who killed Sir Eustace Brackenstall; in "Charles Augustus Milverton," they see a woman empty "barrel after barrel" of her revolver into the black-mailer's body and then grind her heel into his face without feeling that they need do anything about it; in "The Blue Carbuncle," Holmes condones a felony in the hope that he is saving a soul. When the law cannot dispense justice, Holmes does so himself. He is a final court of appeal and the idea that such a court might exist, personified by an individual, was permanently comforting to his readers.

If a man is proclaimed as superior to others, his superiority must be demonstrated. It is a weakness in many of Holmes's disciples that their genius is announced but not proved. Here Doyle is supreme. We learn gradually the astonishing extent of Holmes's knowledge, his monographs on a hundred and forty different varieties of pipe, cigar, and cigarette tobaccos, on the ear, on the Polyphonic Motets of Lassus, his analysis of a hundred and sixty ciphers, his ability to recognize the type of any newspaper at a glance. It is true that we are told about these studies rather than reading them, but the claim made in *A Study in Scarlet* that "by a man's finger-nails, by his coat-sleeve, by his boots, by his trouser-knees, by the callosities of his forefinger and thumb, by his expression, by his shirt-cuffs— by each of these things a man's calling is plainly revealed," is justified again and again. A single instance may be allowed to serve for the dozens in the stories. Given a battered old felt hat of which Watson can make nothing, Holmes is able to deduce that the owner is highly intellectual, was fairly well-to-do but is now poor, and has been going downhill probably under the influence of drink. "This may account for the obvious fact that his wife has ceased to love him." Holmes not only makes these deductions, but explains them in plausible detail. Would it be possible sometimes to reach different conclusions? No doubt, but the pleasure one gets from this opening up of a fine machine so that every cog in it can be seen revolving is hardly to be overestimated. Other writers try to mystify with one conclusion drawn from a fact unnoticed by the reader, where Doyle gives us a dozen, and almost always the deductions are those we might have made ourselves. This is perfectly exemplified in what is perhaps the most famous single short passage of Holmesian dialogue:

"Is there any other point to which you would wish to draw my attention?"
"To the curious incident of the dog in the night-time."
"The dog did nothing in the night-time."
"That was the curious incident."

A baffling fragment? The explanation is perfect. The dog did not bark, although somebody had entered the stables where he was on watch, and had taken out a horse. The significance of the incident is that the intruder must have been somebody well known to the dog. The passage shows, incidentally, a sensibility to phrasing which is not often noticed as one of Doyle's characteristics. Change the words "in the night-time" to what might superficially seem the more natural "during the night," and the sentences run much less happily.

Holmes was very much superior to most of his fellow detectives in his mastery of disguise. In the first of the short stories, he appears as a drunken-looking groom and a Nonconformist clergyman. He can be a tall thin old man, an elderly deformed man able to take a foot off his stature for hours on end—one need not go on. Doyle no doubt took the ideas for some of these disguises from Vidocq, as he took Holmes's style of interpreting thoughts from Poe and the form of some deductions from Gaboriau. The debts were acknowledged, although Holmes himself called Dupin a very inferior fellow and Lecoq a miserable bungler, but out of the borrowings he made something completely his own. Many detectives, when we look at them closely, are not much more than the bag of tricks which their creator has given them as their stock in trade. Like them, Holmes is conceived in outline, with attributes that are really substitutes for characterization—the eagle eye, the misanthropy, the remoteness. It is a mark again of Doyle's skill that Sherlock Holmes comes through to us as a man who genuinely had a genius for his occupation.

THE STORIES AND THEIR AUTHOR

The creator of Sherlock Holmes had other, and as he thought better, claims to consideration as a writer. Arthur Conan Doyle, later Sir Arthur (1859–1930), was one of those all-rounders whose lives blended literature and action in a way that is now very rare. He took himself most seriously as a historical novelist and when, shortly after the publication of *The Sign of Four,* he finished a book and threw the pen across the room with a cry of "That's done it," he was not referring to a Holmes story but to the completion of *The White Company,* the historical novel which ranks with *Micah Clarke* as his best work in this field. The series of Brigadier Gerard stories have a zest and liveliness that keep them marvelously readable, and some of the other books have a feeling for period which is not much inferior to that of Scott. If his belief that *The White Company* "would live and would illuminate our national traditions" has not come true in the sense that the books are not taken seriously by critics, it is because, with all his virtues of lucidity and descriptive power in dealing with action, Doyle did not care to look far into character. The organizing ability shown even in ephemeral work like his history of the Boer War, the analytic skill he showed in examining the cases of Oscar Slater and Edalji, were not accompanied by much depth of imagination. The people in his books and the things that happen to them are conceived on a level not far removed from that of boys' adventure stories. His mind was on the level of Macaulay, not that of Carlyle. The supremacy of the Holmes stories in his work lies in the fact that only in these tales of the Superman who was also the Great Outsider did this intelligent bourgeois find his imagination truly set free.

Doyle was a fine storyteller, and one quality that keeps the Holmes stories alive where so much work by his immediate successors is dead is that they are such good stories. We are hardly ever offered a mere puzzle, but a story about people briefly but vividly seen which encompasses a puzzle. The skill with which Dr. Grimesby Roylott is built up as an infinitely menacing figure in "The Speckled Band" is typical. His actual appearance in the story takes up only a page and a half, yet there are few more convincing characters in this kind of fiction. When the mechanics of the story are examined, we see that an impression of Roylott is first created through Helen Stoner's unwilling description of her stepfather's strength and brutality. Then there is Roylott's visit to Holmes and the poker-bending incident, and finally the visit to Stoke Moran and the creation of a sinister atmosphere through clues like the dummy bell-rope, the saucer of milk, the ventilator, which add to our understanding of Roylott's nature. Consummately skillful writing of this kind marks the best of the stories, and many of them, like "The Musgrave Ritual," are close to the tales of adventure in which Doyle delighted. The stories often begin with the arrival of a client in trouble, and frequently his description of it is marked by a teasingly obscure but not necessarily criminal problem, and by a display of Holmesian intellectual fireworks. In "The Resident Patient," the sparking point for curiosity is the readiness of Blessington to start up Dr. Percy Trevelyan in his own practice; in "The

Red-Headed League," the idea of a league of "all red-headed men who are sound in body and mind"; in "The Missing Three-Quarter," the arrival of the telegram which says: "Terrible misfortune. Right wing three-quarter missing." It may seem that any professional crime writer should be able to arrest a reader's attention in this way, but anybody who has attempted it knows that this is at least as difficult as constructing a satisfactory puzzle.

Sometimes this opening passage leads on to the revelation of a crime committed or in preparation; sometimes it opens out into an adventure story; sometimes it shifts back into the past and an explanation by the visitor. Occasionally Watson apologizes for the small part played by Holmes in a story, emphasizing the fact that what concerned Doyle was the adventure as much as the detection. Some themes are repeated. The purpose of the deception in "The Red-Headed League" is to get the pawnbroker Jabez Wilson out of his shop for a number of hours each day. Mr. Hall Pycroft's curious assignment to mark off all the hardware sellers in Paris in a trade directory in "The Stockbroker's Clerk" is similarly motivated by the need to get him out of London so that a crook may take up the job Pycroft has just been offered, and the theme is repeated again in "The Three Garridebs," where this unusual surname is used to get Nathan Garrideb out of the room which he never leaves except to drive down to Sotheby's or Christie's. Many stories have a particular touch which is wholly Doyle's, like the task set the gull in "The Red-Headed League" of copying out the whole of the Encyclopædia Britannica, and the name invented by Holmes in "The Three Garridebs" to prove that the man who calls himself John Garrideb is an impostor. The trap set is conventional, but the name of the invented character, Dr. Lysander Starr, is peculiarly felicitous. (" 'Good old Dr. Starr,' said our visitor. 'His name is still honoured.' ") Such freshness of detail gives continual pleasure.

So of course does the period atmosphere, which has been much and rightly praised. The London in which Holmes and Watson move, with frequent trips to a Surrey or Hampshire or Devon which prove to be no less sinister ("It is my belief, Watson, founded upon my experience, that the lowest and vilest alleys in London do not present a more dreadful record of sin than does the smiling and beautiful countryside," Holmes says, and the events in "The Copper Beeches" from which this comment is taken are horrible enough), has been described by other writers, but Doyle's world of four-wheelers from which intending husbands disappear, of opium dens lying between slop and gin shops, and of hotels whose expensiveness is shown by their charges of eight shillings for a bed and eightpence for a glass of sherry, remains uniquely flavorsome. We should remember, as most critics do not, that this was not "period" material for Doyle when the first three collections of short stories and three of the four novels were written. He was writing of the world around him, a world somehow transformed by his imagination. People think of Holmes's London as permanently dark and foggy, and one specialist in the stories has said that Holmes and Watson are "wrapped in tobacco smoke and London fog," but the effect is largely created by the tone of Doyle's writing. It is rarely that the "dense drizzly fog" mentioned in *The Sign of Four* or the "opalescent London reek" of "The Abbey Grange" appears in other stories. The weather is described only briefly in most of the stories, in phrases like "a cold, frosty winter's evening," "a close, rainy day in October," or "a bleak, windy day towards the end of March." If we try, again, to see how the magic works, it is difficult to get nearer than saying that it is somehow connected with the personalities of Holmes and Watson. The Baker Street establishment is so firmly realized—the small sitting room with chemicals about everywhere, criminal relics in the butter dish, unanswered letters fixed by a jackknife into the mantelpiece, "V R" done in bullet marks on the wall opposite Holmes's armchair, and Mrs. Hudson equally ready to provide a fresh plate of rashers and eggs or to shift the figure that Holmes has put into his window to lure Colonel Moran—that it pervades the surrounding scene. It is noteworthy that the later stories are less successful in conveying the aura of the Holmesian world, and this is because when *His Last Bow* (1917) and *The Case Book of Sherlock Holmes* (1927) appeared, Doyle was really writing of the past. A few of the stories are set in the twentieth century, but more of them go back to the nineties, and the period details in them are much less convincing.

There are weaknesses in the Holmes stories, caused by casual construction or by contradiction of other material within the canon. The weaknesses of construction are most apparent in the novels. Only *The Hound of the Baskervilles* can be called a coherent story, and even here the problem is not difficult to solve, and the identity of the murderer is revealed two-thirds of the way through. The grip of this novel is exerted in the way Doyle makes us feel the terror and loneliness of the Devon moors, implied in the disturbed feelings of the sober doctor who discovers beside the body of Sir Charles Baskerville "the footprints of a gigantic hound!" But there are flaws in the short stories, too. Some have already been mentioned, but one or two may be added. In "The Norwood Builder," the "charred organic remains" which temporarily persuade both Holmes and Lestrade that Mr. Jonas Oldacre is dead turn out to be rabbit bones, which should surely not have deceived a Great Detective. (In "Wisteria Lodge," set in 1892, bones are examined and immediately pronounced by a doctor—not Watson— to be nonhuman.) Doyle himself remarked on the number of solecisms in "Silver Blaze" that had been pointed out to him by racing men. In "A Case of Identity," we are asked to believe that Mary Sutherland's short sight stopped her from recognizing the stepfather with whom she lived when he presented himself disguised apparently only by tinted glasses, and in "The Man with the Twisted Lip" that Inspector Bradstreet did not spot the red wig, the painted face, the scar running from eye to chin that was presumably also painted, and the twisted lip created by "a small slip of flesh-coloured plaster." Bradstreet was admittedly unobservant, but for such negligence he should have been demoted to sergeant. The reader can make his own list of errors and improbabilities, and his own list, too, of the contradictions in the statements made by and about Holmes and Watson at different times.

Historians of the detective story have been hard upon such casualness. Dorothy Sayers thought that Doyle did not always play fair with the reader, and Howard Haycraft has said that although Holmes and Watson are immortal, it is "no disparagement" to say that the stories are "all too frequently loose, obvious, imitative, trite, and repetitious in device and theme." One would not like to be subject to Haycraft in a disparaging mood: but the answer to be made by those who think more highly of the stories is that Doyle "plays fair" in his deductions more often than any other writer of short stories, in the sense that nine times out of ten we see the clue from which Holmes makes his deductions, and that some of Haycraft's objections are wrong and others are of little importance. The stories are not trite, and they are obvious only in the sense that we can guess the villain, not the means by which the villainy is carried out. A few stories, and more deductions, are derived from Poe and Gaboriau, but almost always Doyle successfully turns the ideas of others to his own original uses, and the repetitiousness mostly comes in the last two volumes of short stories, which are admittedly much inferior to the first three. "The Dying Detective" is extremely feeble, "Thor Bridge" is a very elementary disappearing-weapon story, and "His Last Bow" is a poorly written thriller. One is bound to agree, as Doyle agreed, with the remark that Holmes "may not have been killed when he fell over the cliff, but he was never quite the same man afterwards."

But to give much weight to such criticism is to fall into the error of preferring mechanical technical perfection to skill in storytelling. Many post-Holmes short stories presented better puzzles than any of Doyle's, but almost all were infinitely inferior as stories. Of the fifty-six short stories about Holmes, roughly half are tales which can be read again and again with pleasure, for the creation of a scene and an atmosphere, and for the deductions made by Holmes from evidence presented to the reader. The only other writers of crime short stories whose work can be re-read in the same way, although not for quite the same reasons, are G. K. Chesterton and Stanley Ellin.

THE HOLMES MYTH

Many creators of famous detectives would have killed them off if this had been a practical—that is, financial—possibility.

Conan Doyle was perhaps the first to experience this Old Man of the Sea feeling. He worked on the first set of Holmes stories with care, but he did not take them seriously, and he thought of killing off the detective at the end of the series because "he takes my mind

from better things." At the end of the second collection, he sent
Holmes and Moriarty plunging over the Reichenbach Falls, and
felt a great sense of relief. As he wrote to a friend about Holmes:

> I have had such an overdose of him that I feel towards him as I do
> towards *pâté de foie gras,* of which I once ate too much, so that the
> name of it gives me a sickly feeling to this day.

But it is not so easy to kill a myth. Doyle received hundreds of
letters imploring him to bring Holmes back, and "Let's Keep
Holmes Alive" clubs were started in several American cities. Such
moral pressures were reinforced by offers from magazines of what
were at the time enormous sums of money for a new collection of
short stories. In 1902, after eight years' absence, Holmes reappeared
in what was said to be a pre-Reichenbach novel, *The Hound of the
Baskervilles,* and in October, 1903, the first story in a new series,
"The Empty House," appeared in the English *Strand Magazine* and
the American *Collier's.* Doyle's postcard to his agent, which said
simply "Very well. A.C.D.," meant that he had succumbed to the
lure of an offer of $5,000 from America and a fee of £100 a
thousand words from the *Strand.* "The scenes at the railway bookstalls were worse than anything I ever saw at a bargain sale," an
eyewitness wrote, and Doyle himself remarked that everybody on
the Channel boat was clutching a copy of the magazine. From this
point onward he made no attempt to abandon Holmes, but he still
resented the importance with which the detective's exploits were
regarded. When, a year or two before his death, he was giving a
talk on spiritualism in Amsterdam and was asked to say a few
preliminary words about Sherlock Holmes, his reaction was one of
anger and dismay.

Sherlock Holmes became a myth so potent that even in his own
lifetime Doyle was almost swamped by it, and the myth is not less
potent today. Criminal and emotional problems are still addressed
to Holmes for solution, and pilgrimages are made to his rooms at
221B Baker Street. In the Sherlock Holmes public house, mementos
of his cases are preserved in the bar, and the sitting room at Baker
Street, complete with its occupant, may be regarded while one dines.
There are Sherlock Holmes Societies or Baker Street Irregulars or

Silver Blazers in almost every country in the world except those which are Communist-controlled; there are journals and meetings and dinners and visits to the Reichenbach Falls. Some of this is amusing and perhaps all of it is harmless, although I have an uneasy feeling that the members of these societies are more interested in having fun with Sherlock Holmes than in the merits of the stories.

This feeling is strengthened by some of the literature springing from the inconsistencies already noted in the stories. A typical copy of the *Sherlock Holmes Journal* contains an article about Holmes and the music halls, suggesting that as a young man he had gone "barnstorming round the London halls"; another about Holmes and the stage, in which the theory is put forward that he was "an extremely competent and successful professional actor, probably in the provinces"; three pages on "The Geography of *The Hound of the Baskervilles*"; and discussion of such questions as the possible existence of Colonel James Moriarty, a brother of the Professor. The tone of mock-scholarly facetiousness in such pieces, and in articles speculating whether Watson was a woman, whether Holmes attended Oxford, Cambridge, or both, and where he spent the years when he was supposed to be in Tibet, must make them rank high among the most tedious pieces of their kind ever written. (Perhaps one should make an exception for Vincent Starrett's generally agreeable and informative *The Private Life of Sherlock Holmes*.) And such pieces are not merely tedious. By emphasizing and enlarging the myth of Holmes, they tend to obscure Conan Doyle's real and considerable achievement. Nearly forty years ago, Monsignor Ronald Knox, one of the originators of this sort of scholarship, thought that it was getting out of hand. Certainly what needs to be stressed today is something that should be a cliché, and unhappily is not: that if one were choosing the best twenty short detective stories ever written, at least half a dozen of them would be about Sherlock Holmes.

VI

The Short Story: The First Golden Age

In writing about most of Sherlock Holmes's immediate successors, one has to make a change of gear. The interest of their work lies in the ingenuity with which problems are propounded and solved, rather than in the ability to create credible characters or to write stories interesting as tales rather than as puzzles. The amount of talent working in this period gives it a good claim to be called the first Golden Age of the crime story, but it should be recognized that the metal is nine-carat quality where the best of the Holmes stories is almost pure gold. Yet for those prepared to accept these stories on their own level (as any addict should be) the variety of detectives and ideas offered in them gives enduring pleasure.

At the center of their work was the personality of the detective, who almost always appeared in several series of stories. A number of dichotomies mark these detectives, but the clearest division is between those in the Holmes category of Supermen with no emotional attachments and little interest in everyday life except insofar as it impinges on any particular problem, and the inconspicuous ordinary men who solve their cases by the application of common sense rather than by analytic deduction. The detectives in this second class are private investigators running their own agencies, because that was the fashion of the time, but they often look and sound like policemen. They are Lestrades and Gregsons removed from the official ranks and seen with a friendly eye instead of being made the butts of genius. The Superman is almost always given his accompanying Watson, who may do a lot of the humdrum investigation. The common-sense detective often works alone.

The two most successful Superman detectives of the period were Professor Augustus S. F. X. Van Dusen and Father Brown. Van Dusen was created by Jacques Futrelle (1875–1912), an American born in Georgia, who had a theatrical and journalistic career which was blended with the writing of novels and short stories. Van Dusen's principal appearance is in two collections of stories, *The Thinking Machine* (1907) and *The Thinking Machine on the Case* (1908).* He carries Holmesian omniscience to the point of absurdity. He is introduced to us when he refers contemptuously to chess, saying that a thorough knowledge of the rules of logic is all that is necessary to become a master at the game, and that he could "take a few hours of competent instruction and defeat a man who has devoted his life to it." A game is arranged between the Professor and the world champion, Tschaikowsky. After a morning spent with an American chess master in learning the moves, the Professor plays the game. At the fifth move, Tschaikowsky stops smiling, and after the fourteenth, when Van Dusen says "Mate in fifteen moves," the world champion exclaims: *"Mon Dieu!"* (he is not one of those Russians who know no language but their own) and adds: "You are not a man; you are a brain—a machine—a thinking machine." From this time onward Professor Van Dusen is called the Thinking Machine. In appearance he is dwarfish, with a small white clean-shaven face, long white flexible hands, and a great domed head taking a size-eight hat, under which is a heavy shock of bushy yellow hair.

The whiff of absurdity is strong, but the Thinking Machine stories are almost all ingenious. The usual Futrelle story falls into two parts. In the first a mystery is shown to us, either by third-person narrative or as told to the Thinking Machine. His assistant, the reporter Hutchinson Hatch, does most of the legwork, and the Professor then solves the case. Among the best stories are: one in which

* In England, *The Professor on the Case.*

poison is circulated through the application of a court plaster; another in which a man sees in a crystal ball the picture of his future murder in his own apartment some distance away (the basis of the trick is the creation of a duplicate room in the house where the victim sees the crystal ball); and a third in which a car disappears night after night in a lane which has a policeman at each end. The finest of all the Thinking Machine stories is "The Problem of Cell 13," which begins with an assertion by the Professor that anything can be done by the power of thought. Told that nobody can think his way out of a cell, he replies that "a man can so apply his brain and ingenuity that he can leave a cell, which is the same thing." The story shows him doing just that, with some agreeable mystification in the course of it, and then explaining exactly how it was done. This story has become a classic anthology piece, rather at the expense of some of the others. Futrelle died when the *Titanic* went down. The evidence of his other books does not make it seem likely that his crime stories would have developed any depth of characterization, but within the limits of what he attempted he had a conspicuously original gift.

The short detective stories written by Gilbert Keith Chesterton (1874–1936) were as pungent, paradoxical, and romantic as the novels, poems, literary criticism, and journalism that streamed from his occasionally too ready pen. His essential views about the detective story are set down in the first and best of the several pieces in which he discussed various aspects of the form. It was, he said, a popular realization of the poetry concealed in city life. The detective crosses a London in which "the casual omnibus assumes the primal colours of a fairy ship," and in which the lights of the city are the guardians of a secret known to the writer but not to the reader. "Every twist of the road is like a finger pointing to it; every fantastic skyline of chimney-pots seems wildly and derisively signalling the meaning of the mystery." The detective-story writer should be regarded as the poet of the city, and the detective as a romantic hero, the protector of civilization. "It is the agent of social justice who is the original and poetic figure, while the burglars and footpads are merely placid old cosmic conservatives, happy in the immemorial respectability of apes and wolves.

The romance of the police force is thus the whole romance of man. . . . It reminds us that the whole noiseless and unnoticeable police management by which we are ruled and protected is only a successful knight-errantry."

This was written in 1901, before Father Brown was thought of, and it is admirable special pleading for Chesterton's own detective stories in which reality is made to seem like fantasy and in which Flambeau, the great criminal, soon becomes a detective, like Vidocq. The stories embody also a principle that he announced a quarter of a century later, that "the only thrill, even of a common thriller, is concerned somehow with the conscience and the will." This is true at least of his own very uncommon thrillers, which almost always exemplify a witty paradox about the condition of society or the nature of man. The effect of the Father Brown stories rests partly in the moral point that many of them bring home, but this might appear anodyne but for the witty and subtle way in which Chesterton makes it. He fairly spilled over with good ideas, and they are as evident in his detective stories as in the novels that were the product of his verbal and mental dexterity, like *The Napoleon of Notting Hill* or his metaphysical thriller, *The Man Who Was Thursday.*

Chesterton wrote several other collections of what may loosely be called detective short stories outside the Father Brown series, of which *The Club of Queer Trades, The Man Who Knew Too Much,* and *Four Faultless Felons* all contain good things, but his reputation in this field rests upon the five Father Brown collections. *The Innocence of Father Brown* (1911) was followed by the *Wisdom* (1914), the *Incredulity* (1926), the *Secret* (1927), and the *Scandal* (1935). Father Brown, the dumpy commonplace little priest, with his black hat, dingy umbrella, and collection of brown paper parcels, was based upon Father John O'Connor, parish priest of St. Cuthbert's, Bradford. "The flat hat is true to life, and the large and cheap umbrella was my defence against wearing an overcoat," Father O'Connor has written. "Brown paper parcels! I carried them whenever I could, having no sense of style or deportment."

It may seem odd to class a man who has difficulty in rolling his umbrella and does not know the right end of his return ticket among the Supermen of detection, but Father Brown belongs among them through the knowledge given to him by God. Logicians of the detective story complained with some bitterness that Chesterton outraged all the rules they had drawn up, that he did not tell you whether all the windows were fastened or whether a shot in the gunroom could be heard in the butler's pantry. But the very merit of Chesterton is his ability to ignore such things, to leave out everything extraneous to the single theme he wants to develop, and yet to provide a clue that is blindingly obvious once we have accepted the premises of the story and the character of Father Brown. A dog whines because a stick sinks in the sea, the red light from a closed door looks like "a splash of blood that grew vivid as it cried for vengeance," the priest of a new religion does not look round when he hears a crash and a scream, and these are genuine clues by which we may solve mysteries. And when we have accepted Father Brown, then we are bound to accept also his right to draw religious and social morals from the cases he investigates.

Often the points he is making are beautifully put. In "The Blue Cross," Father Brown identifies a false priest because he attacks reason, which is "bad theology." In "The Queer Feet," the trick of which rests on the fact that a man in evening dress is indistinguishable from the waiter who is serving him, the criticism is social. "Reverend Sir, your friend must have been very smart to act the gentleman," Colonel Pound says at the end of the story, and the priest replies: "Yes, it must be very hard work to be a gentleman; but, do you know, I have sometimes thought that it must be almost as laborious to be a waiter." The paradoxes at their best are perfect. Why does a man wear a startling purple wig? Because by drawing attention to it he diverts any possible curiosity from his presumedly deformed but in fact normal ear. How can a black man conceal himself in a white country? Why, by posing as a soot-masked nigger minstrel.

The Chesterton short stories are a diet too rich for everyday consumption. Two or three, not six or seven, should be read at a sitting. And they have their faults, which spring from the fact that he was never able to take anything that he wrote quite seriously.

Sometimes the detective stories, like his novels, topple into absurdity because the premises of the tale are too fantastic, but this does not happen very often. A comparison with M. P. Shiel's Prince Zaleski stories, which are never plausible even on their own preposterous grounds, shows Chesterton's skill at this sort of tightrope walking. The first two books are on a higher level than the others but, reading them all again before writing about them, it seemed to me still that the best of these tales are among the finest short crime stories ever written. A personal choice would include "The Queer Feet," which has already been mentioned; "The Secret Garden," with its puzzle of two heads and only one body; "The Man in the Passage," in which a superb comic trick is pulled off with a mirror; the logical exercise in "The Paradise of Thieves"; and "The Dagger with Wings," in which a legend is fulfilled when the body of a man looking like an enormous bat is found spread-eagled in unspotted snow. This last story has some loose ends hanging that will not please academics, but after a dozen readings I feel fresh admiration for the cleverness with which the trick is embodied in the legend and for the brilliance of the central picture.

A reading of Chesterton reinforces the truth that the best detective stories have been written by artists and not by artisans. In considering other Superman detectives of the period, we are dealing with journeymen of letters who do not pretend to art. Some had good ideas and some could construct a good story, but they had no ideas as clever as Futrelle's and no poetic inspiration like that which often touched Chesterton. Originality, certainly, must be granted to the Old Man in the Corner invented by Baroness Orczy (1865–1947). He preceded her better-known Scarlet Pimpernel, and appeared in three collections, *The Case of Miss Elliot* (1905), *The Old Man in the Corner* (1909), and *Unravelled Knots* (1926). The Old Man sits in the corner of an ABC teashop consuming glasses of milk and pieces of cheesecake, endlessly tying and untying knots in a piece of string, and giving his solutions of cases that have baffled the police to a girl reporter named Polly Burton, who seems never to have read the newspapers, since the Old Man has to describe the background of every case to her in detail. "There is no such thing as a mystery in connection with any crime, provided intelligence is brought to bear upon its investigation," he says in characteristic Superman style, and he is never seen to move from his seat, although he mentions attending court hearings in several cases. The misanthropic Old Man is concerned solely with demonstrating his own cleverness. He does not care at all about justice, and it is a peculiarity of the stories that in many of them the criminal goes free. "Hang such a man? Fie!" he cries about one murderer, and of another he reflects only that "there goes a frightful scoundrel unhung." In the last story of *The Old Man in the Corner,* it is a presumption that he has himself committed the murder.

Such a character could be a springboard for all sorts of social comments, but these seem never to have been in Baroness Orczy's mind, and apparently she wrote the stories in this way because they absolved her from any need to turn the Old Man's theories into practical proof of guilt. The writing is quite lively and some of the stories contain ideas put to better use by other writers, like that of two men planning a murder so that the man with an obvious motive has an alibi while his apparently uninvolved companion commits the crime, but they too often depend upon police work so inefficient as to make Lestrade look like a genius. Baroness Orczy was also responsible for a woman detective more disastrously silly than most of her kind, *Lady Molly of Scotland Yard* (1910), and for a legal investigator, Patrick Mulligan, who appears in *Skin o' My Tooth* (1928). Lady Molly, really Lady Molly Robertson-Kirk, is "head of the Female Department," and has a husband who is in Dartmoor for murder. She ends up clearing him of the crime after an unexplained five-year delay, and presumably settles down again to domesticity.

Ernest Bramah Smith (1869?–1942), who dropped his commonplace surname for his writings, showed also a stroke of distinct originality in creating the blind detective Max Carrados. The Carrados stories were perhaps a diversion from the mock-Chinese tales about Kai Lung which at one time had an unaccountably large number of admirers, and the blind detective appears in *Max Carrados* (1914), *The Eyes of Max Carrados* (1923), and *Max Carrados Mysteries* (1927). His Watson is an inquiry agent named Louis Carlyle, who changed his name when he was wrongly struck off the solicitorial rolls for falsifying a trust account. Carrados (whose name is really Max Wynn) suffered from a disease called amaurosis, which causes blindness while leaving the external appearance of the eye unchanged. The pair make an agreeable variation on the Holmes-Watson relationship, with Carlyle rather more sophisticated and distinctively characterized than most assistants, and Carrados insistent on the value of having "no blundering, self-confident eyes to be hoodwinked." His supersensitive auditory nerve enables him to hear the cry of a newsboy in the street which is inaudible to other people in a room, and he knows that a man is wearing a false mustache because he carries "a five-yard aura of spirit gum, emphasized by a warm, perspiring skin."

It is a defect of such spectacular discoveries that the reader cannot make them himself, as he can so often make them in the Holmes stories, but the tales about Carrados are well-constructed and interesting. Unlike most crime writers, Bramah sometimes linked his stories to actual social events of the period. Doyle, for instance, although he occasionally dealt with terrorist societies, always placed their activities in some distant country. In "The Knight's Cross Signal Problem," however, the young Indian Drishna responds to Carlyle's indignation about his terrorist act in causing a rail crash by asking: "Do *you* realise, Mr. Carlyle, that you and your Government and your soldiers are responsible for the death of thousands of innocent men and women in my country every day?" A later story, "The Missing Witness Sensation," deals with the kidnaping of a man by Sinn Fein so that he cannot give evidence against them. Carrados handles an unusually wide variety of cases, including in the first volume alone stories about a jewel theft, the railway crash already mentioned, attempted murder, fraud, and the burglary of a safe deposit. Bramah ignored the limiting idea, which had almost become established by the time of his first Carrados book, that every investigation must concern a murder, and the stories are the more interesting for it. Like other Superman detectives, Carrados feels no hesitation about amending the processes of law, in one case to the point of ordering a murderer to commit suicide.

Holmes was a great admirer of Bertillon, but he never concerned himself with fingerprints as he did with tobacco ash, newsprint, and secret writing. Many detectives of this period mention the use of science in solving crimes, but few are seen in the act of using it. The distinction of R. Austin Freeman (1862–1943) is that his Dr Thorndyke is actually seen to be a forensic scientist. His square green box covered with Willesden canvas contains a great variety of materials for the detection of crime. When he says, "Will you give me the Vitogen powder, Jervis," or goes to work on footprints with his plaster tin, water bottle, spoon, and little rubber bowl, we are conscious of watching actual and likely processes of detection. Freeman had a firm basis of medical knowledge, and he put this and the admiration he felt for one of his instructors, the great Victorian expert in medical jurisprudence Dr. Alfred Swayne Taylor, to good use.

For a man who began his literary career late, Freeman produced a great many books. The first of them, *The Adventures of Romney Pringle* (1902), published under the pseudonym of Clifford Ashdown and written by Freeman together with a medical colleague who was also a prison officer, is said to be the rarest book of crime short stories. His début under his own name came with *The Red Thumb Mark* (1907) when he was forty-five years old, and he produced an average of rather more than a book a year up to a short time before his death. Many of them were novels, but is is safe to say that with the exception of one or two, like *Mr. Pottermack's Oversight* (1930), they are markedly inferior to the short stories. With Freeman we confront for the first time the crime writer who produced work of no other kind, and whose talents as a writer were negligible. Reading a Freeman story is very much like chewing dry straw. This is how Thorndyke talks as late as the middle twenties:

"A philosophic conclusion, Jervis, and worthy of my learned friend. It happens that the most intimate contact of Law and Medicine is in crimes against the person and consequently the proper study of the Medical Jurist is crime of that type."

Was ever reader in this manner wooed? If readers were won (and they were), if some remain (and they do), it is because of his accuracy in detail, and because of the originality shown in one collection of short stories. In *The Singing Bone* (1912), Freeman invented what has been called the inverted story. In these stories, we see a crime committed and then watch Thorndyke discover and follow clues that lead to the criminal. There is no mystery, and not much surprise, but the interest of watching Thorndyke at work is enhanced by our own prior knowledge. Freeman never repeated this experiment, which was developed much later and with more skill by Roy Vickers.

It is rather dubiously that one includes Thorndyke among the Supermen, but although he is in character almost anonymous, he has the proper passionless approach to ordinary human affairs. There is less doubt about Uncle Abner, the hero of *Uncle Abner, Master of Mysteries* (1918), by Melville Davisson Post (1871–1930). The stories are set in pre-Civil War Virginia, and Uncle Abner is "one of those austere, deeply religious men who were the product of the Reformation . . . the right hand of the land." He is compared more than once with Cromwell; he carries a Bible in his pocket; he exemplifies the spirit of righteousness in his disorderly society.

The Uncle Abner stories are very highly regarded in America, but comparatively little known elsewhere. No English edition of them has ever been published. This is no doubt because their settings and themes are often distinctively American—"The Edge of the Shadow" contains an argument about the validity of slavery and concerns the murder of an abolitionist, and in the course of "A Twilight Adventure" Uncle Abner stops a lynching for cattle stealing and gives a lecture on the dangers of circumstantial evidence. But the attraction the stories have for Americans simply does not exist for others. To English readers, Uncle Abner is likely to seem a distant and implausible figure, and if one judges in terms of plot the stories have surely been overpraised. They include a far-fetched but ingenious locked-room mystery which has already been mentioned, and a cunning story based on phonetic misspelling, but Uncle Abner's deductions are often of dubious validity, like his conclusion that a man followed the left side of a wall "because his controlling side was on the left—because he was left-handed." Some of the other detectives created by Post, like Monsieur Jonquelle, Prefect of Police of Paris, and Sir Henry Marquis, who appeared in

The Sleuth of St. James's Square and another book, show only that Post was not at home when he was abroad.

The detective as ordinary man is embodied in the Martin Hewitt stories written by Arthur Morrison (1863–1945). The first series of them ran in the *Strand* during 1894, and they were illustrated by Sidney Paget, who had also interpreted the appearance of Holmes. In looks and behavior, Hewitt represents a conscious reaction—and the first reaction, as the date shows—from the Superman detective. Hewitt is a "stoutish, clean-shaven man, of middle height and of a cheerful, round countenance" who "maintains that he has no system beyond a judicious use of ordinary faculties." The first and best of the three Hewitt collections contains some cases with interesting ideas in them, like "The Stanway Cameo Mystery," in which a dealer discovers that the cameo he has sold is a forgery, and steals it back again to save his reputation. There is another story about jewels stolen by a carefully trained parrot, and "The Loss of Sammy Throckett," which deals with the kidnaping of a runner expected to win a handicap race in the North of England, contains sociologically interesting details. But Morrison, who was a journalist and short-story writer concerned with actual poverty and crime (he wrote an admirable book about London slum life, *Tales of Mean Streets,* at the time he was producing the first Hewitt stories), seems always to have been disturbed by the idea of treating crime light-heartedly, and the later collections are rather humdrum.

The stories about Paul Beck and his son, by M. McDonnell Bodkin (1850–1933), do not deserve the total neglect into which they have fallen. Bodkin was an exuberant Irish barrister, and for a short time a Nationalist M.P., who became a judge in the County of Clare. His first detectival creation, Paul Beck, is described as a "stout party in grey" who "don't seem particular bright." He has a ruddy face, curling light brown hair, a chronic look of mild surprise in his light blue eyes, and the appearance of a milkman rather than a detective. Beck does not profess great intelligence. "I just go by the rule of thumb, and muddle and puzzle out my cases as best I can." In saying this, he hardly does himself justice, for *Paul Beck, the Rule of Thumb Detective* (1898) shows him exercising a good deal of native wit, even though the famous detective Murdock Rose is scornful about him. The book had a very good press, and Beck was favorably compared with "the late lamented Sherlock Holmes." *Dora Myrl, the Lady Detective* (1900) was no less absurd than other stories of the time about women detectives, who retained an impossible gentility of speech and personality while dealing with crime. In *The Capture of Paul Beck* (1909), Dora and Beck end up married after being on opposite sides in a case, and *Young Beck, a Chip of the Old Block* (1911) introduces their son, also Paul. These stories are unusual, in that they are mostly based on young Paul's life at university and just after leaving it, in company with his friend Lord Kirwood, son of the Secretary of State for Foreign Affairs, who is among the sillier Watsons. The cases of Paul, Jr., have great freshness. They include one of the finest card-cheating stories ever written, and one in which Bodkin made good use of his knowledge of the House of Commons. The Becks, senior and junior, are possibly the best Plain Man detectives of their era.

Other Supermen and Plain Men, although not very many of the latter, were at work in the field of the short story during this period, but there seems no need to particularize any of them, except perhaps the prolific Dick Donovan, the pseudonym of J. E. Preston Muddock (1843–1934), who spanned in a curious way the gap between the detective proper and the great flood of penny-dreadful figures headed by Sexton Blake, and including Nelson Lee, Dixon Hawke, and Falcon Swift, which began in imitation of Holmes—but of course an active nonanalytical Holmes always chasing or being chased by a super-villain—in the nineties. In America, a similar development was taking place, as Miss Joan M. Mooney has shown in a valuable, detailed discussion of the Nick Carter and Old Cap Collier stories. The crudity of the few penny dreadfuls I have read precludes them from consideration, but Donovan is a different matter. His plots are often absurdly melodramatic, but the level of his writing is sometimes reminiscent of rather inferior Trollope. He wavers between the undistinguished but readable:

> In personal appearance he was the true stamp of a thorough English gentleman. It might be that there was just a very faint tinge of port wine in the well-rounded cheeks, for if there was one thing that he was more partial to than another it was good old crusted port.

and the totally preposterous:

"What devil was it that prompted me to listen to your honeyed words, to drink in your gilded lies? Can you undo what has been done! Can you restore to me my girlish innocence?"

The most nearly acceptable Donovan is in the novels told in the third person, some of them recounting the exploits of other detectives like Calvin Sugg, a typical post-Holmes figure, who speaks at least six languages fluently and has been given innumerable medals by various governments, but the most popular were the short stories in which Donovan boastfully recounts his own exploits. Like Holmes, he was thought to be a real person, and received many letters, including one from a woman in Brighton who asked him to shadow her husband. Muddock in his autobiography notes regretfully the preference for his detective stories over his other writings, and says: "I have never been in full sympathy with my Donovan work."

There are two writers still unmentioned whose work should be included in relation to the short story of the time, although what they wrote was nearer to the thriller than to detection. The Arsène Lupin stories of Maurice Leblanc (1864–1941) and the Raffles tales of E. W. Hornung (1866–1921) represent the last flicker for a long time of the criminal-hero tradition. *Arsène Lupin, gentleman-cambrioleur* (1907) introduces him as the leader of a gang of thieves, who masquerades in various disguises and outwits the police of every country, impersonating an English detective at Scotland Yard, making a fool of Holmlock Shears (Herlock Sholmès in the original), and taking charge of the search for Lupin in the Vidocq manner, while posing as the chief of the Sûreté. Lupin is a rogue rather than a villain, and in the later stories he is often on the side of law and order. The short stories about him come off better than the rambling novels, although there is something irritatingly slapdash about them all.

A. J. Raffles is a much more interesting character, even if the interest is partly sociological. Raffles is, on the surface, an image of a perfect English gentleman. He is captain of the school cricket team and later becomes the finest slow bowler of his decade (an amateur, naturally). Apart from playing cricket all the summer, he leads a life of apparent idleness. Apparent: for he really makes a living as a burglar, and *Raffles, the Amateur Cracksman* (1899) records his adventures in collaboration with Bunny, who has worshiped Raffles since fagging for him at school. In one very curious story, Bunny dresses as a woman, and there are suggestions of a platonic homosexual relationship between them.

The series, which includes the later *Raffles* (1901) and *A Thief in the Night* (1905), shows the public-school ethos turned round, with the traditional virtues of sticking to your chums and doing the decent thing used in the service of theft. Raffles sometimes does the decent thing by conventional standards, as on the occasion when he sends a gold cup stolen from the British Museum back to the Queen, and on another occasion he explains to Bunny that it is not a betrayal of hospitality to steal the jewels at Lord Amersteth's house, because he has been "asked for my cricket, as though I were a pro." It is less easy to excuse his conduct in jumping overboard when things become desperate, leaving Bunny to face a long prison sentence, or on the occasion when he burgles the house in which Bunny's girl lives. Bunny's own ethical code is also distinctly odd. After a little initial reluctance, he enters wholeheartedly into burglary, but he refuses to stoop to "personal paragraphs and the baser journalism."

Hornung, who also wrote some indifferent detective and adventure stories, had no satirical intentions. He was Conan Doyle's brother-in-law, and Doyle strongly disapproved of the whole idea of Raffles, saying, "You must not make the criminal a hero." Since Raffles is seen through the worshiping Bunny's eyes, he undoubtedly is a hero, although Bunny often says things like "Raffles was a villain, when all is written," and promises to "paint in every wart." The stories are always lively, although occasionally absurd, and both Raffles and Bunny come through very clearly. They are also often intentionally funny. Hornung was a dexterous punster, as is shown by his remark that "though he might be more humble, there's no police like Holmes," and the Raffles stories contain one excellent pun. When Raffles and Bunny pay a visit to the "Raffles Relics" in Scotland Yard's Black Museum, they see the spectacles and jimmy of Charles Peace, and the master murmurs: "The greatest of the pre-Raffleites." Hornung never sees Raffles as ar enemy of the class in which he had been brought up, as an earlier writer would have done, but as a man who adheres to the standard: of this class even though he is a crook. For him, as for Bunny, Raffles's sins are canceled out by his heroic death in the Boer War

The Golden Age of the short story, which began with Holmes, ended with the First World War. The Holmes stories are the best things in the period, but they are not the only things worth remembering. Most of the short story's better practitioners in these years turned to detection as a relief from other work, and partly for this reason much of what they wrote retains its freshness. They enjoyed using a form which, still in its infancy, offered infinite opportunities for variation, and there is a gaiety in the often unsophisticated capers they cut which was slowly lost by the writers who followed them.

VII

The Rise of the Novel

One has to be careful to discover, and not to impose, a pattern in the shape of any sort of literature. Although the short story was the dominant form in crime fiction for roughly thirty years, novels were of course being written during this period. The decline of the short story's popularity, which became sharply noticeable after World War I, corresponded to the novel's rise, and both of these were linked with social, technical, and economic changes. The emancipation of women which took place during the war played a large part in the creation of a new structure in domestic life, particularly in Europe, through which women had more leisure and many of them used it to read books. It is often said that detective stories are mostly read by men. There seems to be no statistical basis for this statement, and probably it was true only up to the middle twenties. The rise of the large circulating libraries, associated in Britain particularly with the names of Boot's the chemists and W. H. Smith the book and newspaper wholesalers, greatly changed middle-class reading habits.

There was a branch of Boot's or Smith's in every town of any size, and every branch had its library from which books could be borrowed either on annual subscription or by paying a few pennies a book. News agents and stationers started their own little libraries, often obtaining stock from a central wholesaler and charging twopence a week for all except the most recent books, so that these became known as "twopenny libraries." Some of the twopenny libraries stocked chiefly the thrillers and Westerns that remained staple reading for the male working class, but many others were used overwhelmingly by women. Supply again followed their demand for books that would reinforce their own view of the world and society: long untroubling "library novels," light romances, detective stories. Many of the detective stories were written by women, and essentially also for women.

At the same time, changes in the style of urban living and in the nature of travel greatly affected magazine sales. More and more people traveled by car, and read nothing at all on the journey. Railway journeys became shorter, and men no longer queued at railway bookstalls to buy the latest issue of the *Strand* or any other magazine. They were more likely to be reading a newspaper on their way home from city to suburb, or a book from the circulating library on a journey from town to town.

I have been outlining this process in Britain, but something similar to it took place in many other countries. The effects were gradual, and the way in which social and mechanical change altered reading habits has not yet been studied in close detail. In relation to the detective story, these changes implied the replacement of the short story by the novel.

UP TO RINEHART AND CHRISTIE

The basic problem of authors writing novels during the era of the short story's supremacy was that if a mystery could be stated and solved in a few thousand words, there seemed no reason for expanding it to a novel ten times as long. Often they made a slightly uneasy attempt to guy the whole form. A typical example of this is George R. Sim's *The Case of George Candlemas* (1890) in which Sir Arthur Strangeways answers an agony-column advertisement because he longs so much to be a detective, and lands himself in all sorts of ludicrous mischief. *The Big Bow Mystery* (1892), by Israel Zangwill (1864–1926), is also much more nearly a parody than has been acknowledged. The novelette, written in a fortnight to meet a sudden demand from the London *Star,* is a mystery in which a man is found with his throat cut in a room locked, bolted, and "as firmly barred as if besieged." The detective is the murderer, and he committed the crime after the opening of the door, dashing across the room while another man was present and cutting the sleeping victim's throat without leaving more than a trace of blood. The solution of the locked-room mystery in *Le Mystère de la Chambre Jaune* (1907) is no less preposterous, although this once-famous book was called by John Dickson Carr's mouthpiece Dr. Fell, "the best detective tale ever written." Here the explanation involves a nightmare, the accidental firing of a revolver, and a whole concatenation of co-incidences. Leroux's book, which appeared as *The Mystery of the Yellow Room* in America in 1908 and in Britain a year later, contains a number of ingenious touches, but it shows the French abandonment of the last traces of Gaboriau's realism in dealing with the police.

That the line between the comic and the serious in the detective story is a fine one is shown by the most famous novel of these years, *Trent's Last Case* (1913). Its author, Edmund Clerihew Bentley (1875–1956), made his living as a journalist, and was for more than twenty years chief leader writer on the *Daily Telegraph.* Bentley had a talent for light humorous writing, and invented the tart little four-line verse known as the clerihew. In 1910, he thought that "it would be a good idea to write a detective story of a new sort." The book would be light-hearted, because Bentley disliked both the egotism and the seriousness of Holmes. The detective also was to be treated lightly, and perhaps for this reason was originally called Philip Gasket. In tune with this was the "most pleasing notion of making the hero's hard-won and obviously correct solution of the mystery turn out to be completely wrong," so that the whole thing would be "not so much a detective story as an exposure of detective stories." Bentley started with the last chapter, in which Gasket is staggered by the revelation of what really happened, and worked backward from this, revising the plot several times while walking from his Hampstead home to his Fleet Street office. The final result seemed to him poor, and when John Buchan, who was at that time reader for Nelson's, accepted the book, Bentley thought that he was offering far too much money. With Gasket changed to Trent, it was published in England, and in America under the title *The Woman in Black*. Its success was immediate, not as an "exposure" of detective stories, but as light entertainment.

Writing elsewhere about *Trent's Last Case,* I have said that it is difficult now to understand the high regard in which the book was held, and that "the writing seems stiff and characterless, the movement from one surprise to another, and the final shock of revelation, rather artificial." Perhaps it is a sign of the benevolence of age that this judgment now seems too severe. I think it remains true, though, that the book falls into two parts which are not very well connected. It was dedicated to Chesterton, and Bentley shared at this time Chesterton's radical dislike of the rich, and particularly of rich speculators. The opening treats the death of the millionaire Sigsbee Manderson with an almost savage irony, stressing that "to all mankind save a million or two of half-crazed gamblers, blind to all reality, the death of Manderson meant nothing." His epitaph is provided by the editor of the newspaper, who looks at the large broadsheet announcing "Murder of Sigsbee Manderson" and says: "It makes a good bill."

This ironic note recurs occasionally but is not maintained, and Manderson after being introduced with such a flourish becomes more shadowy as the story proceeds. The major part of the book deals with Trent's investigation and his (as it proves erroneous) discovery of what really happened. Much of this is ingenious, although it depends upon some actions that seem very unlikely, like an innocent man's removal of a denture from the dead Manderson's mouth. Of more importance is the fact that the detection wavers uneasily between a desire to treat the whole thing as a joke and Bentley's impulse to write seriously about the fact that Trent falls in love with the woman whom he supposes to be involved in the murder. There is a similar uncertainty in the treatment of Trent, who, as Bentley said, "is apt to give way to frivolity and the throwing about of absurd quotations from the poets at almost any moment" and yet, since he is the hero, cannot be regarded as a figure of fun. But perhaps this is still pressing too hard on a book that was acclaimed everywhere as something new in detective stories. The other works in which Trent appears, published more than twenty years later, showed only that Bentley was not able to adapt himself to the further development of the form.

The difficulties that confronted the writer of detective novels at this time are shown also in the construction of *At the Villa Rose* (1910), the first detective story by A. E. W. Mason (1865–1948). Mason, like Doyle, was an extrovert personality who found in the detective novel an outlet for dark imaginings that had no place in dashing historical romances like *The Four Feathers*. In characterization, *At the Villa Rose* is greatly superior to Bentley's book, and it has an ingenious plot with a firm though distant basis in two actual murder cases. Mason was determined, however, to "make the story of what actually happened more intriguing and dramatic than the unravelling of the mystery and the detection of the criminal." Accordingly, the criminal is revealed not much more than halfway through, and the rest of the book elucidates what really happened in terms of what the criminal and his accomplice say under examination by the magistrate. The essential element of suspense is largely lost through the adoption of this technique. Mason did not make the same mistake again, but because of it a book which might have been a landmark trails off disappointingly. Yet *At the Villa Rose* can still be reread with a pleasure largely associated with the detective, Inspector Hanaud of the Sûreté, and his Watson, Mr. Ricardo. Both are original creations. The stout broad-shouldered Hanaud, who looks like "a prosperous comedian," carries out quite a lot of closely argued detection, and the uxorious wine-loving Ricardo is one of the few Watsons to emerge as a distinct personality.

A book that must be mentioned at this point, although it is outside the detective canon, is *The Three Impostors,* by Arthur Machen (1863–1947). Neglected at the time of its publication in 1895, but for the last few years available in Britain, this is the finest of Machen's tales of terror, a sort of *New Arabian Nights* with the diabolism of the nineties replacing Stevensonian cheerfulness. The opening line: "And Mr. Joseph Waters is going to stay the night?" (there are few crime novels with a more tantalizing and disturbing opening line) leads into a series of cunningly interwoven tales, each extremely ingenious, the whole ending with the appalling discovery made by Machen's ingenuous amateur investigators in a decayed suburban house. It cannot be denied that the book is imitative of Stevenson, but this artificial flower of the nineties has a genuine poisonous scent. By its side, such a book as *The Lodger* (1913), the attempt made by Mrs. Belloc Lowndes (1868–1947) to convey the terror of the Jack the Ripper murders, looks forced and meretricious. Machen's horrific imaginings were real to him; Mrs. Lowndes's are designed to give the reader an entirely comfortable shiver.

It is this kind of shiver one gets, certainly, from the books of Mary Roberts Rinehart (1876–1958) and Carolyn Wells. These were stories written to a pattern. All of them deal with crime, and the crime is almost always murder. There is a detective, but his activities are often less important than those of the staunch middle-aged spinster, plucky young widow, or marriageable girl who finds herself hearing strange noises in the night, being shut up in cupboards, overhearing odd and apparently sinister conversations, and eventually stumbling upon some clue that solves the mystery. Much of what happens in these stories occurs by chance, and the mystery is prolonged only by the obstinate refusal of the characters to reveal essential facts. Mrs. Rinehart's books in particular became those of the Had I But Known school, the absurdities of which were wittily summed up by Ogden Nash:

> Sometimes it is the Had I But Known what grim secret lurked
>   behind the smiling exterior, I would never have set foot
>   within the door;
> Sometimes the Had I But Known then what I know now, I could
>   have saved at least three lives by revealing to the
>   Inspector the conversation I heard through that fortuitous
>   hole in the floor. . . .

And when the killer is finally trapped into a confession by
    some elaborate device of the Had I But Known-ers some
    hundred pages later than if they hadn't held their
    knowledge aloof,
Why, they say, Why, Inspector, I knew all along it was he,
    but I couldn't tell you, you would have laughed at me
    unless I had absolute proof.

These are the first crime stories which have the air of being
written specifically for maiden aunts, and they exploited a market
which, with the spread of library borrowing, proved very profitable. From Rinehart's second book and first success, *The Circu-
lar Staircase* (1908), at the climax of which spinster Rachel
Innes finds herself shut up with the murderer in a small secret
room behind the great old chimney piece ("I knew he was creep-
ing on me, inch by inch"), the formula of needless confusion and
mock terror did not change. The settings became more varied,
yet also more enclosed. As one commentator has said, "It does
not really matter much to the world view which emerges whether
the backdrop is New York City or Connecticut, a town or a
country house, the stability and balance most usually associated,
sentimentally at least, with an agrarian order are assumed." People in the books die, but this is not important, because in relation
to the real world none of them was ever alive. Nobody is ever
doing any work, although suspects may be labeled solicitor, doctor, chauffeur.

Sometimes the confinement of the society in which violence
takes place is carried to fantastic lengths. Rinehart went on writing until a year or two before her death, and *The Album* (1933)
is typical of her later novels. It deals with five families living in
Crescent Place, "a collection of fine old semi-country houses, each
set in its own grounds," insulated from the city outside by an
entrance gate marked *Private,* "so that we resemble nothing so
much as five green-embattled fortresses." The action literally
never moves outside the Crescent. Reporters and photographers
cause no trouble after an initial visit, and make no attempt to
gain access to the houses, although four murders are committed,
the first with an axe and the last involving a headless trunk. Within

this totally closed circle, none of the characters works, although one apparently did, since we are told that "he had given up even the pretence of business since the depression, and spent a good bit of time tinkering with his car in the garage." Even such tinkering is unusual, for there are cooks, a gardener, a chauffeur, various helpers. These people really have nothing to do, apart from being suspected of murder. The murderer, naturally, is one of them. Her actions, when her identity is revealed, are outrageously unlikely.

Rinehart's work was naive, but in some ways her world was that of the detective novel after World War I, as it is discussed in the next chapter. The main line of development, however, was marked clearly by the appearance in 1920 of Agatha Christie's first novel, *The Mysterious Affair at Styles*.

Agatha Christie's entry in *Who's Who* does not reveal the year of her birth, but this is now admitted to have been 1890. Her background, she says vaguely, was that of "English country life." She was brought up by her widowed mother, and had no formal education, either at school or at home. She published a book of poems, and had vague aspirations toward a career as a singer or pianist which ended when she realized that she would be too nervous to play in public and that her voice was not strong enough for opera. After writing two or three novels which she says were "long and confused" and were rejected by publishers, she decided to try her hand at a detective story. The influences working on her were "the pattern of the clue" and "the idiot friend" as developed in the Holmes stories. She worked during the war in a hospital and so obtained some knowledge of poisons, which she put to use in the story written in odds and ends of leisure time over a period of eighteen months. It was turned down by three publishers, and kept by the Bodley Head for nine months. John Lane then agreed to publish the book, which sold about 2,000 copies. She made £25 out of the British publication, and had to wait for ten years before it appeared in the United States.

The Mysterious Affair at Styles is not one of Agatha Christie's best detective stories, although it is based upon a characteristically cunning idea and contains some of those equally characteristic sleights of hand by which the reader is deceived into making what prove to be unjustifiable assumptions. It ushered in a very distinctive detective, the Belgian Hercule Poirot, whose appearance impresses one as being rather like that of Humpty Dumpty with a mustache, and a Watson of extreme stupidity in Captain Hastings. It revealed a gift for writing light, agreeable, and convincing dialogue, and the plot was constructed with firmness and coherence. Yet these things had been done before. Agatha Christie's book is original in the sense that it is a puzzle story which is solely that, which permits no emotional engagement with the characters. Bentley wavered into seriousness against his original intention; it is possible to be disturbed about the fate of Mason's Celia Harland; the reader's identification with the principal character is a prerequisite of enjoying Mrs. Rinehart. Christie's first book is notable because it ushered in the era during which the detective story came to be regarded as a puzzle pure and complex, and in which interest in the fates of the characters was increasingly felt to be not only unnecessary but also undesirable. It was the beginning of what came to be known as the Golden Age.

VIII

The Golden Age: The Twenties

LAYING DOWN THE RULES

Up to the middle twenties, there had been little serious consideration of crime stories as a particular kind of literature, and no attempt had been made to assess the detective story as something having rules which could be strictly formulated and which it was important to observe. By the end of the decade, however, a body of criticism had been produced which tried to lay down the limits within which writers of detective stories ought to operate.

Some of this work has already been mentioned, but to understand what happened to crime fiction between the wars, it is necessary to consider the rules in more detail. The attitude from which they sprang was that the detective story was a kind of game played, as Knox put it, between "the author of the one part and the reader of the other part." When one talked about rules, he went on, it was not "in the sense in which poetry has rules . . . but in the sense in which cricket has rules—a far more impressive consideration to the ordinary Englishman." (Knox was writing for his countrymen, but one supposes that he expected foreigners also to obey the rules, even though they did not understand cricket.) To infringe the rules was, to say the least, extremely bad form.

Starting from the assumption that the detective story was a game, the rules had two purposes, first to describe the nature of the game and then to show how it should be played. What made a detective story distinct from other superficially similar forms of literature? Well, clues had to be provided, and it was necessary that the detective should draw from them rational and inevitable conclusions. Any conclusions reached purely by instinct, through accident or through coincidence, showed a failure on the part of the author and were unfair to the reader. S. S. Van Dine, writing in his own person as Willard Huntington Wright, regarded an author who deceived the reader in this way as no better than a practical joker, and said that "if the detective does not reach his conclusions through an analysis of clues, he has no more solved his problem than the schoolboy who gets his answer out of the back of the arithmetic."

The detective was the vitally important figure. What sort of person should he be? Freeman, deprecating the "vast amount of rushing to and fro of detectives or unofficial investigators in motor cars, aeroplanes or motor boats," stressed that the connoisseur looked for "an exhibition of mental gymnastics," which was obviously best provided by an intellectual or scientific detective like his own Thorndyke. Wright agreed that the chief interest of the story should be mental analysis and was equally scornful of detectives continually in physical danger, although he regarded Thorndyke as "an elderly, plodding, painstaking, humorless and amazingly dry sleuth." (Sayers thought him probably the handsomest detective in fiction.) Wright said that the detective must be "a character of high and fascinating attainments—a man at once human and unusual, colourful and gifted," by implication resembling his own Philo Vance. Although most detectives during the twenties continued to be rather eccentric amateurs they were less anti-social than Holmes, and Sayers noted in 1928 a tendency to produce detectives remarkable only for their ordinariness, like Freeman Wills Crofts's Inspector French.

And then, what kind of crime should the detective investigate? There was a great shift here from the short stories that were frequently concerned with some sort of fraud. Wright, often the most extreme of these theorists, said that the crime simply must be murder because "three hundred pages is far too much pother" for interest to be maintained in any mere fraud or deception. One of the early historians, E. M. Wrong, also thought that murder must come first, chiefly because "it involves an intenser motive than any other peace-time activity." The other legislators tacitly agreed, without expressing themselves so definitely. Nobody, rather curiously, expressed a preference for murder on the ground that its punishment when detected was in many countries the irrevocable one of death.

The legislators turned to the criminal. It was agreed that he must be introduced early in the story and must not turn up three-quarters of the way through, as sometimes happened in early detective stories. He must not be the detective, or at least not the official detective. This rule was often infringed, most notably in Leroux's *Mystery of the Yellow Room* and in Bernard Capes's neglected tour de force *The Skeleton Key* (1919). He must not be a servant, because this was "a too easy solution" and "the culprit must be a decidedly worth-while person" (Wright). Servants, except as servants, were really not worthwhile. It was taken as a matter of course in Golden Age detection that murder most often took place where servants were around, but no servant could ever be guilty of more than petty theft or attempted blackmail. There were a few exceptions to this rule, in which somebody might *pretend* to be a servant, but they were rare. Nor could the murderer be a professional criminal. It was necessary, in fact, that he should be part of the same social group that contained the other suspects. He might be professionally linked with them in the capacity of doctor or solicitor, or he might have the socially ambiguous position of a secretary. John Dickson Carr, writing in 1935, thought that statistics would show the secretary to be still the most common murderer in crime fiction, although no doubt members of the murderee's family would have come first if they had been admitted as a category. And it was accepted that the motives for all crimes should be personal, and within that context rational. They should not be committed for reasons of state or on behalf of theoretical principles or by somebody merely insane. It was permissible that the people in a story should *think* that a crime was irrational, or had been carried out by an international spy who was selling secrets, but the reader knew that there would always turn out to be a personal motive.

There were rules about the story itself rather than the characters, some flippant and others serious. If scientific devices were used, the reader must be given a hint of their nature. Some deprecated Thorndyke's investigations, on the ground that you would be no wiser after he had shown you his discoveries, unless you happened to know the effect of belladonna on rabbits or had "an intimate acquaintance with the fauna of local ponds." Undiscovered poisons were ruled out, and so were supernatural solutions. Insistence that the writer must play fair with the reader was universal, and Knox, in deploring the use of secret passages, virtuously pointed out that when he had introduced one, he had been "careful to point out beforehand that the house had belonged to Catholics in penal times." Knox, never one to resist facetiousness, thought also that no Chinaman should appear in a story, a remark unintelligible except on the basis that he would not be a likely member of any English murder group. In America, Earl Derr Biggers's Charlie Chan offered not merely a Chinese character, but a Chinese detective.

Other rules were more seriously conceived. The importance of unity of mood was stressed and Wright was the first to lay down firmly the rule that there must be no love interest, because through it such unity was damaged. This rule was often broken, but in relation to sex the Golden Age detective story was strikingly inhibited. Money and sex are two main motives for murder, but although this was acknowledged in theory, in very few of these stories are the characters seen in depth, rather than as puppets in a game of murder. To see them in depth would have been against the rules. As Sayers said, these people lived "more or less on the *Punch* level of emotion," and if they were to be considered more seriously their emotions would "make hay of the detective interest," which was the truly important thing. E. M. Wrong was even clearer about it when he said that "what we want in our detective fiction is not a semblance of real life . . . but deep mystery and conflicting clues."

Sexual feeling was not the only aspect of life ignored in these stories. The period in which they were written was one in which the number of unemployed in Britain rose to three million and remained near that mark for a decade; in which boom in America was succeeded by slump, and slump by depression; in which dictatorships rose to power. It was a period that ended in a long-expected war. These things were ignored in almost all the detective stories of the Golden Age. In the British stories, the General Strike of 1926 never took place, trade unions did not exist, and when sympathy was expressed for the poor it was not for the unemployed but for those struggling along on a fixed inherited income. In the American stories, there were no bread lines and no radicals, no Southern demagogues or home-grown Fascists. The fairy-tale land of the Golden Age was one in which murder was committed over and over again without anybody getting hurt.

And why not? one of the ghosts of those past Golden Age critics might say. *Don't we always escape in fairy tales from what is disagreeable in life; isn't that their very purpose? Must we always be worrying about the state of society?* But the point is that these were very special fairy tales, and that social and even political attitudes were implied in them. It is safe to say that almost all of the British writers in the twenties and thirties, and most of the Americans, were unquestionably Right Wing. This is not to say that they were openly anti-Semitic or anti-Radical, but that they were overwhelmingly conservative in feeling. It would have been unthinkable for them to create a Jewish detective, or a working-class one aggressively conscious of his origins, for such figures would have seemed to them quite incongruous. It would have been equally impossible for them to have created a policeman who beat up suspects, although this was the time when American newspapers wrote about the third degree. Acknowledging that such things happened, they would have thought it undesirable to write about them, because the police were the representatives of established society, and so ought not to be shown behaving badly. And although an unemployed man might be seen sympathetically if he was trying to be helpful to his social betters, he was usually regarded as somebody who just refused to work. The social order in these stories was as fixed and mechanical as that of the Incas. We are very far in these books from the social radicalism of Chesterton, and a long way even from passages like Bentley's denunciation of Sigsbee Manderson. Golden Age writers would not have held it against Manderson that he had become rich by speculation, although they might have regretted his brashness and vulgarity.

Our approach to the crime story is so different from that of the most characteristic Golden Age writers that it is hard now to believe that all this ever happened. The Detection Club, founded in 1928 with Chesterton as president, still exists, but it is no longer confined, as it once was, strictly to writers of pure detective stories, and members no longer "solemnly swear never to conceal a vital clue from the reader" at their initiation. As many of them write thrillers rather than detective stories, such an oath would be meaningless. There is no limit to folly, but it seems surprising that the intelligent men and women who devised the rules did not see that they were limiting the scope and interest of their work. The puzzle of Who and Why and How remains a vital element in most crime fiction, but to abjure voluntarily the interplay of character and the force of passion was eventually to reduce this kind of detective story to the level of a crossword puzzle, which can be solved but not read, to cause satiety in the writers themselves, and to breed a rebellion which came sooner than has been acknowledged.

Nevertheless, for several years the rules received at least lip service, and it was discovered that detective stories were extremely easy to write. If none of the skills of a novelist was needed, if all one had to do was to construct a puzzle and then set down the events relating to it in a bald featureless narrative, why then almost anybody with time to spare and paper available might try his hand. In the great flood of British and American detective stories that began after World War I, as H. R. F. Keating has recently said, "dullness in everything except the riddles was the rule." In these years, the detective story reached peaks of ingenuity that have never since been attained and are now rarely attempted; and, sometimes in the same book, it dropped into abysses of absurdity and dullness that have never again been plumbed.

MISTRESSES AND MASTERS

In retrospect, four names stand out in the twenties, those of Agatha Christie, Dorothy Sayers, and Anthony Berkeley in Britain, that of S. S. Van Dine in America. Ellery Queen and John Dickson Carr belong properly to the thirties, although both published their first books before the end of the decade.

Agatha Christie's career moved in a steady but unspectacular way until 1926, when *The Murder of Roger Ackroyd* appeared. A second impression was called for within a few weeks, and the book was already a success when, seven months after its publication, she disappeared. This happened at a critical emotional period in her life, and after a nationwide search she was discovered in a famous spa suffering from amnesia. The affair undoubtedly helped the sale of her books, but the important point is that *Roger Ackroyd* was already successful. A work so notably original in its field could not have failed to find a wide audience.

In an obvious sense, the book fits comfortably within the conventions that have been outlined. The setting is a village deep in the English countryside; Roger Ackroyd dies in his study; there is a butler who behaves suspiciously but whom we never really suspect, and for good servant measure a housekeeper, a parlormaid, two housemaids, a kitchenmaid, and a cook. We are offered two of the maps that had by now become obligatory, one of the house and grounds, the other of the study. So far so conventional, but we notice at once the amused observant eye which makes something interesting out of the standard material. It is a mark of the best Golden Age writers that they were unable to stick to those injunctions about subduing the characters. The narrator's sister Caroline, good-natured but intensely inquisitive, a retailer of one ridiculous rumor after another, is a genuine comic character done with affectionate ridicule. The detective is Poirot, who in the best Holmesian style asks obscure questions that turn out to be meaningful, like his concern here with the color of a suspect's boots.

Every successful detective story in this period involved a deceit practiced upon the reader, and here the trick is the highly original one of making the murderer the local doctor, who tells the story and acts as Poirot's Watson. (Original with Christie, that is, for in an earlier book she had made a gesture toward the same device.) Once the trick has been accepted, the use of it is exquisitely fair, but should it be accepted? It certainly outraged one of the commandments in Knox's Detective Decalogue, which said that the thoughts of the Watson must not be concealed, and Wright thought it "hardly legitimate," although it was defended by Dorothy Sayers. Christie's best books, apart from this one, came in the thirties and later, but *Roger Ackroyd* is the first book to show her finest skills at full stretch, together with her characteristic zest.

Similar zest and gaiety, erring at times in the direction of flippancy, marked also the early work of Anthony Berkeley Cox (1893–   ), who wrote first as Anthony Berkeley and later as Francis Iles. His full achievement as Francis Iles is discussed in the next chapter, but as Anthony Berkeley he was responsible in the twenties for one of the most stunning trick stories in the history of detective fiction. *The Poisoned Chocolates Case* (1929), which began as a short story and was then enlarged into a novel, is equally cunning and irreverent—irreverent in the way it cocked a snook at the pedantic solemnity which had by then invaded not merely writing about the detective story, but the actual books. His novel, woven very loosely round the Detection Club which Berkeley had recently founded, offers six separate solutions to the question: who sent the poisoned chocolates that killed Joan Bendix? One of these solutions is proposed by Roger Sheringham, the amateur detective who appears in most of Berkeley's early books. Like Trent, Sheringham was conceived almost as a joke, a caricature of an offensive acquaintance. He was taken seriously by readers, however, so that Berkeley had "to tone his offensiveness down." None of the other early stories is equal to *The Poisoned Chocolates Case,* but all have a liveliness that keeps them fresh even today.

Of Dorothy (Leigh) Sayers (1893–1957) it is not easy to write fairly. For her wholehearted admirers, a diminished but still considerable band, she is the finest detective-story writer of the twentieth century; to those less enthusiastic, her work is long-winded and ludicrously snobbish. The early books are as ingenious as the later ones, and differ from them chiefly in her attitude to Lord Peter

Wimsey. It is from a point of view a long way short of idolatry that they are discussed here.

Her merits were rare among the crime writers between the wars. Her mind was clear and incisive, and she had read very widely in crime literature. Her introductions to the first two volumes of *Detection, Mystery and Horror,* published in 1928 and 1931,* show an acute intelligence at work. She was the first writer to place five of Poe's stories rather than three within the canon, the first to acclaim the merits of Le Fanu in this field. Everything she says calls for respect, even though some of it may prompt disagreement. And in reading her novels and short stories it is impossible not to admire the careful craftsmanship with which they have been made. Her plots are organized with care; the details she produces about a means of murder are often original and always carefully researched. She took pains to make sure that the details in her stories were right, or at least she tried to make sure, not always with success. In the best of her early novels, *Unnatural Death* (1927), murders are committed by the injection of an air bubble into an artery, which stopped the circulation and so caused an apparently natural death. A medical opinion given a few years later was that although the entry of air into the circulation *may* cause death, this "would be unlikely with a hypodermic syringe, which rarely holds more than 2-3 cc." It would be pernickety, though, to condemn a book which is a compendium of clever touches (who else has thought of making not one set of false footprints, but three, as the villain does here?) on such a ground. The method was at least possible, and it would be ungenerous to demand certainty. *The Unpleasantness at the Bellona Club* (1928) is partly concerned with the decision about an inheritance involved by the question of whether General Fentiman or Lady Dormer was the first to die, and similarly cunning strokes can be found in most Sayers books.

The case against Dorothy Sayers rests chiefly upon the same evidence that admirers would cite in her favor. It is based upon the way in which she wrote, and upon the character of her detective.

* In America, these short-story collections were called *The Omnibus of Crime.*

Edmund Wilson called a later novel, *The Nine Tailors,* "one of the dullest books I have ever encountered in any field," and there can be no doubt that by any reasonable standards applied to writing, as distinct from plotting, she was pompous and boring. Every book contains an enormous amount of padding, in the form of conversations which, although they may have a distinct connection with the plot, are spread over a dozen pages where the point could be covered in as many lines. This might be forgivable if what was said had some intrinsic interest, but these dialogues are carried on between stereotyped figures (her English yokels are particularly to be deplored, with facetious professional men running them close) who have nothing at all to say, but only a veiled clue to communicate. These people, like the clubmen in the *Bellona Club* or the minor upper-class characters in *Clouds of Witness** are indeed conceived in the terms of a sketch for *Punch,* and *Unnatural Death* shows her flinching away from anything more serious. The multiple murderess here detests men (she shows an "uncontrollable revulsion of the flesh" when kissed by Wimsey) and has distinct power over clinging women. She is clearly a lesbian, but because of Sayers's inability to convey this, the portrait of her is inadequate. Of course the conventions of the time did not permit description of physical lesbian acts, but there is something coarsely wrong about the way in which this woman first tries to murder Wimsey and then desperately attempts to force herself to make love to him.

It would be charitable to think that Wimsey, like Sheringham, was conceived as a joke, but unhappily there is every indication that Sayers regarded him with the most tender feelings. Lord Peter, the second son of the Duke of Denver, is a caricature of an English aristocrat conceived with an immensely snobbish loving seriousness. His speech strongly resembles that of Bertie Wooster, slightly affected by Arthur Augustus d'Arcy in the *Magnet.* He sometimes wears a monocle, or at least this is a fact sometimes mentioned, and it would seem that it may have been either a real monocle or a powerful magnifying lens. He drops the last letters of words, and says things like "I'll drop in on you later and we'll have a jolly old pow-wow, what?" and asks of a man following him, "Is the fellow a

* In America, *Clouds of Witnesses.*

sahib?" At times his self-conscious humor is excruciating, in passages like this one where he addresses himself for the benefit of Detective Inspector Parker:

"Even I am baffled. But not for long! (he cried, with a magnificent burst of self-confidence.) My Honour (Capital H) is concerned to track this Human Fiend (capitals) to its hidden source, and nail the whited sepulchre to the mast even though it crush me in the attempt! Loud applause. His chin sank broodingly upon his dressing-gown, and he breathed a few guttural notes into the bass saxophone which was the cherished companion of his solitary hours in the bathroom."

One is not surprised that the family motto is "As my Whimsy takes me." The Wodehouse note is repeated in the Jeeves-like Bunter, Wimsey's "confidential man and assistant sleuth," whose conversational style is made clear on the first page of *Clouds of Witness*: " 'Good morning, my lord. Fine morning, my lord. Your lordship's bath-water is ready.' "

All this might be more endurable if Wimsey ever appeared to have the knowledge of history, antiques, music, gastronomy, and other matters that he is said to possess, but these qualities are asserted rather than demonstrated, and when demonstration is attempted it is sometimes wrong. When Wimsey tells Parker that he should ask Bunter "to give you a bottle of the Château d'Yquem —it's rather decent," he does so in apparent ignorance of the fact that this very sweet wine is not an all-purpose tipple. (In the same spirit, Thorndyke orders a bottle of Barsac before considering what he is going to eat.)

In America, during the same decade, S. S. Van Dine produced a similar monster of snobbish affectation in Philo Vance. Willard Huntington Wright (1888–1939), who used the name of S. S. Van Dine for his crime stories, was a journalist and art critic who wrote under his own name a number of books, including a study of Nietzsche and an interesting but commercially unsuccessful novel called *The Man of Promise* (1916). He turned to serious reading of crime stories during a long period of illness, and used a pseudonym for his first crime story, *The Benson Murder Case*

(1926), because he thought that although British novelists could write detective stories as a sideline without damaging their reputations, "Being an American, I rather feared ostracism if I boldly switched from esthetics and philologic research to fictional sleuthing." He hid therefore behind "an old family name and the SteamShip initials." Van Dine plotted his criminal career carefully, beginning with the submission of three very long synopses which were immediately accepted, and planning to abandon crime stories after writing six of them in as many years. In the event, the books were so overwhelmingly successful and, together with the films made from them, brought in so much money that Wright-Van Dine wrote nothing else. Howard Haycraft says that his second book, *The Canary Murder Case* (1927), "broke all modern publishing records for detective fiction."

It is difficult now to grasp the extent of Van Dine's success in America, and to a much lesser extent in Britain. Ian Fleming affords a modern parallel, although the devices of publicity were used more obviously in his case. Van Dine's second book was on the American best-seller lists for months, and the third was even more successful. It was said that he had lifted the detective story onto the plane of a fine art, and by his own account he was the favorite crime writer of two Presidents. Wright, a self-conscious aesthete with an admiration for the Nietzschean superior man, was delighted, but the pleasure was not unalloyed. His fate is curiously foreshadowed in that of Stanford West, the hero of his only novel, who sells out by abandoning the unpopular work in which he searches for "a sound foundation of culture and aristocracy" and becoming a successful novelist. The title of an article he wrote at the height of his fame, "I Used to Be a Highbrow and Look at Me Now," reflects both his pleasure, and his regret that he was no longer regarded seriously as a writer.

Philo Vance, who might be called Wimsey's American cousin, was Wright's wish-fulfillment projection. He is "a young social aristocrat" who spent some time at Oxford and later "transferred his residence to a villa outside Florence," although all his cases take place in urban America. Just under six feet tall, slender, sinewy, and graceful, he has what was even at the time a slightly outdated

Byronic charm. "His chiselled regular features gave his face the attraction of strength and uniform modelling," although "a sardonic coldness of expression precluded the designation of handsome." Like Wimsey, he wears a monocle and drops the "g" at the end of words like "amazin' " and distressin',", and he has a ludicrous manner of speech, represented by remarks like " 'I note that our upliftin' Press bedecked its front pages this morning with head-lines about a pogrom at the old Greene mansion last night. Where-fore?' " He has an encyclopedic knowledge about absolutely everything, or at least about everything related to the cases in which he is concerned, a knowledge supported by a tremendous apparatus of footnotes. This learning is continually and unnecessarily ob-truded, so that he answers a question from the woodenheaded Sergeant Heath about what he has been doing by saying: " 'I've been immersed in the terra-cotta ornamentation of Renaissance façades, and other such trivialities, since I saw you last.' " He expresses always a languid world-weary superiority to the crimes he investi-gates and solves.

All this may sound intolerable, but there is something more to be said. Van Dine's erudition, at least in matters connected with art, painting, music, and comparative religion, was real where Sayers's was defective. Partly in consequence of this, and partly be-cause he took such pains with the idealized self-portrait, Vance does come through as a personality of real intellectual attainment in a way that Wimsey does not. In the early books, his knowledge is directly related to the cases in which he is involved, and informa-tion is given which enables the intelligent reader to follow the deductions. And it should also be said that the best of the Van Dine stories are models of construction. Utterly remote from real life, they remain fascinating by strict adherence to the rules of their own dotty logic, and through their creator's self-absorbed immer-sion in his own work. There is a sort of grand imaginative folly about the best books, *The Greene Murder Case* (1928) and *The Bishop Murder Case* (1929), which carries us along once the prem-ises of the story are accepted. In the first of these stories, a whole series of murders is carried out, which prove to have been copied from material in a great crime library. Do the crimes seem im-possible? Van Dine is able to show that every one of them can be paralleled in Hans Gross's great handbook on criminal investigation. *The Bishop Murder Case* is an even more astonishing performance. Again there is a series of murders, apparently the work of a maniac who bases himself on nursery rhymes, so that Johnny Sprig is shot through the middle of his wig and Cock Robin is killed by an arrow. Are the crimes meaningless? Obscure intellectual clues are remarked by or planted on Vance, connected with chess, Ibsen's plays, mathematical theories. In the end, the murderer dies when Vance swaps the poisoned drink prepared for him, after distracting attention by exclaiming in admiration at sight of a Cellini plaque (" 'Berenson told me it was destroyed in the seventeenth century' "). When District Attorney Markham says that this death was murder, the detective's reply is characteristic. " 'Oh, doubtless. Yes—of course. Most reprehensible . . . I say, am I by any chance under arrest?' " In *The Scarab Murder Case* (1930), Vance dispenses the justice of Superman in a similar way, by arranging that the murderer shall be killed, since there is no chance of his legal conviction.

Ogden Nash summed up later feelings about Vance in two lines:

> Philo Vance
> Needs a kick in the pance.

No doubt. Yet admiration should not be withheld from these two books at least. In their outrageous cleverness, their disdainful disregard of everything except the detective and the puzzle, they are among the finest fruits of the Golden Age.

HUMDRUMS, FARCEURS, AND OTHERS

The plan of the house indicating where the body was found, the map of the grounds showing the garden and the summerhouse were standard accessories to the story of the period, and in many British books a timetable appeared, too. This timetable, often of a railway or bus journey, was offered in preparation for the breaking of an alibi, and it was used in greatest detail and most often by Freeman Wills Crofts (1879–1957), who put his knowledge as a railway engineer to frequent although hardly varied use. In a Crofts story, the murderer can often be identified at an early point by his

apparently unbreakable alibi, which is then broken by dogged
Inspector (later Superintendent) French. Crofts's first book, *The
Cask* (1920), which traces back in elaborate detail the way in which
a cask came to contain gold coins and a woman's hand instead of
a piece of statuary, has a grip and a cleverness that he never quite
repeated. His plotting became increasingly mechanical, particularly
after the appearance of the plodding French in his fifth book.
Crofts knew nothing about Scotland Yard, and did not think it
important that he should learn the details of police procedure. He
succeeded so well in making his detective commonplace (in fact,
police detectives are markedly colorful characters) that he became uninteresting. For those who want to encounter the plodder at
his best, *Inspector French's Greatest Case* (1925) and *Inspector
French and the Cheyne Mystery* (1927)* can be recommended.

Crofts was not just a typical, but also the best, representative
of what may be called the Humdrum school of detective novelists
whose work poured from the presses during the decade, and indeed
for long afterward. Most of them came late to writing fiction, and
few had much talent for it. They had some skill in constructing
puzzles, nothing more, and ironically they fulfilled much better than
Van Dine his dictum that the detective story properly belonged in
the category of riddles or crossword puzzles. Most of the Humdrums
were British, and among the best-known of them were Major Cecil
Street, who used the name of John Rhode; R. A. J. Walling; and
J. S. Fletcher. The collaborative Humdrum of G. D. H. and Margaret
Cole should be mentioned, because the Coles were both deeply in-
volved in the Labour movement, and G. D. H. Cole was a famous
figure within it, yet their books ignored the very existence of the
social realities with which in life they were so much concerned.
American Humdrums were fewer and rather less alkaline than their
British counterparts, chiefly because the crime story in the United
States remained in its infancy before Van Dine.

More lively than the Humdrums were the Farceurs, those writers
for whom the whole business of fictional murder, and of writing
murder stories, was endlessly amusing. These were almost wholly
British, partly because the writing of such stories demanded a degree

* In America, *The Cheyne Mystery*.

of sophistication that American writers did not possess during this decade, and partly because Britain between the wars was such a safe country in which to live. If you lived in Chicago, or even in Paris, during the twenties, you were much less likely to treat murder light-heartedly than if you lived in London.

One of the most talented Farceurs was Philip MacDonald (189?–   ), who introduced Colonel Anthony Gethryn in *The Rasp* (1924). MacDonald was one of those writers who find it easy to think of an idea but hardly ever manage to carry through a fully coherent plot. A restless but careless experimenter, he belongs in spirit to the twenties, although two of his best stories, *Rynox* (1930) and *X. v. Rex* (1933), were written in the following decade. *Rynox* begins with an epilogue in which nearly £300,000 is delivered in used pound notes to the Naval, Military and Cosmos Assurance Company, and then traces the means by which this has happened, with occasional asides from author to reader. In *X. v. Rex,* written under the pseudonym of Martin Porlock, there is a most elaborate description of the police measures taken in an attempt to trap an "invisible man" mass murderer, and the way in which he evades them. (One murder is carried out by a sandwich man, firing under cover of his board.) The build-up in this story is most tantalizingly done, although the climax, as often with MacDonald, is rather a letdown.

Monsignor Ronald Knox (1888–1957) is the super-typical Farceur of the decade, one who never allowed into his half-dozen detective stories the faintest breath of seriousness, to disturb the desperate facetiousness of his style. *The Viaduct Murder* (1925), with its amateur investigator who gets everything wrong, owes a good deal to Bentley, but a more characteristic book is *The Footsteps at the Lock* (1927), one of those stories in which a man who is presumed dead turns out to have staged his own disappearance. Knox was fascinated by the Holmesian apparatus of clues and deductions, as MacDonald was fascinated by methods of murder, and neither of them bothered much about concealing the identity of the easily spotted villain.

Probably the most entertaining book of this kind written during the twenties is *The Red House Mystery,* the only detective story of

A. A. Milne (1882–1956). More than twenty years after the book's publication in 1922, Raymond Chandler made an attack on it which successfully convicted Milne of characteristic Farceur-like carelessness in plotting, and of condoning some outstanding improbabilities. Chandler's attack is devastating—it should be said that the sort of analysis he makes would be damaging to many Golden Age detective stories—yet I was able to reread the story without much loss of pleasure, and even with some admiration of Milne's skill in skating over thin ice. Rex Stout seems to be right in pinning the word "charming" to the book's light, easy way with murder, its dexterous shifts of suspicion and emphasis. There are improbabilities that have to be ignored as Milne ignores them, but the charm remains potent.

Improbabilities were not confined to Farceurs. The crime stories written by Eden Phillpotts (1862–1960), under his own name and that of Harrington Hext, were among the most ridiculous of the time. Two examples will be sufficient. In *The Grey Room* (1922), people who sleep in this room die because the heat of the mattress releases a Borgia poison contained in fifty miles of wire put between the flock mattress and its satin casing. There is no need even for the victim to sleep on the mattress, for in one case a hot-water bottle placed in the bed does the trick. In a Harrington Hext book, *The Thing at Their Heels* (1923), a Radical clergyman (any Radical is automatically to be suspected in this era) kills four people so that the family estate can descend to him and become a home for outcasts.

Among the principal achievements of the decade were A. E. W. Mason's second and third detective stories, *The House of the Arrow* (1924), and *The Prisoner in the Opal* (1928). Mason was a member of the Detection Club, but he had little patience with the attempt to draw up a set of rules and little liking for the way in which he saw the detective story going. He put his position clearly a few years later in a radio interview, when he said that the question was whether the detective novel was to consist "simply of a conundrum and its answer," or whether, as he preferred, it should "present one facet of a story which shall seek to enchant the interest of its readers on the different ground of the clash of its characters and the diverity of their interests." These two books fulfill such requirements. They are both good detective stories and they are also among the best of his novels, containing a genuine *frisson* of terror given through use of the detective form. Given our present degree of sophistication, the puzzle in *The House of the Arrow* is rather easy to solve, but this fact affects very little the pleasure one has in reading the book, and *The Prisoner in the Opal* is one of the few crime stories to make successful use of devil worship and the Black Mass. Hanaud and Ricardo reappear, skillfully interwoven into the pattern of the stories, and the quality of the detection in both books is of high quality. Mason's last two crime stories, *They Wouldn't Be Chessmen* and *The House in Lordship Lane,* show his powers in decline.

Before the end of the twenties, a certain weariness with mechanical ingenuity was beginning to be apparent. Van Dine, appearing in his own person as Wright, declared in 1927 that only the "inept and uninformed author" would any longer use such "fashions and inventions of yesterday" as the cipher message containing the solution, the murder committed by an animal, the phonograph alibi, the discovery of a totally distinctive cigarette, the forged fingerprints, the dummy figure, the dagger or other sharp instrument shot from a machine, the locked-room murder committed after somebody had entered the room. A rebellious note was struck, too, as well as a weary one. In 1930, Anthony Berkeley said, in the preface to what was actually a disappointingly conventional book called *The Second Shot*:

I am personally convinced that the days of the old crime-puzzle, pure and simple, relying entirely upon the plot and without any added attractions of character, style, or even humour, are in the hands of the auditor; and that the detective story is in the process of developing into the novel with a detective or crime interest, holding its readers less by mathematical than by psychological ties.

Both Wright and Berkeley were to be proved truthful prophets, although both underestimated the tolerance of readers, the skill of new writers in burnishing up dingy devices so that they shone freshly, and the ability of established ones to adapt their techniques.

IX

The Golden Age: The Thirties

NEW BLOOD

When one looks at the Golden Age in retrospect, the developing rebellion against its ideas and standards is clearly visible, but this is the wisdom of hindsight, for during the thirties the classical detective story burgeoned with new and considerable talents almost every year. Just before the decade began, Ellery Queen and John Dickson Carr published their first books, and in the middle of it Michael Innes and Nicholas Blake brought a fresh style and approach to the form. Margery Allingham and Ngaio Marsh used the standard formula in a way rather different from that of Christie and Sayers, and in America a fleet of women writers played their own variations on the theme. The French detective story, which had been quiescent for years, was triumphantly revived by a Belgian, Georges Simenon. In numbers also, the detective story grew enormously during the thirties. Haycraft has some interesting figures about the number of crime stories mentioned in the American *Book Review Digest*. No more than a dozen were reviewed in 1914, a figure which had grown to 97 in 1925 and to 217 in 1939. These figures say nothing about the number of books actually published, of which there are no details available, but, as he says, the increase is probably "rel tive and representative." In Britain as in America, no details are available in actual figures, but it is safe to say that if 1914 is taken as a basis, the number of crime stories published had multiplied by five in 1926 and by ten in 1939.

In dealing with the mass of stories published in the thirties, and the greater number appearing with every year up to the present time, I have by wish and necessity been selective rather than comprehensive. It should be understood that in the thirties, and later still, many Humdrums continued to write, and some new ones appeared. Perhaps the only one who need be mentioned individually is Arthur William Upfield (1888–1964), who created the half-caste detective Napoleon Bonaparte. The "Bony" books have the advantage of an original detective, whose tracking skills are again slightly reminiscent of Fenimore Cooper, and of the unusual Australian setting. The earlier ones are well told in a straightforward way, the later marked by some curious stylistic affectations, but the characters apart from Bony are uniformly wooden, and none of the books really moves out of the well-worn Humdrum tracks. Apart from Upfield, there were in the thirties many reasonably competent writers who produced work thinly echoing that of the major practitioners, but this is a history and not a catalogue, and the history of the crime story is that of its major talents. Of these the two new and most notable in the first half of the thirties were John Dickson Carr and Ellery Queen.

John Dickson Carr (1905–   ), who also uses the pseudonym of Carter Dickson, is unique among crime writers in his unswerving devotion to one form or another of the locked-room mystery. In his first crime novel, *It Walks by Night* (1929), the essential elements of every Carr puzzle are laid out by the French detective Bencolin:

"The murderer was not hiding. . . . There is no possibility of false walls, for you can stand in any door and test the entire partition of the next room. Tear open floor or ceiling, and you will find only floor or ceiling of the next room. . . . In short, there are no secret entrances; the murderer was not hiding anywhere in the room; he did not go out by the window; he did not go out by the salon door. . . . Yet a murderer *had* beheaded his victim there; we know in this case above all others that the dead man did not kill himself."

In The Hollow Man (1935),* Carr offers in one chapter, through his detective Dr. Gideon Fell, a splendidly lively and learned discussion of locked-room murders and their possible solutions under seven different classifications, with some sub-divisions relating to methods of tampering with doors. In his dozens of books, Carr/Dickson has rung the changes on the possibilities with astonishing skill. Often his postulates are improbable, but the reader rarely feels them to be impossible, and the deception is built up, sustained with teasing hints that can be interpreted in half a dozen different ways, and at last revealed, with staggering skill. The best Carr/Dickson is the most ingenious, and my vote would go to The Hollow Man itself, one of the books which, as Dr. Fell says, "derives its problem from illusion and impersona-tion." (The kind of improbable postulate I mean, which doesn't affect enjoyment at the time but may do so afterward, is shown here by the evidence of three witnesses, all of whom accept the in-accurate time shown by a street clock. Did nobody possess a wrist-watch?). The conjurer's illusion is marvelously clever. But almost every one of the early books has its passionate admirers. Among those most praised by most people are The Arabian Nights Murder (1936), The Burning Court (1937), The Black Spectacles (1939),† and the Carter Dickson The Judas Window (1938). To these I would add two favorites of my own, one Carter Dickson called The Ten Teacups (1937),‡ and one John Dickson Carr, The Emperor's Snuff Box (1942). For almost twenty years, Carr's fertility seemed endless. He wrote an average of two or more books a year, every one of them playing a fresh variation on the locked-room theme. Perhaps because there is after all a limit to such variations, perhaps because the formula itself is now badly worn, his recent books are much inferior to the early ones.

The trouble with exploiting such a formula is that everything else becomes subservient to it, or at least that is what has happened with Carr. He was strongly influenced by Poe and Chesterton. (Dr. Fell with his great bulk, his cane, his eyeglasses on a black ribbon,

* In America, The Three Coffins.
† In America, The Problem of the Green Capsule.
‡ In America, The Peacock Feather Murders.

flowing cloak, and rumpled hair is a very Chestertonian figure.) His books are full of reference to macabre events and possibilities, and of Chestertonian paradox, but in the later work especially these are mere stage trappings. There is genuine feeling in some of Chesterton's short stories, but very little in any of Carr's writing after his first half-dozen books. Since the whole story is built round the puzzle, there is no room for characterization, and the limitation of these clever stories is clearly expressed in the fact that what one remembers about them is never any of the people, but simply the puzzle.

Carr is an American writer who is often regarded as British, partly because of his rumbustiously Anglo-Saxon tone and partly because many of his best books have an English setting. There is no doubt about the American origins and manner of Frederic Dannay (1905–   ) and Manfred B. (Bennington) Lee (1905–1971), two cousins who under the name of Ellery Queen combined in one of the most successful and lengthy collaborations in literary history. Like Carr, they were unusual in coming to crime writing as young men, and like him they showed for many years an agreeable zest. The early Queen stories, and also those written under the name of Drury Lane, showed some debt to Van Dine. In Wright's stories, S. S. Van Dine appears as the recorder of Vance's cases, and Ellery Queen added a grace note of a similar kind by making the author identical with the detective. It was my impression that in the early books Ellery Queen himself had many of Vance's characteristics, but although he speaks with a drawl, calls his father "pater," and is given to airing bits of out-of-the-way knowledge, I found in a recent rereading that the resemblances are only superficial. Ellery is an amateur investigator—and in fact a detective-story writer—always at hand when his father, Inspector Richard Queen, is confronted by a difficult case.

The word "ingenuity" gets a good deal of work in these chapters about the Golden Age, and certainly one would not wish to avoid it in writing of the early Queen novels. The ingenuity is of a kind quite different from Carr's, resting in a relentlessly analytical treatment of every possible clue and argument. In these early books, a "Challenge to the Reader" appears some three-quarters of the way through, in the form of a statement saying that the reader has now been presented with all the clues needed to solve the case, and that only one solution is possible. The rare distinction of the books is that this claim is accurate. These are problems in deduction that do really permit of only one answer, and there are few crime stories indeed of which this can be said.

Again, which of the Queen novels containing this challenge is the best must be largely a matter of individual taste. My own favorite is *The Greek Coffin Mystery* (1932), with its brilliant surprise ending, but almost equally good are *The Dutch Shoe Mystery* (1931), which has a perfect piece of extended reasoning about the shoes left by the murderer, *The French Powder Mystery* (1930), in which you have to wait until the last line for the solution, and *The Chinese Orange Mystery* (1934), with its turned-round clues. Judged as exercises in rational deduction, these are certainly among the best detective stories ever written.

Yet something has been lost to achieve this rational perfection, and, as with Carr, what has been sacrificed is the sense that the author has any feeling for the people in his story. More sensitive than Carr, or less persistently adherent to a formula, Dannay and Lee gave up the Challenge and the close analysis of clues, and made Ellery a less omniscient and more human figure, in search of a wider significance and more interesting characterization. Perhaps their immense reading in the field of crime stories made them dissatisfied with what they were doing, perhaps they felt that they had worked out this particular vein. In any case, their first ten books represent a peak point in the history of the detective story between the wars.

Among the most extraordinary performances of these years were the three "Obelist" stories (an obelist is "one who harbors suspicion") of C. Daly King (1895–1963). King was a psychologist who wrote a book called *Beyond Behaviorism* and another on *The Psychology of Consciousness*. Psychologists enter most of his stories, and in *Obelists at Sea* (1933) four of them, all belonging to different schools, investigate a murder at sea. At the end of each book, King provided a "clue finder," showing by page references that "the arch-criminal hereinbefore has been suggested by sundry indications," as he coyly put it. The most remarkable of his books, one with a gloss of slightly meretricious cleverness, is *Obelists Fly High* (1935), in which a famous surgeon, flying to operate on his brother the American Secretary of State, receives a death threat which is carried out on the plane. The book begins with a shooting-it-out epilogue between the police guard of the surgeon and an unnamed villain, and ends with a prologue which reveals a wholly unsuspected murderer. The glitter is meretricious because the solution outrages our capacity for belief. Nobody, however, could deny the originality of the obelist stories. King's other work was much inferior to them, and with the coming of the war he gave up writing crime stories.

It looked at one time as though the work of Rex (Todhunter) Stout (1866–   ) might similarly represent a peak, in the creation of the most original and plausible Holmes-and-Watson pair. He began to write crime stories late in life, after the production of some interesting but commercially unsuccessful novels, and *Fer-de-Lance* (1934) introduced his puffing, grunting Montenegrin-born heavyweight detective Nero Wolfe, and Wolfe's tough, sometimes aggressive assistant Archie Goodwin. Stout may have begun with the intention of guying a little, in the gentlest way, the whole detective form. Wolfe sits in his oversize chair, unable to cross his legs because they are so fat, taking trips in the elevator up to his collection of ten thousand orchids in the plant room on the roof, and solving crimes without moving from the house. Goodwin, a barbarian man of action ("I do read books, but I never yet got any real satisfaction out of one"), is Wolfe's eyes and legs for anything that takes place outside the old brownstone on West Thirty-fifth Street.

Plotting was not Stout's strong suit, and Wolfe's solutions were sometimes arbitrary or instinctive, but in *Fer-de-Lance, The League of Frightened Men* (1935), and other early books, notably *The Red Box* (1937), the dialogue crackles, Archie dashes around and almost falls in love, and Wolfe is built up into a slightly comic but always impressive figure. But as time went on and the books piled up, Wolfe had sometimes to be taken away from home, and the problems involved in all series characters who appear in a lot of stories became evident. These are, of course, all the greater when the characters are built up from a few superficial attributes, like love of beer and orchids and a gourmet's appreciation of food. Slowly, slowly, the Wolfe stories have declined. The decline became steep after the end of the forties, which still contain some books very near to Stout's best work, like *The Silent Speaker* (1946) and *The Second Confession* (1949). Stout himself is the Grand Old Man of American crime fiction, still full of liveliness and charm now that he is in his middle eighties.

During the thirties, the style of the detective, and particularly of the amateur detective, changed. The habit of disguise finished with World War I. Very few detectives who made their appearance after that time attempted to change their appearances. The tradition of omniscience was maintained in Dr. Fell, in the barely distinguishable Sir Henry Merrivale, who is Carter Dickson's investigator, and in Ellery Queen, but the detectives springing from the new talents of Margery Allingham, Ngaio Marsh, Nicholas Blake, and Michael Innes behaved more like normal human beings, and were capable of making mistakes. This change was accompanied by a cautious drawing of the blinds that are kept permanently down in the house of classical detection, so that a little light from the outside world peeped in. The work of Margery Allingham (1904–1966) and the New Zealander Ngaio Marsh (1899–   ) often viewed the social scene with gently ironic eyes. The first novel in which Allingham's talents are really on display, *Death of a Ghost* (1934), contains a lively picture of the hangers-on feeding on the posthumous fame of a great Victorian and Edwardian artist, and Ngaio Marsh's *Death in Ecstasy* (1936) goes into considerable detail about one of those semi-dotty semi-erotic mystical cults that are commonplace today. Other early Allinghams used a publishing house and smart Mayfair as backgrounds, and Marsh put her knowledge of the theatre into *Vintage Murder* (1937). Of course all crime stories have some background setting, but whereas in a wholly classical novel like the first Queen, *The Roman Hat Mystery,* the theatre where the crime takes place is devised as a puzzle box, Allingham and Marsh comment upon the affectations of near-artists or the pretensions of theatricals.

They found it difficult, however, to combine this sort of thing with writing a detective story. The first forty-odd pages of *Death of a Ghost* have amusing things to say about artists and critics. Then comes the murder, and all this is forgotten in the need to discover clues and investigate suspects. In Marsh's work of this period, there are often long and tedious post-murder examinations of suspects. Both writers were to refine their technical skills in later books. In the meantime, they were known chiefly for their detectives, whose characters testified to that Anglo-American snobbery upon which Sayers played so successfully. Margery Allingham's Albert Campion is lank, pale, fair-haired, spectacled, and "the general impression one received of him was that he was well-bred and a trifle absent-minded." He is indeed well-bred, having close connections with the upper reaches of the peerage, and perhaps distant ones with royalty. His servant, Magersfontein Lugg, is a comic Cockney described in an early book as "a Vulgarian in the service of Mr. Campion." Ngaio Marsh's Inspector (later Superintendent) Roderick Alleyn, although a professional detective, is by no means of humble birth. His mother is Lady Alleyn, a breeder of Alsatians, and Alleyn is very much at home in places where most professional detectives would feel uneasy. Both Allingham and Marsh were intending to draw naturalistic portraits, but the result is simply that their detectives are less distinctive and interesting than Vance and Queen, although it is true that they may be regarded as less objectionable.

Cecil Day-Lewis (1904–   ), poet and now Poet Laureate, who began in 1935 to write detective stories under the name of Nicholas Blake, brought to the Golden Age detective story a distinctly literary tone, and also in his early books a Left Wing political attitude. Both of these things were unusual at the time. I can remember still the shock I felt when on the first page of Blake's first book, *A Question of Proof* (1935), T. S. Eliot's name was mentioned. (I should be prepared to offer odds that there are less than a dozen crime stories written during the decades between the wars in which the name of any modern poet appears.) And most of the new writers, like the old ones, had at least implicit Right Wing sympathies. Their policemen were all good, their radicals bad or silly; they took the existing social order for granted. None of them would have produced a book like Blake's second, *Thou Shell of Death* (1936), in which a national hero based perhaps on T. E. Lawrence is the murderer, nor certainly would the solution to the mystery have been produced by Nigel Strangeways's recognition of a quotation from the Jacobean dramatist Tourneur. Strangeways was a real innovation, a truly literary detective rather than one of those given quotations to spout. The best of his prewar cases, and perhaps Blake's most successful book, is *The Beast Must Die* (1938), a clever variation of the Ackroyd trick.

Probably the most engaging thing about these early books of Blake's is their bubbling high spirits, the obvious pleasure he got from playing with detection. One should not exaggerate his political concern or the literary character of his work, for these things are apparent chiefly in contrast to the attitudes of his detectival colleagues. Michael Innes, the pseudonym of John Innes Mackintosh Stewart (1906–   ), certainly gave his books a much thicker coating of urbane literary conversation, rather in the manner of Peacock strained through or distorted by Aldous Huxley. The Innes books were immediately acclaimed as something new in detective fiction from the publication in 1935 of *Death at the President's Lodging,* a title with misleading implications for the United States, where it was rather tamely renamed *Seven Suspects.* The *Times Literary Supplement* said that he was a newcomer who at once took his place in the front rank and, with the publication of *Hamlet, Revenge!* (1936), called him "in a class by himself among writers of detective fiction."

There was actually nothing very new about Innes's approach. J. C. Masterman, in *An Oxford Tragedy* (1933), had produced very much the same kind of "don's delight" book, marked by the same sort of urbanity. But Innes is the finest of the Farceurs, a writer who turns the detective story into an overcivilized joke, by a frivolity which makes it a literary conversation piece with some detection taking place on the side. There is no greater quotation spotter or capper in crime literature than Inspector (later Sir John) Appleby, and few Innes characters of this period will flinch at playing a parlor game which involves remembering quotations about bells in Shakespeare. Appleby, when confronted by the "fourteen bulky volumes of the Argentorati Athenaeus," murmurs: "The Deipnosophists . . . Schweighauser's edition . . . takes up a lot of room. . . . Dindorf's compacter . . . and there he is." Appleby shows off, not out of sheer pretentiousness like Wimsey or Vance, but from genuine high spirits. The Innes stories cannot compare as puzzles with the work of Van Dine or Queen. Their strength is in their flippant gaiety, and perhaps the best of them all is *Stop Press* (1939), in which he dispenses with the almost obligatory murder, and keeps the story balanced on little jets of unfailingly amusing talk.

The crime stories of C. H. B. (Clifford Henry Benn) Kitchin (1896–1967), in particular *Death of My Aunt* (1929), have attracted a small band of fervent admirers. Perhaps the best of them is the last, *Death of His Uncle* (1939), in which, although we are likely to discover the truth before his stockbroker investigator, there is a good deal of pleasure to be obtained from the always urbane and at times elegant writing. Kitchin did not, however, bring anything new to the crime story although he has his place as a minor, amiable Farceur.

Just before the war, John Strachey wrote an article for the *Saturday Review of Literature* in which he picked out Innes, Blake, and Allingham as the "white hopes" of the British detective story. It was an intelligent choice, but in fact only Allingham was able to develop her talent further in the postwar world. Blake slowly lost the zest of his early writing, and only *Minute For Murder* (1947), *End of Chapter* (1957), and his fictional reconstruction of an Edwardian murder case, *A Tangled Web* (1956), have the quality of his prewar books. Innes has written some fine thrillers, but his more nearly orthodox crime stories are no longer conversation pieces fizzing with wit but overcomplicated and often extremely improbable tales. Appleby, too, is now more likely to discuss the weather than to expand on Schweighauser and Dindorf. Among the later books, *A Private View* (1952) and *The New Sonia Wayward* (1960) can be recommended, but they are minor achievements compared with his first four novels. Neither Innes nor Blake really represented a new departure, as they seemed to do at the time. Their innovations, compared with those of Francis Iles, were superficial rather than radical.

VAN DINE, SAYERS, CHRISTIE: TWO STORIES END

The detective, then, was still there and still very often an amateur, but even in the work of long-established practitioners like Sayers and Christie he was changing. Against all her previously stated principles about love affairs in detective stories, Dorothy Sayers gave Lord Peter a wife and built a whole book around his falling in love with her. Agatha Christie got rid of Poirot's Idiot Friend Captain Hastings, and modified the little Belgian a great deal because she felt him to be increasingly absurd. She also refused after the early thirties to allow him to appear on the stage, and actually wrote him out of a book in which he had been the central character when she made it into a play.

Philo Vance, however, could not change. Wright had laid down the laws that relate to detective stories and their investigators, and Vance adhered to them. He became not less but more erudite, talking often about subjects that had little to do with the case in hand. His affectations and eccentricities were not softened like those of other Great Detectives, but became more pronounced. With this went an increasingly bizarre choice of subject, an increasing strain in the treatment. The decline in the last six Vance books is so steep that the critic who called the ninth one more stitch in his literary shroud was not overstating the case. Films of the books continued to be made (no less than eight actors played Vance on the screen, including William Powell, Paul Lukas, Warren William, and Basil Rathbone), but the popularity of the books had greatly faded by the time Wright died of a thrombosis in 1939. He died rich but, as he bitterly recognized, no longer much respected. The last line of his single straight novel, after the hero has settled for comfort and easy fame instead of hard integrity, is: "Behind his smile was a sense of unutterable and tragic irony." Willard Huntington Wright must have recognized that irony.

The development of Dorothy Sayers can be charted best from an essay she wrote in 1937, in which she says that she had always wanted her books to be "novel[s] of manners instead of pure crossword puzzle[s]," so moving back to the tradition of Collins and Le Fanu. She had "indulged in a little 'good writing' here and there" and had been encouraged by its reception. With this encouragement, she had introduced a love element into *Strong Poison* (1930), produced a "criticism of life" in *Murder Must Advertise* (1933), and at last in *Gaudy Night* (1935) had as she thought succeeded in "choosing a plot that should exhibit intellectual integrity as the one great permanent value in an emotionally unstable world" and so managed to say "the thing that, in a confused way, I had been wanting to say all my life."

There is a breath-taking gap here between intention and achievement. Wimsey remains essentially unchanged. He still says things like "What-ho! that absolutely whangs the nail over the crumpet," and a snobbishness outrageous even for Sayers has provided him with a pedigree and a family history which, together with a long biographical note, act as preface to the new editions of each book. The books themselves show, with the exception of the lively *Murder Must Advertise,* an increasing pretentiousness, a dismal sentimentality, and a slackening of the close plotting that had been her chief virtue. *Gaudy Night* is essentially a "woman's novel" full of the most tedious pseudo-serious chat between the characters that goes on for page after page. Mrs. Q. D. Leavis seems perfectly right in placing this later Sayers beside Marie Corelli and Ouida, and in saying that she performed the function of "giving the impression of intellectual activity to readers who would very much dislike that kind of exercise if it was actually presented to them." Sayers is hardly likely to have agreed with this attack, but after *Busman's Honeymoon* (1937), which was frankly subtitled "A love story with detective interruptions," she turned away from the hero of whom she had said, "I can see no end to Peter this side of the grave." In the last twenty years of her life, she wrote no more detective novels. When, a few years before her death, her American publishers asked for a new introduction to accompany an omnibus volume, she refused it, saying that she had written the books only to make money and had no further interest in them.

One moves with pleasure from these records of disillusionment to one of success. During the thirties, Agatha Christie produced, year after year, puzzle stories of varied ingenuity and constant liveliness. Her skill was not in the tight construction of plot, nor in the locked-room mystery, nor did she often make assumptions about the scientific and medical knowledge of readers. The deception in these Christie stories is much more like the conjurer's sleight of hand. She shows us the ace of spades face up. Then she turns it over, but we still know where it is, so how has it been transformed into the five of diamonds? It is on her work during this decade, plus half a dozen of her earlier and later books, that her reputation chiefly rests, perhaps most specifically upon *Peril at End House* (1932), *Lord Edgware Dies* (1933),* *Why Didn't They Ask Evans?* (1934)† *The ABC Murders* (1936) and *Ten Little Niggers* (1939).‡ There were some mis-hits in her very considerable output at this time, but she succeeded wonderfully often in her two objectives of telling an interesting story about reasonably plausible characters and of creating a baffling mystery. Her work stayed at its peak until roughly the end of World War II. Since then it has shown a slow decline, although she is alone among Golden Age writers in remaining as readable as ever and in her capacity sometimes still to bring off a staggering conjuring trick.

ACHIEVEMENTS AND LIMITATIONS

Very many Golden Age writers whose work was once highly regarded remain undiscussed, including Josephine Bell, Gladys Mitchell and E. R. Punshon in Britain, Mignon G. Eberhart, Conyth Little, §Mabel Seeley, Helen Reilly, and Elizabeth Daly (most of whom carried on and occasionally improved the Rinehart formula) in America. The list could easily be lengthened. But the most notable practitioners have already been examined in detail, and the period can properly be judged by them.

Their achievement can be seen at its best in the close plotting of the early Queen, Van Dine, and Sayers stories, the cunning tricks of Christie, the locked-room deceptions of Carr, the literary ease of Innes and Blake. If we consider the crime story only as a puzzle, nothing written during the last twenty years comes within trailing distance of the best Golden Age work, although it should be said

---

* In America, *Thirteen at Dinner*.
† In America, *The Boomerang Clue*.
‡ In America, *And Then There Were None*.
§ In America, *Constance and Gwenyth Little*.

that little attempts to do so. If we consider it as a frivolous entertainment, nothing has been produced that is the equal of early
Innes. There are no trick stories nowadays as good as those of
Christie and Carr, certainly not the stories now being written by
those two practitioners.

In constructing the detective story as a perfect mechanism, however, the Golden Age writers sacrificed almost everything else for
the sake of this perfection. Their work pandered to the taste of
readers who wanted every character degutted so that there should
be nothing even faintly disturbing about the fate of victims or murderers. To insulate your writing totally from life permits the creation of a kind of art, but enjoyment of it has limitations as great
as those in the closed world of Restoration comedy. Indeed they are
greater, for crime stories must inevitably be "about" life in a way
that a play need not be, and if the effect is wholly artificial, in the
end we dissent from what is being offered us. The Golden Age was
not the main highway of crime fiction that it looked at the time,
but a minor road full of interesting twists and views which petered
out in a dead end.

A curious experiment by the thriller writer Dennis Wheatley with
the planning cooperation of J. G. Links, which began in 1936 with
the publication of the "murder dossier" *Murder off Miami,** blew
the gaff on the artificial nature of the Golden Age story, although
this was not the authors' intention. These "murder dossiers" were
artifacts rather than books. They contained "real" clues in the
shapes of such things as hair, matches, poison pills, in transparent
envelopes, along with photographs of the characters and the scene
of the crime. The text came in the form of telegrams, letters,
memoranda, police documents, and reports, all reproduced in
facsimile. The dossiers were produced in loose-leaf form with
ribbon bindings, except for the first one in America. The solution
of the problem depended on the illustrations. In the first dossier,
the presence of the wrong kind of toothbrush on the washstand and
the fact that one character's coat did not fit very well had to be
spotted, and another is based on a variation of the Roger Ackroyd
device. A close study of the family tree which is reproduced at the

* In America, *File on Bolitho Blane.*

start of *The Malinsay Massacre* reveals that the storyteller himself is the logical murderer. Attention is diverted from this by the fact that the text consists largely of letters written to the murderer, so that he is being told about what has happened and seems to be outside suspicion.

The first dossier sold 80,000 copies in Britain at the very low price of three shillings and sixpence. The second and third were less successful but still sold well, but the fourth, *Herewith the Clues,* was an almost complete failure. In America only the first two were published under the names Wheatley and Links, and in other countries, too, they had less success than in Britain. The sudden end of the dossiers, which are now collectors' items, reflected partly the coming of the war and partly increased costs, but principally the fact that it was almost impossible actually to read them. There was in the nature of things no characterization of any kind, and interest rested solely in the comparison of the texts with the visible clues in an attempt to discover discrepancies. The whole thing was, as Milward Kennedy said in the *Times,* nothing more than a game, and a game that could be played with full enjoyment only once. Once the gimmick of the visual clues and the letter facsimiles lost its impact, the stories could be recognized as frankly dull, and nobody would be inclined to "read" one of these dossiers a second time. But then the orthodox detective puzzles of the time were only similarly bloodless and characterless games of a more sophisticated kind, after all.

Something of this was understood by the late thirties. When Sayers said that "after a time . . . the writer gets tired of a literature without bowels," she was perfectly right, although she mistook an aristocratic pedigree for bowels. Allingham, Queen, Stout, Blake, Innes all recognized that the old order had to change and tried to change with it, but they carried with them the ball and chain of detective heroes who could not be sacrificed because of their popularity. There was also a ground swell of conscious objection to the rules and to the game, which has already been mentioned.

X

The Golden Age: Rebellion

THE BRITISH

The promise of "a novel with a detective or crime interest" made by Anthony Berkeley was fulfilled by his alter ego Francis Iles. In *Malice Aforethought* (1931) and its equally brilliant successor *Before the Fact* (1932), there is no puzzle of the classical kind. From the start, the villain is plain to us and his intentions are known. The problem is whether he will be able to carry them out successfully. What was new about the books may be expressed in the first sentences of *Malice Aforethought:*

It was not until several weeks after he had decided to murder his wife that Dr. Bickleigh took any active steps in the matter. Murder is a serious business.

Everything is laid out, the doctor's plans, their fulfillment, the police investigation. Some critics have said that a similar approach was made earlier, by Mrs. Belloc Lowndes and by Austin Freeman in his "inverted" stories, but Iles's method is so much more subtle that his work is really not comparable. The fascination of these two books lies in the interplay of character, the gaps between plot and execution, and in the air of suburban or small-town normality with which Iles invests the whole thing. The slow revelation of the villain's character in *Before the Fact* is beautifully done, and the books show very clearly that the naming of the criminal in the last chapter is not the only way of surprising the reader. Iles was a very clever writer, and the only criticism that might be made of these outstandingly original books is that they have just occasionally an air of contrivance out of keeping with their generally realistic tone.

The third Iles book, *As for the Woman* (1939), was interesting, but less successful than the first two. Announced as the first volume of a trilogy, it has had no successor. During the thirties, Cox also wrote several Anthony Berkeley books. One of them, *Trial and Error* (1937), exploits a variation of the Iles theme in the sense that we see Mr. Todhunter, who has only a few months to live, deliberately planning and apparently carrying out a murder. Too flippantly conceived to be on quite the same level as the Iles stories, this is still a highly enjoyable book with several characteristically clever twists and turns.

The Iles books were admired, although the masterly way in which they broke away from the conventions of the detective story was not fully appreciated. Iles had several followers, who faithfully copied his avoidance of the classical puzzle and tried hard to catch his particular blend of cynicism and realism, but for the most part succeeded only in being casual about murder. Among the most interesting of them were Richard Hull, the pseudonym of Richard Henry Sampson (1896–   ), and Anthony Rolls, the name under which the historian and belle-lettrist Colwyn Edward Vulliamy (1886–1971) wrote crime stories. In *Murder of My Aunt* (1934), the best of Hull's books, an epicene young man tries to kill his aunt, first through an apparent car accident, then by arson, and finally with poison. The joke has become labored long before the end, in which she foreseeably murders him. Rolls's *The Vicar's Experiments* (1932)* is about a clergyman who suddenly begins to suffer from homicidal delusions, believing that he has "been chosen by the Inscrutable Purpose to be the destroyer of Colonel Cargoy." A good deal of what follows is very amusing, but the story falters sadly once suspicion of the clergyman has been aroused. The weakness of Iles's followers was that they found it almost impossible to

---

* In America called *Clerical Error,* and later reissued under this title in Britain, with Vulliamy acknowledged as the author.

resist being facetious, whereas the master himself wrote about murder in a manner blending the detached interest of a recording angel and the impersonality of a court reporter. Rolls's later books, published twenty years and more after *The Vicar's Experiments,* did not repeat its success, and Hull had declined into a comparatively conventional writer by 1950, when his last book appeared.

Something of Iles's realism, although not his humor, is present in *A Pin to See the Peep-Show* (1934) by F. (Fryniwyd) Tennyson Jesse (1889–1958). Taking the famous Thompson-Bywaters murder case as a basis, she produced a soundly realistic crime novel which is especially good in showing the romantic Edith Thompson, renamed Julia Almond, as she becomes more and more completely caught in a web of fantasy.

The best book written under the influence of Iles—the influence was less direct and so the story more original—was *Verdict of Twelve* (1940), by Raymond Postgate (1896–1971). Stories about juries tend to have a dismal similarity (the favorite plot finds jurymen who tried some ancient murder case being killed off one by one), but Postgate's puzzle, set in terms of the characters of the jury members and their reactions, remains fresh on a second or third reading. A certain diffusion of interest between the jury and the case they are trying is the only weakness of a highly accomplished first crime story, which had two slightly disappointing successors.

Altogether the Iles school, including its founder, showed a certain lack of staying power. Iles's own long-term effect upon the crime story was permanent and important, but for the time being his influence faded.

THE AMERICANS

Some of these British writers were not far removed from their Golden Age contemporaries, and Iles in his Berkeley incarnation was firmly within it. The writers of what used to be called the American hardboiled school made a complete break with all that.

Their tough detectives were born in the American pulp magazines that flourished in the twenties. They inherited the radical feeling occasionally found in the dime novels (but not in the British penny dreadfuls), and their rise reflected the increasing violence of American society and the misery of the Depression years. The writers for these pulp magazines had no artistic intentions. They wrote in a way that implied a wholly different ethos from that of the Golden Age detective-story writer. The hardboiled dick did not inhabit the same world as the Great Detective. Where the Great Detective avoided and often scorned violence, to the hardboiled dick it was as natural as drinking. "Many people have their little peculiarities. Mine was holding a loaded gun in my hand while I slept," says Carroll John Daly's Race Williams, said to be the first hardboiled dick. Williams used his gun very often, mostly against other gunmen, explaining, "You can't make hamburger without grinding up a little meat." The Great Detective's language was affected or colorless; that of the hardboiled dick was pungent as cigar smoke or garlic. The Great Detective was omniscient and believed in the supreme power of reason. The hardboiled dick moved instinctively, was as fallible as the next man, and put faith in his gun. His rise came with the increasing corruption of American society, shown in the power of gangsters and their acceptance by many who were socially respectable, the collapse of any accepted moral code.

There were a great many pulp magazines, but much the most notable was *Black Mask* during the reign of Captain Joseph T. Shaw, from 1920 to 1936. Shaw was clearly an editor of genius. As he told his authors, he wanted stories of violent action directly told, and he eliminated everything unconnected with the physical excitement he demanded as rigorously as Ezra Pound blue-penciled the adjectives in the early work of Ernest Hemingway. Shaw believed also, however, in contrast to Golden Age writers, that "action is meaningless unless it involves recognizable human characters in three-dimensional form." The stories in *Black Mask* had a corporate style, whether they were written by Daly, by Erle Stanley Gardner under his early pseudonym of Charles M. Green, by George Harmon Coxe, Raoul Whitfield, Lester Dent, or even by Raymond Chandler, whose first story, "Blackmailers Don't Shoot," was published by the magazine in 1933. Shaw was lucky enough, however, to find in Dashiell Hammett one writer of immense natural talent, a talent that was first trimmed to fit the requirements of the magazine and then expanded in at least two of the century's finest crime novels.

Samuel Dashiell Hammett (1894–1961) was one of those independent freewheeling hard-living radicals who seem to Europeans typical of one kind of American. He left school at thirteen and had all kinds of jobs, including for eight years that of a Pinkerton detective. In his witty notes "From the Memoirs of a Private Detective," he says that he was once falsely accused of perjury and had to perjure himself to escape arrest, that he knew a detective who attempted to disguise himself and was taken into custody by the first policeman he met, that a chief of police gave him a complete description of a man down to a mole on his neck but forgot to mention that he had only one arm, and commented:

That the law-breaker is invariably soon or late apprehended is probably the least challenged of extant myths. And yet the files of every detective bureau bulge with the records of unsolved mysteries and uncaught criminals.

Raymond Chandler, writing in 1944, said that Hammett "gave murder back to the kind of people that commit it for reasons, not just to provide a corpse; and with the means at hand, not with hand-wrought duelling pistols, curare, and tropical fish." This is only half true, or is not true in its implication that Hammett wrote realistically in a documentary sense. What his stories have, even the earliest and least of them, is a flavor wholly individual. This flavor comes partly from the bareness of a style in which everything superficial in the way of description has been surgically removed, partly from his knowledge of actual criminal investigation, and partly from the wistful cynicism with which he wrote. Few of the early short stories about a fat middle-aged detective called the Continental Op get further than this. They are remarkable in the way they are written, but not in the things they say. Their tersely casual characterization is attractive in a gritty way, but they are not often really memorable. Hammett's achievement rests upon his five full-length stories, *Red Harvest* and *The Dain Curse* (both 1929), *The Maltese Falcon* (1930), *The Glass Key* (1931), and *The Thin Man* (1934).

The first lines of *Red Harvest* show how far removed the story
was in tone and feeling from any contemporary detective story
British or American:

I first heard Personville called Poisonville by a red-haired mucker
named Hickey Dewey in the Big Ship in Butte. He also called his
shirt a shoit. I didn't think anything of what he had done to the city's
name.

The corruption of the city is conveyed on the same page in a view of
its policemen which would not have appealed to Sayers or to Queen:

The first policeman I saw needed a shave. The second had a couple
of buttons off his shabby uniform. The third stood in the centre of
the city's main intersection—Broadway and Union Street—directing
traffic, with a cigar in one corner of his mouth. After that I stopped
checking them up.

The narrator in this story is the Continental Op, who within hours
of his arrival is plunged into a blood bath of battles between rival
gangsters. The police, of course, are crooked almost to a man, and
in one comic sequence a gang boss whose house is under siege gets
away by sending a couple of men out with bribes and then driving
away in a Police Department car. The Continental Op plays off one
gang boss against another, does his share of killing, destroys them
all, and leaves Poisonville a clean town. This world of total violence
was not far removed from that in some parts of urban America, and
Hammett does not make the gang bosses glamorous or the Continental Op a crusader. The bosses are scum on top of the stew; the
detective observes certain elemental decencies and loyalties, that is
all. Sam Spade in *The Maltese Falcon,* Ned Beaumont in *The Glass
Key* are nearly but not quite dishonest. In the end, they answer the
demands of some kind of justice, rather than those of love or friendship.

With all his innovations of form and language, Hammett kept
the puzzle element from the orthodox detective story. Who gunned
down Spade's partner Miles Archer in an alley, killed Taylor Henry
in China Street, caused the disappearance of the thin man Clyde
Wynant? The problems are composed just as skillfully as those in an
orthodox detective story, but in the best of Hammett they are the

beginning and not the end of the book's interest. *The Maltese Falcon* and *The Glass Key* offer a gallery of characters and scenes unexcelled in the crime story, all of them seen with a Dickensian sense of the truth in caricature. One portrait must stand for twenty, that of Caspar Gutman in *The Maltese Falcon:*

The fat man was flabbily fat with bulbous pink cheeks and lips and chins and neck, with a great soft egg of a belly that was all his torso, and pendant cones for arms and legs. As he advanced to meet Spade all his bulbs rose and shook and fell separately with each step, in the manner of clustered soap-bubbles not yet released from the pipe through which they had been blown. His eyes, made small by fat puffs around them, were dark and sleek. Dark ringlets thinly covered his broad scalp. He wore a black cutaway coat, black vest, black satin Ascot tie holding a pinkish pearl, striped grey worsted trousers and patent-leather shoes.

In *The Glass Key,* the theme is again that of the gangster-ruled town, seen this time not in terms of pure violence but of personal integrity. Paul Madvig is a half-honest gang boss, a backslapper not very quick on the uptake. Ned Beaumont, his much more intelligent sidekick, is devoted to him. As James Sandoe has said, the book is not only a detective story but "an exceptionally delicate scrutiny of friendship under curious conditions." The women in the book are painfully real, where Miss Wunderly in *The Maltese Falcon* is still a bit of a pipe dream. Some of the tricks and strategies, like those in the chapter where Beaumont destroys the feeble editor of the *Observer,* are deeply memorable. The prose is more subtle and complex than that of the short stories or of *Red Harvest,* which was thought by André Gide to have given pointers to Hemingway and Faulkner.

The Glass Key is the peak of Hammett's achievement, which is to say the peak of the crime writer's art in the twentieth century. Constant rereading of it offers fresh revelations of the way in which a crime writer with sufficient skill and tact can use violent events to comment by indirection on life, art, society, and at the same time compose a novel admirable in the carpentry of its structure and delicately intelligent in its suggestions of truths about human relationships. As a novel *The Glass Key* is remarkable, as a crime novel unique. It was succeeded by *The Thin Man,* a continuously charming and sparkling performance, which was still for Hammett a slight decline. And that was the end. The books were filmed; the production of *Thin Man* comedy thrillers, with William Powell and Myrna Loy, became for a time a minor industry. Hammett went to Hollywood and wrote no more books. His whole writing career, outside of screen work in Hollywood, covered only ten years and the novels only five.

The brevity of his career as a writer springs from the fact that for Hammett, much more than for most men, his books were a minor offshoot of his hard, reckless life. His drinking from the twenties onward, one of his friends told me, was explicable "only by an assumption that he had no expectation of being alive much beyond Thursday." He regarded *The Glass Key* as his best book, but thought little of any of them, and refused to allow the short stories to be reprinted even in the poverty of his last years. He went to prison during the witch hunt of the fifties, because he refused to reveal the names of contributors to the funds of a Communist-front organization. He may not have been a card-carrying Communist, but Lillian Hellman says that although he was "often witty and bitingly sharp about the American Communist Party . . . he was, in the end, loyal to them." By his own standards Hammett was perhaps a failure, but they are standards far removed from those we use in dealing with almost all other crime writers.

The Glass Key can stand comparison with any American novel of its decade. It can stand comparison, for example, with *Sanctuary* (1931). The principal contribution made to the crime story by William Faulkner (1897–1962) was perhaps his short stories about Gavin Stevens, which are mentioned later on, but the novels are always hovering on the edge of crime fiction, although only *Sanctuary* and possibly *Intruder in the Dust* can really be classed as crime novels. *Intruder in the Dust* (1948) has the apparatus of an orthodox detective story—a murder, a substitute body, an empty coffin, Gavin Stevens as investigator—but the true interest for Faulkner lies in the relationship between the town's whites and the Negro who is accused of murder. *Sanctuary* is another matter. Before writing it, Faulkner said much later, he asked himself what would sell ten thousand copies and then "invented the most horrific tale I could imagine and wrote it in about three weeks." That "about three weeks" was not accurate, and there was no need to have been so deprecatory, for the book is not just a potboiler. With its terrified heroine-victim and its voyeuristic villain, it is a shocker, which perhaps provided the germ of *No Orchids for Miss Blandish,* but unlike most other shockers it is a book really *written,* and the theme gives Faulkner's thick curdled prose a distinct air of menace. With its romanticism about sexual violence, *Sanctuary* looks forward to much that has been disagreeably developed by later crime writers (as *The Glass Key* is in one aspect a precursor of the realistic crime stories of the sixties), but what a French critic has called Faulkner's "technique of hallucination" makes the book memorable and suffuses it with a queer sort of poetry.

Few of Hammett's contemporaries—that is, of those whose approach to crime writing resembled his—had a distinctive talent. Cornell Hopley-Woolrich (1903–1968), who wrote under the names of Cornell Woolrich, William Irish, and George Hopley, was associated with rather than allied to the school of Hammett. He invented plots which dazzle by their ingenuity in the half-light of evening, but when the morning comes seem rather contrived. *Phantom Lady* (1942), one of the Irish products, shows his talent for plotting and melodrama, and *The Bride Wore Black* (1940), by Cornell Woolrich, is also ingenious. *The Postman Always Rings Twice* (1934), by James M. (Mallahan) Cain (1892–   ), is a taut tart tale of sex and money told with an absolute concentration on the bare, relevant material of crime. W. R. Burnett (1899–   ) is a pedestrian writer with a considerable knowledge of the criminal scene which he put to good use in *Little Caesar* (1929), *The Quick Brown Fox* (1942), and particularly *The Asphalt Jungle* (1949). (But a comparison of the efficient *Little Caesar* with *Red Harvest* helps to show why Hammett was supreme in this field.) Jonathan (Wyatt) Latimer (1906–   ) had an irresponsible gaiety that marks out his work from the ordinary competent hardboiled novel. All the Latimers of this period are very similar, with his first book *Murder in the Madhouse* (1935) setting the tone of casually accepted corruption that informs also *The Lady in the*

Morgue (1936) and the savage and, for its time, sexually outspoken *Solomon's Vineyard* (1941). After this book, Latimer became submerged in Hollywood, where his talent was buried.

It would be easy to add to this list, and Raymond Chandler did so once in a letter to me listing his favorite crime writers, but of course much the most notable of them after Hammett was Chandler himself. Raymond Chandler (1888–1959) came late to the writing of crime stories. He was in his forties when, after the ruin in the Depression of the small oil companies with which he was associated, he began to read pulp magazines and "decided that this might be a good way to try to learn to write fiction and get paid a small amount of money at the same time." His early short stories are almost indistinguishable from much of the other material in *Black Mask,* although a good deal is made of them now. His reputation, like Hammett's, rests on his novels. There were seven, beginning with *The Big Sleep* (1939), published when he was fifty years old.

Chandler had a fine feeling for the sound and value of words, and he added to it a very sharp eye for places, things, people, and the wisecracks (this out-of-date word seems still the right one) that in their tone and timing are almost always perfect. "Did I hurt your head much?" Philip Marlowe asks a blonde in *The Big Sleep* after he has hit her with his gun. She replies: "You and every other man I ever met." It is impossible to convey in a single quotation Chandler's almost perfect ear for dialogue, but it comes through in all the later books whether the people talking are film stars or publicity agents, rich men, gangsters, or policemen. To this is joined a generous indignation roused in him by meanness and corruption, and a basic seriousness about his violent entertainments. The actual plotting of the books improved greatly as he became more sure of himself. In the first two or three stories, that joke about solving plot problems by having a man come in the door with a gun is not too far away from the truth, but the plots of *The Little Sister* (1949) and *The Long Goodbye* (1953) are as smoothly dovetailed as a piece of Chippendale. Yet plotting was never something he really enjoyed. Nothing could better indicate the difference between Chandler and a typical Golden Age writer than the fact that for the Golden Age writer the plot is everything and the writing might often be done by computer, whereas Chandler thought that "plotting may be a bore even if you are good at it" but "a writer who hates the actual writing to me is simply not a writer at all." And we do read Chandler first of all for the writing, and afterward for the California background, the jokes, the social observation, the character of Marlowe. The plots are firm and adequate, but they are not what we take away from the books.

It must be said that in the inevitable comparison between Hammett and Chandler, Chandler comes off second best. There was a toughness in Hammett that Chandler lacked, and did not appreciate. It comes through in his remark that the Hammett style could "say things he did not know how to say or feel the need of saying" and that "in his [Hammett's] hands it had no overtones, left no echo, evoked no image beyond a distant hill." Chandler set himself to remedy this, and to create in the private detective Philip Marlowe a man who should be "a complete man and a common man and yet an unusual man . . . to use a rather weathered phrase, a man of honour." Yet the detachment in Hammett that seemed to Chandler inadequate was really a mark of strength. Chandler's long, famous rhetorical invocation to his dream detective hero which begins, "Down these mean streets a man must go who is not himself mean, who is neither tarnished nor afraid," is too long to quote in full, but after reading it one can hardly be surprised that Marlowe was originally called Mallory. Sam Spade and the Continental Op have their crude code of ethics, but they are rough people doing dirty work. We can believe that private detectives were something like this. Philip Marlowe becomes with each book more a piece of wish-fulfillment, and idealized expression of Chandler himself, a strictly literary conception.

All this has to be said, yet Chandler was a very good writer, a good critic of the work he liked, and a sensitive, intelligent man. He wrote his own epitaph as a writer, too modestly but with fair accuracy, in one of his witty letters: "To accept a mediocre form and make something like literature out of it is in itself rather an accomplishment. . . . Any decent writer who thinks of himself occasionally as an artist would far rather be forgotten so that someone better might be remembered." Chandler's best work runs no risk of being forgotten.

Hammett wrote a scathing review of Van Dine's first novel, but he had no real interest in the form of the crime story. Chandler had. "It is the ladies and gentlemen of what Mr. Howard Haycraft calls the Golden Age of detective fiction that really get me down," he says in "The Simple Art of Murder," the most powerful attack ever made on the classical detective story. By this time, it is true, he was knocking at an open door, for the limitations of the Golden Age's arbitrary conventions had been realized by several critics. Three years before Chandler's article appeared in 1944, Philip Van Doren Stern had made many of the same points more gently in an article called "The Case of the Corpse in the Blind Alley":

The great need of the mystery story today is not novelty of apparatus but novelty of approach. The whole genre needs overhauling, a return to first principles, a realisation that murder has to do with human emotion and deserves serious treatment. Mystery story writers need to know more about life and less about death—more about the way people think and feel and act, and less about how they die.

These words could serve as both an obituary for the Golden Age and an introduction to the best crime stories of the following years.

XI

Simenon and Maigret

The case of Georges Simenon (1903–   ) requires a separate chapter. He is the only European crime writer (if we regard
Britain as an offshore island) to have become famous outside his
own country since Gaston Leroux and Maurice Leblanc. He is
certainly much more than a crime writer, and is regarded by his
greatest admirers as a novelist comparable with Balzac. He wrote
for many years an average of six short novels a year, books so
varied in subject, setting, and characterization that nobody could
possibly call them production-line articles. Yet in spite of this
variation his work is so even in tone and manner that there is
not much question of talking about an early or a late style. What
is attempted here is not an estimate of Simenon's stature as a
novelist but an assessment of the Maigret stories, which number
seventy-odd at present. Some of his other books are much more
important, but most of them do not come within the canon
of the crime story, even though they are often concerned with
criminal matters. A book like *L'Homme qui regardait passer les
rains* (*The Man Who Watched the Trains Go By,* 1942) is very
much a study in character first, a crime story second, even though
Sergeant Lucas from the Maigret stories has strayed into it and
become a Superintendent.

The first thing an English reader is likely to notice about the

Maigret saga is the contrast between the realism of the charac
terization and background and the sensationalism of the plots
In *Le Fou de Bergerac* (1932), translated as *The Madman o
Bergerac* (1940), Maigret dives out of a train after a man whe
has occupied the upper bunk in his sleeping berth, is shot by him
taken to the little town of Bergerac, and spends the rest of th
story recuperating in a hotel room and trying to discover th
apparent madman, who has killed two women by use of a lon;
needle stuck through the heart and has attacked a third. Maigre
knows that the murderer is one of the people who visited his hote
room, because he has carelessly dropped his railway ticket in th
passage outside. The origins of the crime prove to lie far back ii
the past, in an extraordinary tale revealed casually at the end o
the book about a doctor working in an Algiers hospital who dis
covers that his villainous father is there, and has been condemne
to death for his crimes. The doctor saves his father by burnin,
down part of the hospital and substituting another body for tha
of his father. This doctor later establishes himself as a respectabl
figure in Bergerac. The "madman" is in fact the father, now ;
psychopath, who has paid unwelcome visits to his son, murderin,
a woman each time. After the second of these murders, the docto
kills his father and empties his pockets of identification material
but carelessly drops the railway ticket outside Maigret's door.

Why should a plot of Simenon's be singled out for its improba
bility, it may be asked? What is a touch of arson, a body substi
tution, a psychopath who stabs with needles, compared to a locke
room? One is disconcerted by things in Simenon that can be take
for granted in John Dickson Carr, just because Simenon's charac
ters are convincing as real men and women. If they were card
board cutouts, one would mind much less what sort of conduc
was attributed to them. The art of Simenon lies in making th
implausible acceptable. Consider the opening of another earl
story, *Le Pendu de Saint-Pholien* of 1931 (Maigret and the Hun
dred Gibbets), in which Maigret follows a man over Franc
and to the Dutch-German border simp y because he sees hir
stuffing a large sum of money into an envelope and posting i
The man is shabby, and carries a cheap fiber suitcase, so wh;

s he doing with so much money? Maigret manages to buy an identical case which he stuffs with newspaper, exchanges the cases at a railway station, and is in the next hotel room when the man shoots himself after discovering the exchange. Looked at in any reasonable light, the detective's behavior is highly improbable. The astonishing thing is that in reading all this is made acceptable, and both *Le Pendu de Saint-Pholien* and *Le Fou de Bergerac* are extremely interesting and convincing stories. In the latter, there are bits of characteristic deadpan humor in the original police belief that Maigret is himself the man they are looking for; the relationship between the doctor, who has something to hide, his wife, and his mistress is sketched with easy mastery; and the feeling of a French provincial town as sensed, although not seen, by Maigret while he fidgets in bed is perfectly done. This early Maigret is a typical story, similiar in its merits and weaknesses to others. The settings never fail, giving always an impression of personal involvement with Paris or Antibes, a shop by the Belgian frontier or a *guinguette* by the Seine. The weather is described with such vigor and pleasure that it is, again, as though the writer were actually soaking up the rain or sun that he is writing about. Simenon's susceptibility to physical experience of this kind is greater than that of any other contemporary novelist. And the characters grow in this thick soil of sensuous experience; they fit perfectly into sleazy or criminal city life, a small town's close provincialism, or the uneasy potential violence of a port. They take color and conviction from their surroundings, and there seems absolutely no limit to the kinds of people Simenon knows, and into whose personalities he can enter. Well, perhaps there is. Has he produced a convincing Englishman?

The surroundings and the weather and the people are filtered to us always through the personality of Maigret. When we get a powerful sense of holiday life in *Liberty Bar* (1932), it is because Maigret has this feeling; when in *Maigret et la vieille dame* (1953 in France, 1958 in Britain as *Maigret and the Old Lady*) Valentine Besson is presented as a charming old lady, this is because she is being shown through Maigret's eyes. I do not think it has been noticed that never in these stories does Simenon stand back and write in the third person. Everything that happens is as Maigret sees it, or as it is told to him. He really *is* the stories, in a way that is not true of any other detective. As John Raymond has said in his study of Simenon, "Each case is less a problem to resolve than a drama to be understood, with Maigret himself playing each part." Obviously some of the stories are better than others and my own feeling is that the early tales, which often find Maigret mixed up with professional criminals, are preferable to the sometimes ramblingly philosophical books of recent years, but the important thing is Maigret himself. We know him better, in the sense of knowing him all round, than we know any other detective, certainly better than we know Sherlock Holmes.

If a single story had to be chosen to represent the finest qualities of the Maigret stories without any of their defects, it might be *Mon Ami Maigret* (published 1949 in France, 1956 in Britain as *My Friend Maigret*). Here he takes the chance to get away from rainy Paris to the heat-soaked island of Porquerolles in the Midi. An old crook has been murdered, it is thought because he boasted that Maigret was his friend. Accompanied by a Scotland Yard detective who has come to study Maigret's methods (but, as Maigret says, he has no methods), he goes to Porquerolles and there shows his gift for absorbing like a sponge the nature of the people who live on the island, and concealing behind his apparently sluggish enjoyment of the local food and drink the capacity for interpreting behavior which is his greatest detectival asset. The crime proves to be a product of that total nihilistic rejection by some of the young of any standard of behavior which Simenon was contemplating long before the days of student revolt, and there is some fine characterization. The crook's former girl friend, who was once helped by Maigret and is now the madame of a brothel, is particularly good. The Scotland Yard man is merely sketched, but Maigret's uneasiness in his presence provides some passages of unstrained comedy. There are no coincidences, no improbabilities. This is certainly one of the half-dozen best Maigret stories.

Our knowledge of Maigret in the accounts of his cases is supplemented by *Les Mémoires de Maigret* (1950)—in Britain

Maigret's Memoirs (1963). This very witty book tells us not only of the detective's childhood, courtship, and early career in the Paris police, but also of his slight resentment of the simplifications made by Simenon in writing about him. The author, it seems, at first took some liberties and presented what was almost a caricature of the real Maigret, who very rarely wore a bowler hat and does not remember "the famous overcoat with the velvet collar" of the early stories, although he admits that he may have at one time possessed it. Such a piece of writing, at once plausibly extending the myth of Maigret and stressing its artificiality, is a world away from the tediums of Holmesiana. But mostly, of course, Maigret comes to us through the various aspects of his personality shown to us in the cases, and this is not just a matter of a few obvious symbols like a pipe and a liking for apéritifs.

This son of a bailiff is never at ease with aristocrats, or for that matter with politicians, as he is with children, criminals, and bourgeois of the lower class, and with professional men like doctors and solicitors. There are certain kinds of people about whom his understanding is limited—artists, scientists, eccentrics generally. His instinctive respect for but also distrust of the rich is shown in *L'Affaire Saint-Fiacre* (1933), in Britain *The Saint-Fiacre Affair* (1940). If he solves the cases in which such people are mixed up, it is through his gift of empathy combined with the sudden moments of instinctive understanding that come to him. The personage created by Simenon, through stroke after stroke in book after book, has a plodding energy and endless patience. He is not of great intellectual stature, but has flashes of what can only be called artistic penetration, through which he understands ways of life alien to his own. We do not know how he votes, but are sure that it will always be for stability rather than for change. We do not know his sexual habits, but they will certainly not be markedly unusual. Maigret is a typical bourgeois, but with a breadth of sympathy that most bourgeois lack. He is one of the most completely realized characters in all modern fiction. It is partly because he already existed fully as a person that he has been shown so successfully on the TV screen.

The Maigret stories stand quite on their own in crime fiction, bearing little relation to most of the other work done in the field. (Simenon is not much interested in crime stories, and has read few of them.) The bases of the stories are often slight, almost anecdotal. There are no great feats of ratiocination in them, and the problems they present are human as much as they are criminal. The ambience of the stories is wonderfully real, the characters are true and often memorable, yet we are not often emotionally moved by them. Maigret's detached sympathy becomes our own, and like him we do not care to dig too deeply into the roots of crime; we are ready to move on to another case. Simenon is an undoubted master of the crime story, but his mastery rests primarily in the creation of Jules Maigret.

XII

"Mr. Queen, Will You Be Good Enough to Explain
Your Famous Character's Sex Life, If Any?"

Looking back at the decade that began with the 1939–1945
war, it can be seen as one of a desperate struggle by established
crime writers to adapt to new conditions and ways of feeling.
The war was a watershed in the history of the crime story, sep-
arating not only the world of housemaids and nurses from that of
daily helps and *au-pair* girls, but also the world of reason from
that of force. The conscious assumption of the classical detective
story was that human affairs are ruled by reason. Crimes were
committed by individuals, small holes torn in the fabric of society.
The individuals were discovered, the holes mended by the detective who represented the force of order, and he did this through a
process of reasoning. Such beliefs were buttressed by the existence
of the League of Nations, and most Golden Age crime writers
adhered, consciously or otherwise, to the slogan of the Beaver-
brook press that there would be no war in Europe, this year or
next year either. The war forced upon them the acknowledgment
that quite a different world existed, one in which force was supreme and in which irrational doctrines ruled more than one
nation. It was a world much more like that of *Red Harvest* than
that of *Gaudy Night* or *The Greek Coffin Mystery*. Naturally the

writers did not think of it in those terms, but with the end of
the war efforts to adapt to the world of the welfare state and the
atomic bomb became intense.

The great problem for established writers was what could be
done with the Great Detective, who in a symbolic sense had
failed to prevent the war and in a realistic one appeared more
absurd as scientific and forensic aids to detection became more
refined and more important. The idea of the British Superintendent
or the American Chief of Police pleading with the languid investigator to spare a little time from his research into Transyl-
vanian folk songs to solve a problem that had baffled the best
police brains of Scotland Yard or New York looked increasingly
ridiculous, yet how could "Ellery Queen" sacrifice Ellery Queen
or Margery Allingham give up Albert Campion? And there were
other incongruities, equally painful to face. Hammett, when introducing Ellery Queen to a lecture audience, began by asking:
"Mr. Queen, will you be good enough to explain your famous
character's sex life, if any?" Such a question could not have been
asked before World War II. Holmes could then be accepted as a
misogynist, Poirot as an aging bachelor, Queen as a figure susceptible to feminine beauty but above or outside emotional en-
tanglement; but with the acceptance during the fifties and sixties
of the fact that everybody has some kind of real and/or fantasy
sex life, such easy answers would no longer do. It now appeared
suggestive of impotence to fall in love with lovely ladies in a
purely platonic way like Ellery; there seemed something sexually
ambiguous about the household of Nero Wolfe and Archie Goodwin. Without going into more details, it is clear that Hammett's
question showed up sharply the totally mythical nature of the
Great Detective. Queen's response was to say that a wife, mistress,
or even physical love affair planted on Ellery after all these years
would upset readers. This was no doubt true, but the difficulty remained, and was recognized.

The solutions attempted varied with individual writers. Some
ignored the problem altogether. John Dickson Carr's Gideon Fell
and H. M. came puffing and wheezing into the postwar world,
creaking like antique engines on a grass-grown track. Ellery re-

tained his virginity but lost his pince-nez, and occasionally even lost his father, as his exploits took place more frequently in the small town of Wrightsville, with its "complacent elms, wandering cobbles, and crooked side-streets nestled in the lap of a farmer's valley and leaning against the motherly abdomen of one of New England's most matriarchal mountain ranges," where his arrival as a house guest was likely to be the signal for the commission of one or more murders. Very intelligently, Dannay and Lee used this change in locale to loosen the structure of their stories. More emphasis was placed on personal relationships, and less on the details of investigation. For a time, this worked well. *Calamity Town* (1942) and *The Murderer Is a Fox* (1945) are two books in which the transition from one kind of crime story to another is successfully managed, although a feeling lingers that they would be even better books if Ellery did not appear in them. In later stories, however, fantastic ingenuity takes over at the expense of characterization, as in *Ten Days' Wonder* (1948), where the crimes follow the Ten Commandments, or *Double, Double* (1950), where the pattern of a nursery rhyme runs through a series of murders. One can admire the ingenuity, and yet sense that there is something wrong about the way in which Queen is turning back to Van Dine and abandoning the possibilities glimpsed in the first Wrightsville books.

Poirot was modified in a rather similar way. His mustaches and his language were trimmed, and he became, as Christie put it, "more and more of a private investigator and less of an engaged enquiry agent." With that her public rested content, and if the author herself was slightly dissatisfied, she found solace in the activities of her second string, Miss Marple, who has placidly knitted her way through a good many cases since her first appearance in 1930. To an outside eye, Miss Marple seems more unreal than Poirot, but in spite of an inevitable faltering of invention, Agatha Christie managed the problem of adaptation better than most of her contemporaries.

Some writers went no further than smoothing down the rough edges of their detectives, and making them more nearly commonplace. Patrick Quentin's theatrical producer Peter Duluth and

Edmund Crispin's Professor Gervase Fen are not detectives, but people to whom things happen. Agreeable characters and perceptive men, they are still only shadows of the Great Detectives of the past, just as Nigel Strangeways and Nero Wolfe in their later incarnations were only a thin echo of the men they had been before the war. But what was the point of having an amateur detective at all if he was not to be in some way exceptional? The thought must have occurred to Margery Allingham, who used considerable skill in changing Campion from the near-Wimsey or near-Wooster figure of the early books into a character altogether more serious and mature. In *Coroner's Pidgin* (1945), the intelligence behind his apparent vacuity is stressed:

> There were new lines in his over-thin face and with their appearance some of his old misleading vacancy of expression had vanished. But nothing had altered the upward drift of his thin mouth nor the engaging astonishment which so often and so falsely appeared in his pale eyes.

Campion played a smaller part in these later books, where her Stevensonian feeling for adventurous romance with a hint of horror in the background was given full play. *More Work for the Undertaker* (1948) shows her moving away from the orthodox crime story while retaining its puzzle element, and in the best of all her books, *The Tiger in the Smoke* (1952), she broke away completely from the old conventions to produce a thriller of the highest quality about a hunted man and his hunters. Yet one feels in these books, as in the best of the later Queens, that good as they are they would have been better still without the detective, who belonged to an earlier time and a different tradition.

Ngaio Marsh has never gone so far as Allingham in attempting to write novels with a detective element, rather than detective stories. Her capacity for amused observation of the undercurrents beneath ordinary social interchanges is so good that one had hoped for something more than she has ever tried to do. The first half of *Opening Night* (1951)* gives a brilliant picture of the intrigues taking place before the opening of a new play. All this is, as it should be, preparation for the murder that

* In America, *Night at the Vulcan*.

is to take place, and after the murder we hope that the book will remain in the same key and that the problems will be resolved as they began, in terms of character. To our disappointment, however, Marsh takes refuge from real emotional problems in the official investigation and interrogation of suspects. The temperature is lowered; the mood has been lost.

Patrick Quentin and Edmund Crispin have already been mentioned. Quentin's story shows a very interesting and typical development. Richard Wilson Webb and Hugh Callingham Wheeler (1912–   ) collaborated as early as 1931 in books written under the names of Q. Patrick and Jonathan Stagge. These were competent, but in no way exceptional, Golden Age crime stories. Patrick Quentin seems to have been a name invented to provide another pseudonym, but almost from the first the Quentin books were distinctly better than those of Patrick or Stagge. All of them had "Puzzle" in the title, and *Puzzle for: Fools, Players, Puppets, Wantons, Fiends, Pilgrims* appeared in the space of a few years. Then in the late forties the Puzzle stories and Peter Duluth, their appropriately light-hearted central character, were abandoned, together with the other pseudonyms. The later Quentin books, some of them written by Wheeler alone after the death of Webb, are more serious in tone and more subtle in approach. There is no investigator of any kind. The books don't dig quite deep enough to be called serious crime novels, but all of them are alert studies of people who commit crimes for plausible reasons. On their own level, these stories are believable, where a book like *Ten Days' Wonder* is not. It is not easy to pick out particular Quentins when the level is so even, but *The Man with Two Wives* (1955) and *The Wife of Ronald Sheldon* (1954)* are two of his best books.

The Crispin story shows the difficulties of a writer emerging at the end of the war who adhered by sympathy to Golden Age standards. Robert Bruce Montgomery (1921–   ), who uses the name of Edmund Crispin for crime stories, is the last and most charming of the Farceurs. His first book, *The Case of the Gilded Fly* (1944),† was written when he was still an undergraduate. Crispin's master was, and remained, Michael Innes in the eight

---

* In America, *My Son the Murderer*.
† In America, *Obsequies at Oxford*.

novels and one collection of short stories that he produced at the rate of one a year until 1953. Since then he has been silent, although there have been rumors of a new book and chapters of it have even been visible in typescript. Crispin's work is marked by a highly individual sense of light comedy, and by a great flair for verbal deception rather in the Christie manner. If he never gives the impression of solid learning that can be sensed behind Innes's frivolity, he is also never tiresomely literary. At his weakest he is flippant, at his best he is witty, but all his work shows a high-spiritedness rare and welcome in the crime story. His third book, *The Moving Toyshop* (1946), which is about a toyshop that really does seem to move mysteriously from one part of Oxford to another, is probably his best, although his Shakespearean excursion, *Love Lies Bleeding* (1948), is delightfully funny and witty. In recent years, Crispin has offered some compensation for his silence as a crime novelist by producing knowledgeable and tolerant criticism of current crime stories.

Nothing is more indicative of the changed atmosphere in which the new writers worked—writers, that is, who produced their first books near the end of the Golden Age or later—than the abandonment by most of them of the series character who appeared in a succession of books, and gave readers the comfortable pleasure of asking for a book not by the author's name but by that of his hero or detective. Of course the series character continued and continues to exist, and he appears in the work of a few postwar writers of quality, but he is no longer an almost essential ingredient of a crime writer's success. The reaction against the prewar Superman detective was partly political, prompted by distrust of all Supermen, and partly based upon the writers' feeling that they had something of interest to say which would be hampered rather than helped by the development of a single character. As the American critic Anthony Boucher said: "It is all but impossible for any writer above the hack level to write about people and problems without implying some set of values, some ethical standard." It has already been said that an ethical standard was implicit in the social values taken for granted by Sayers, Christie, Rinehart. (And it should perhaps be emphasized again that such names stand for dozens of their epigones, like Anthony Gilbert and Georgette Heyer in one country, Ursula Curtiss and Mabel Seeley in another.) Such social values demanded the solution of problems by a detective, either amateur or professional. The attitudes of the new writers were different. They wanted to combine popular entertainment with a study of "people and problems," and often they felt that an investigator was out of place.

There disappeared with the Great Detective much other impedimenta of the Golden Age, the accessories that had enhanced his feats. By 1950, there were few drawings of the grounds and the house, with the body shown in copse or library; stories based on the elucidation of alibis through timetables had vanished; nobody was dealing in unknown poisons; and methods of murder had become noticeably less bizarre. This happened gradually, and as late as 1955 Ngaio Marsh's *Scales of Justice* offered a map, but nowadays you might read a hundred crime stories without finding a drawing of the manse or the manor house, and without discovering any murder weapon more arcane than knife or revolver. The new writers were inclined to ask Why rather than How, and their Why was often concerned with the psychological make-up and social background of killer and killed.

This was true even of a writer like Cyril Hare, whose work would have fitted comfortably into the Golden Age pattern if he had begun to write a few years earlier. Cyril Hare was the pseudonym used by Alfred Alexander Gordon Clark (1900–1958), a barrister who was on the staff of the Director of Public Prosecutions during World War II, and later became a County Court Judge. Hare showed from the first an agreeable liveliness in writing dialogue, and an unusual capacity for using his legal knowledge. In his fourth book, *Tragedy at Law* (1942), his gifts coalesced, and the account of the life of a judge on circuit is done with a sense of comedy and a feeling for character that keep one totally absorbed in the misadventures of the Honourable Sir William Hereward Barber, Justice of the King's Bench Division of the High Court of Justice. The mystery is interesting, too, but what holds us from the start is the account of the legal world that Hare was able to see with detachment and intimate affection. He never again quite equaled this book, the first half of which is outstanding among portraits of legal life in crime fiction, but all his work is marked by careful plotting and a nice ear for conversation.

In the late fifties, I produced the dubiously useful list of the Hundred Best Crime Stories already mentioned, for an English Sunday paper. They were dismayed when many of the selections proved to be out of print, and although I insisted upon some of my unobtainable selections (what was the good of choosing books which readers couldn't buy, the paper not unreasonably asked), I agreed after prolonged arguments to make some substitutions which seemed harmless at the time but look regrettable now. The list was also partly cooperative, in the sense that I approached several critics and asked them to select their favorite recent crime stories. Among them was Howard Haycraft, historian and devotee of the classical detective story. It is a striking confirmation of the decay in the classical form that the only postwar writer thought by Haycraft worthy to enter the canon was Elizabeth Mackintosh (1897–1952), who wrote plays under the name of Gordon Daviot and crime stories as Josephine Tey. Her first crime story, *The Man in the Queue* (1929), introduced the slight, dapper Inspector Grant, and for its time and of its kind was an unusually interesting performance, although it depends upon the supposition that a man stabbed in a theatre queue will not cry out, or even know what has happened, before he collapses a minute or two later. Other Teys were published intermittently, and all have something original about them, in particular *The Franchise Affair* (1948), which translates the eighteenth-century disappearance of Elizabeth Canning into modern terms, and then offers an explanation which really applies to the modern fiction rather than to the eighteenth-century case, and is somehow a little disappointing after the sparkling beginning in which the mystery is set out.

The book selected by Haycraft as her best, with the agreement of several other critics, was a freakish performance called *The Daughter of Time* (1951). In this, Grant, immobilized after falling through a trap door, provides with the help of an American student a solution to the mystery of the Princes in the Tower on the

lines that they were murdered at the instance not of Richard III
but of Henry VII. There is nothing new about this theory, as
the student discovers at the end of their research, and Grant's
almost total ignorance of history is the most remarkable thing
about the book. The pleasure taken by critics in the very slow
unfolding of a thesis already well known suggests a similar ignorance on their part. But even more to the point is the fact that
this amateur rehashing of a well-known argument, interspersed
with visits from friends to the detective's bedside, is, as one might
expect, really rather dull.

Whatever one thinks about the merits of Josephine Tey, her most
praised work was not only preoccupied by the past but also belonged to it. The anticipatory notes of the coming themes were
struck in four books published during the forties. The themes
they announce are those of the realistic and even brutal novel
about real-life crime; the story which is based upon a setting conceived in such detail and with such firmness that the ambience
seems to dictate the crime; and the novel which uses a criminal
theme as a means of investigating the nature of human psychology.
One of these books was English, the other three American, and
none of them would have been written before the war.

A Case to Answer (1947) was much the best of the three crime
novels written by Edgar Lustgarten (1907–   ). Like Hare,
Lustgarten had a professional knowledge of the law, which he
used to emphasize the sordidness of his theme. Hare would never
have contemplated as a possible subject the murder and mutilation
of a prostitute in Soho and the trial of the respectable young
businessman accused of her death, but if he had done so one may
be sure that the detective puzzle would have been at the heart of
the story. Lustgarten gives us instead an account of the evidence
at the trial. Such concentration on a single scene can become wearisome, and this difficulty is evaded rather than solved by some
lively but largely irrelevant sketches of judge and counsel. The
book is no masterpiece, but at the time it had the jarring impact
of something unpleasant but real in contrast to the mild fading
pleasures offered by most current detective stories. The ending,

which implies that the wrong verdict has been reached, also seemed shocking. In this suggestion that the operations of justice are fallible, *A Case to Answer* was an original book, one giving notice of things to come.

In the Depression years, Kenneth (Flexner) Fearing (1902–1961) was a poet whose rolling lines of despair, protest, and Whitmanesque optimism have still not been valued at their proper worth. Among his few crime stories, *Dagger of the Mind* (1941) was much admired by Chandler, but *The Big Clock* (1946) is his principal contribution to crime fiction. Like many American writers before and since, Fearing had worked on *Time* magazine, and an organization very similar to that of Henry Luce is really the book's chief character. The various periodicals run by the organization are invented with a lot of felicitous detail, and the device is perfectly worked into the plot by which George Stroud of "Crimeways" is given an assignment to find the missing witness he knows to be himself. We are never in any doubt that the megalomaniac proprietor, Earl Janoth, is the murderer of his slightly lesbian mistress. The excitement of the story springs from the way in which Stroud manages to mislead his own investigators, although as point after point involving him is discovered the net moves in always more closely. *The Big Clock* has an air of conviction which comes from Fearing's close observation of the background. The film made from the story, with Charles Laughton as Janoth and Ray Milland as the technically innocent but morally null hero, was, for once, not a travesty of the book.

"Like an athlete who runs her first mile in 3.59 and then retires, Helen Eustis asserts that her first mystery novel was also her last," Anthony Boucher wrote in 1958, adding that the "one and only Eustis whodunit is a highpoint in modern murder." The title of *The Horizontal Man* (1946) comes from Auden—we are a long way in feeling, although not in years, from the time when it was a surprise to find Eliot's name mentioned in a crime story. The book begins with the murder of Kevin Boyle, a full-time professor of English and part-time poet on an American campus, by a woman who loves him. The puzzle is: find the lady. Helen Eustis offered in her only crime story a murder mystery which Boucher called "the

trickiest bit of strict 'fair play' since Dr. Sheppard told of the murder of Roger Ackroyd," but she gave a good deal more than that.
The Horizontal Man is a very intelligent novel, and also (this is
what the story depends on) a successful dive into the waters of
abnormal psychology. If Lustgarten's book gave us murder as it
often sordidly is, and Fearing's showed the kind of surroundings
nurturing a tension that can lead to violence, Eustis investigated the
personality patterns that can lead to crime. All these books use the
sexual motive in a way from which Golden Age writers would have
flinched. The writers were implicitly asking, as earlier crime novelists would not have cared to do, for a freedom of comment equal to
that of any other novelist.

The same can be said of John Franklin Bardin, an American
writer so little known in his own country that I have never been
able to find anybody there who has read his books. The first Bardin
crime story, *The Deadly Percheron* (1946), is a sort of exercise in
Surrealist logic. *The Last of Philip Banter* (1947) is equally remarkable in the way it creates and maintains a mood of menace.
His third and finest book, *Devil Take the Blue Tail Fly* (1948), is
a psychological study. At first sight, it may seem to go no further
than Helen Eustis, but its treatment of a similar theme has a greater
depth of understanding. The book is, so far as I know, unique in
modern crime fiction in showing a world seen solely from a schi-
zoid's point of view. From the opening, when Ellen Purcell wakes
on the morning of her discharge from hospital and finds the friendly
nurses strangely reluctant to turn their backs, to the last terrifying
pages, the vision of the world and what happens in it is wholly hers.
This memorable novel was a failure in England, where the earlier
books had been much praised, and it did not find an American
publisher until the late sixties. With its failure, Bardin began to
publish a series of crime novels under the name of Gregory Tree,
but these slickly sophisticated books lack altogether the imaginative
intensity of the earlier work. He has produced nothing in the crime
field, either as Bardin or as Tree, for the past fifteen years.

With work of this kind, the crime novel had become something
different, in form as well as in content. It is true that the detective
story was not dead. Edmund Crispin observed with gentle mockery

in 1959 that although people had been pronouncing "the doom of the detective story" for a long time, the writers survived. "Mrs Christie still has butter to put on her bread. Mr. Carr seems confident of being able to continue supporting his wife and family. There is happily no hint from America that Mr. Queen is feeling the pinch." He went on to suggest that "the drifting, opportunist variety of writer" (a label which I fear he might have pinned on the four just under discussion) had now abandoned the detective story in favor of "the thriller, or the so-called psychological crime tale, or the *soi-disant* 'naturalistic' murder story," and that the detective story would be all the better for this detachment of "its catchpenny hangers-on." That was thirteen years ago, and perhaps Crispin would not write in quite the same terms today, but his choice of names is significant. All were pillars of the Golden Age establishment, and nobody would deny that they have retained, and in at least one case increased, their following. Nobody would deny, even, that detective stories continue to be produced by new writers in Britain, and to a lesser degree in America. The point is that in plotting and execution almost all recent detective stories are feeble things compared with the older ones. If Crispin had been asked to name half a dozen new and talented adherents to what he himself called the "artificial, contrived and fantastic" standards of the classical detective story, he might have found it difficult, and a dozen would certainly have been beyond him. From a time that one could roughly put at the end of the forties, new writers have shied away from this particular kind of fantasy. In the last twenty years, the crime novel has returned to its origins. Its variety of approach and style is very great, embracing at one end the police novel and at the other the more or less fantastic spy story. Somewhere in between lie stories about crime of a more or less naturalistic kind.

The approach common to these books involved the cutting of the bonds by which detective-story writers had confined themselves— or, to put it in another way, the abandonment of everything that had been regarded by the Golden Age writers as good taste. It could no longer be assumed that policemen were by definition honest, or that they would never work over a suspect. They were shown as human beings like others, embodying a justice that was itself much flawed. There is a passage in Chandler's *The Lady in the Lake* which is both an excellent piece of writing and a summary of what many writers felt about policemen as a group:

> They had the calm weathered faces of healthy men in hard condition. They had the eyes they always have, cloudy and grey like freezing water. The firm set mouth, the hard little wrinkles at the corners of the eyes, the hard cruel and meaningless stare, not quite cruel and a thousand miles from kind. The dull ready-made clothes, worn without style, with a sort of contempt; the look of men who are poor and yet proud of their power, watching always for ways to make it felt, to shove it into you and twist it and grin and watch you squirm, ruthless without malice, cruel and yet not always unkind. What would you expect them to be? Civilisation had no meaning for them. All they saw of it was the failures, the dirt, the dregs, the aberrations and the disgust.

By contrast with the policemen, the behavior of the private detective may be tough, but is based on ethical standards. As Spade says to Brigid O'Shaughnessy, alias Miss Wunderly, when she asks if he would have given her up to the police if the falcon had been real and not a fake: "Don't be too sure I'm as crooked as I'm supposed to be. That kind of reputation might be good business—bringing in high-priced jobs and making it easier to deal with the enemy." And as he says to her a little earlier about the killing of his partner Miles Archer: "It happens we were in the detective business. Well, when one of your organisation gets killed it's bad business to let the killer get away with it. It's bad all round—bad for that one organisation, bad for every detective everywhere." Such are the modest standards by which the Hammett detective lives.

By the sixties, American writers had gone far beyond Hammett and Chandler in their readiness to draw crooked or sadistic cops. Samples of both appear even in work so tied by the conventions of a series as Ed McBain's 87th Precinct stories. British writers were slower to treat the police in this way, and in 1960 the American publisher of Julian Symons's *The Progress of a Crime* expressed a certain amount of shocked surprise at the police treatment of suspects. Five years later, no publisher, and few readers, would have felt any sense of shock, and a detective now may be a Jew or a

Negro, a homosexual or a womanizer who sleeps with his more attractive suspects. It is a long way from Marlowe, who rejected all sexual temptation until he met Linda Loring.

The treatment of sex has changed as much as the treatment of the police. Murder might have been associated with rape before the war, but the rape would have been mentioned delicately. "Any sign of—interference?" the police investigator occasionally asked, and if the surgeon shook his head, he might well "sigh with relief." Today all this has changed. Rape is now perhaps more frequently encountered in books than it is in life, at least in Britain, and semen tests on clothing or in vagina are often given in detail. Transvestism, lesbianism, or homosexuality may be made the basis of stories, and blackmail by means of pornographic films or photographs is commonplace, with the pictures sometimes described. (Even such an old-fashioned writer, in this sense, as Carr once made use of sex photographs of a girl taken at her lover's request as a plot feature.) Detailed accounts of sex acts are still less frequent in the crime story than in ordinary novels, and four letter words are less used, but the situation is wholly different from that prevailing a few years ago when several English publishers turned down Nicolas Freeling's first book, *Love in Amsterdam,* because it was thought to be too sexually outspoken, and it was commonplace for words and passages to be queried on the ground that they would be disliked by many readers. "Is it really necessary to use the word 'shit' in a piece of light entertainment meant for family reading?" was an actual query put within the last decade by a publisher to an author. Very few words or phrases would be thought objectionable today.

In dealing with violence, crime writers were always allowed more freedom, even though such violence has obvious associations with sex. The pleasure found by Mickey Spillane's Mike Hammer in crunching his heel into the faces of men and occasionally beating up women who are on the "wrong" side has often been remarked on and reproved, but it is nothing new. Sapper's *Bulldog Drummond* (1920) finds Drummond forcing the villainous Lakington into a bath of acid from which he emerges with his clothes burned off and "mad with agony." In *The Black Gang* (1922), two Jews working in the service of revolution, "a little flashily dressed, distinctly addicted to cheap jewellery," are told by the masked Drummond, "My friends and I do not like your trade, you swine" before being beaten "to within an inch of their lives" with the cat-o'-nine-tails. In 1939, the critic John Mair summed up the casualties in James Hadley Chase's first book, *No Orchids for Miss Blandish:*

Guys rubbed out	22 (with a rod, 9; with a tommy-gun, 6; with a knife, 3; with a blackjack, 2; by kicking, 1; by suicide, 1)
Guys slugged bad	16 (in the face or head, 15; in the guts, 1)
Guys given a work-over	5 (with blunt instruments, 3; with a knife, 1; with burning cigarettes, 1)
Dames laid	5 (willing, 3; paid, 1; raped, 1)

The central feminine character in Latimer's *Solomon's Vineyard* can only get sexual pleasure after being hit, and one of the men obtains it only during the act of murder. In M. Scott Michel's *Sweet Murder* (1945), Wood Jaxon, the Marlovian private eye, is tied spread-eagled to a bed while an immensely strong and tall but girlishly pretty homosexual thug jams the lighted end of a cigarette into his mouth, lets it burn out on his chest, and beats him up again and again. These instances could be multiplied. Violence, much of it deliberately sadistic, had been an element in the thriller long before James Bond and Mike Hammer. The change is that a scene of violence may now be found in any kind of crime story, not just in the thriller.

It is not very profitable to welcome or regret this freedom of expression on ethical grounds. When C. H. B. Kitchin suggested in one of his detective stories that "a historian of the future will probably turn, not to blue books or statistics, but to detective stories if he wishes to study the manners of our age," he was writing just before World War II and was far from having Mike Hammer in mind, but what he said remains true. The crime story reflects the prevailing ethic of its period in the attitude adopted by its writers toward police and criminals, crime and punishment. Because crime literature is based on giving the public what it wants, crime writers are more than usually sensitive to shifts of taste. This sensitivity is mostly unconscious; they simply find themselves in tune with a considerable section of the reading public on any given subject. To ask whether Agatha Christie would have written differently if she had been born half a century later is like asking whether a modern Shakespeare would have written in blank verse. The questions beg themselves by their absurdity. Nobody born in 1940 could possibly have thought like Agatha Christie, and so would not have written like her. To put the point in reverse, many recent crime writers would have written different kinds of books, or perhaps would not have written at all, a few years earlier. The present period has encouraged their talents, as it has discouraged those who feel a wistful yearning for the Golden Age.

Yet there is something more to be said. It may not be true that life imitates art, as Wilde suggested, but all literature takes color from its social surroundings and at the same time gives them a further element of meaning. Hammett and Chandler did not breed a class of young men who wanted to be Spades and Marlowes. What happened is that the sensibilities of these two writers produced such archetypal figures out of the American air, and fed them into the public consciousness through literature. Their acceptance by a large audience then helped to change the response of that audience, not just to private eyes but to the very nature of crime. This is one way in which popular art works, and the conditions of the fifties and sixties encouraged the production of crime and spy stories which were able to use crime literature as a form of popular entertainment to make moral or social comments about society. In the last twenty years, many of the best crime stories have returned to the spirit of the ancestor who preceded Poe: William Godwin.

XIII

The Short Story's Mutations

DECLINE

In *Queen's Quorum*, the "History of the Detective-Crime Short Story as Revealed by the 106 Most Important Books Published in This Field Since 1845," published in 1951, there is no hint of the short story's replacement by the novel as the dominant crime-fiction form, nor of its decline in quality. There is instead a triumphal progress from the "Second Golden Era" to "The First Moderns," "The Second Moderns," and then "The Renaissance." Such conclusions do more credit to Ellery Queen's enthusiastic heart than to his analytical head. The Golden Age showed an immediate decline in the quality of short stories, and eventually in their number.

One reason for this has already been mentioned. The losses in circulation suffered by the kind of magazine that had nurtured the short detective story were slow but steady. The *Strand* clung for years to the formula that had brought success, which, as its historian has admitted, involved ignoring during the twenties "the new poor, the decline of the larger country houses, the General Strike," and anything else that readers might find uncomfortable. The last Doyle story appeared in April, 1927, and although crime stories continued to appear they were with a few exceptions much inferior to those that had been published before World War I, or even to the Four Just Men tales that had been published during its course. The *Strand* relied upon the formula of frivolity that had served it so well in the Victorian and Edwardian years, and perhaps the magazine was not helped by the retention of an essentially Victorian editor, Greenhalgh Smith, until 1930. The circulation fell to 80,000 during World War II, and although its appearance was modernized, the paper that had grown up with Sherlock Holmes had no real reason for existence in the age of Philip Marlowe. By the time the last number appeared in March, 1950, the flow of new short stories had almost stopped. It is typical of the magazine's backward look that, long before the end, they used a Sherlock Holmes story written in imitation of the master by Ronald Knox, and illustrated in the manner of Sidney Paget.

In the United States, the short story as a commercial article was replaced by serialized novels. The *Saturday Evening Post* had run the Thinking Machine and the Father Brown stories as series before World War I, but in 1927 the serialization of Frances Noyes Hart's *The Bellamy Trial* provided a signpost to the future. The *Post* went on to publish a great many serializations of crime novels by Rinehart, Christie, Stout, and others during the interwar years. In 1927 also, *Scribner's* managed temporarily to check a steady decline in circulation with publication of Van Dine's *The Canary Murder Case*. In the same years, these and other magazines carried comparatively few short stories of the classic Holmes length.

To say that the serialized novel had become more important for magazines than the short story is not to say that short stories were no longer written or that they failed to find print, only that there was a decreasing demand for them. In America the pulp magazines which relied on short stories flourished in these years, and there was a considerable development also of the "short short story," of 2,000 words or less, which could easily be read in bus or train on the way home. Such a length gave no room for development of plot or character, or for anything more than the making of a single ingenious point; for instance, that a man supposedly deaf has heard a casual remark made in another room; or that a man who claims to have been cut off from all communication during the past week knows the result of a football match that took place two days ago. Anecdotes of this kind can be entertaining both to write and to read, but a diet based on them soon becomes tiring.

Yet the short story's decline in these years was not only a matter of changes in editorial requirements. Crime-fiction writers soon realized for themselves that the plot construction of a short story could be almost as demanding as that of a novel, and was far less rewarding. Perhaps one should not put too much stress on purely financial considerations. Allingham, Berkeley, Carr, Queen, Sayers, Van Dine (the names are taken almost at random) accustomed themselves to the leisurely pace of a novel, its accumulation of suspense and doubt, the final revelation and explanation that might take up some thirty pages. It is not surprising that some crime writers never attempted the short story, and that few between the wars made it a major part of their work. The remarkable thing is that some of these stories were so good. Their merits are not those of Doyle in development of scene and character, or of Chesterton in revealing truths by paradox. The writers of short stories between the wars attempted no more than the statement of a puzzle and its solution by decent detective work. Within these limits, the short stories particularly of Queen, Sayers, and Carr give a great deal of pleasure. Indeed, in some ways the short story is better suited than the novel to this kind of writing. That final snap of surprise can bring just as genuine a gasp of pleasure after a short period of suspense as after a long one.

This is notable especially in the case of Ellery Queen. The best of his short stories belong to the early intensely ratiocinative period, and both *The Adventures of Ellery Queen* (1934) and *The New Adventures* (1940) are as absolutely fair and totally puzzling as the most passionate devotee of orthodoxy could wish. At least one of the stories in the first book, "The Adventure of the Bearded Lady," is a perfect example of this kind of problem story, baffling in its components but simple when they are put in their right places. Half a dozen others are almost equally good, and every story in these books is composed with wonderful skill. Some of the later Queen stories are interesting, but generally they do not come up to those in the first two collections, because the structure is looser and there is not much compensation in the way of greater depth. Most of Carr's stories are compressed versions of his locked-room novels, and at times they benefit from the compression. Probably the best of them are in the Carter Dickson book, *The Department of Queer Complaints* (1940), although this does not include the brilliantly clever H. M. story "The House in Goblin Wood" or a successful pastiche which introduces Edgar Allan Poe as detective.

Dorothy Sayers's short stories treat their subjects with an ease that most of the novels lack, and they are free from the worst excesses of Wimsey. Within the space of thirty pages, there is mercifully no room for Wimsey-Bunter dialogue, although there is still some stuff that must seem strange to those who regard Sayers as a semi-realistic writer. "Go back to your War Office and say I will not give you the formula" cries a French Royalist Count to Wimsey. "If war should come between our countries—which may God avert!—I will be found on the side of France." This is from a preposterous but rather enjoyable story called "The Bibulous Business of a Matter of Taste," in which three Wimseys appear at a French château and have their credentials tested by a prolonged session of vintage and date naming. The collection that contains this story, *Lord Peter Views the Body* (1928), includes also the genuinely terrifying "The Man with the Copper Fingers" and "The Adventurous Exploit of the Cave of Ali Baba," which opens with a newspaper account of Wimsey's death, followed by his enlistment in some unspecified secret society. *Hangman's Holiday* (1933) includes the clever "The Image in the Mirror" and a funny, quite uncharacteristic Sayers (no detective appears in it) called "The Man Who Knew How." *In The Teeth of the Evidence* (1939) offers two good stories in which Wimsey appears rather mutedly and several odds and ends, including the delightful "The Inspiration of Mr. Budd." Altogether, the short stories suggest that Dorothy Sayers might have been a better and livelier crime writer if she had not fallen in love with her detective.

These were worthy books by writers whose short stories were subsidiary to their novelistic talents. The same can be said of the short stories written by other crime novelists. The Poirot and

Miss Marple short stories are far inferior to the novels, and so are Allingham's stories about Mr. Campion. Several collections produced by Humdrums are no improvement on their longer work. Some other books mentioned in *Queen's Quorum* are either production-line work by writers who were at their best no more than efficient or, like the stories of Louis Golding and Damon Runyon, are remote from the ordinary concerns of the crime story. If the mere fact that a story dealt with a crime and its punishment was sufficient, then a miniature masterpiece like William Gerhardi's "A Bad End" or a collection like Ambrose Bierce's *Can Such Things Be?* could not be ignored, but the real interest of these stories lies elsewhere.

After World War I, there were few writers for whom the short story was a natural medium of expression, as it had been for Doyle, Chesterton, and Futrelle. Most often praised among them is H. C. Bailey (1878–1961), whose first collection of stories about Reggie Fortune appeared in 1920. It was followed by several other books of short stories and some Fortune novels, as well as novels about a sanctimonious and scoundrelly lawyer named Joshua Clunk. The Fortune stories were so successful that in the early thirties Bailey was regarded as one of a semi-mythical "Big Five" among English detective-story writers, the others being Christie, Crofts, Freeman, and Sayers. They are now so disregarded that all the books are out of print, although single stories may occasionally be found in anthologies. For those like me who find Fortune intolerably facetious and whimsical, and the stories always affected, sometimes silly, and at times obscure, this unanimity of disregard will seem perfectly justified. In case injustice may be done here, it should be recorded that other critics have found that Bailey had "a pretty sense of puzzle" (Sandoe) and that few writers produced "puzzles more elaborately conceived or genuinely mystifying" (Haycraft).

The Solange Stories (1931) of F. Tennyson Jesse are sometimes mentioned as highly individual performances, but although they have a lucid and lively introduction dealing with her development of a woman detective with a special warning sense of evil, the stories themselves are disappointingly thin. Perfectly readable, but also disappointing after the praise lavished on them, are C. Daly King's collection of stories about *The Curious Mr. Tarrant* (1935) and the stories about Henry Poggioli in *Clues of the Caribbees* (1929), by T. S. (Thomas Sigismund) Stribling (1881–1965). Poggioli is an instructor in psychology at Ohio State University who becomes involved in cases set in Haiti, Martinique, and parts of the West Indies. The stories themselves are slight, although they gain something from the originality of the settings. In the longest of them, Poggioli is called in as "the great American voodoo inspector" to demonstrate to Haitian Negroes that voodooism is nothing more than a superstition, and in "A Passage to Benares" he is a murder suspect. It is suggested, indeed, that he has been hanged before the murderer's confession, although he survived to have more adventures recorded in *Ellery Queen's Mystery Magazine.*

These are the best work in a thin time. They represent a sharp descent from the great days of the short story. But, as always, there are felicities scattered along the way in the form of single tales. Among them are Aldous Huxley's "The Gioconda Smile," a poisoning story based rather distantly upon an actual murder trial; Thomas Burke's chilling "The Hands of Mr. Ottermole"; and "The Perfect Murder," by Stacy Aumonier, a writer whose few genuine crime stories are all well worth reading.

REVIVAL

The short story's revival is linked directly with America, and partly with Hammett, Chandler, and their followers. Although the Continental Op stories were inferior to Hammett's novels, and although many of Chandler's stories are the work of a man learning his craft, they gave a lead in theme and language to other writers. Take the first line of a Hammett story, a line like "It was a wandering daughter job," or the evocation of the flavor of the desert town of Corkscrew in the story of that name, and you are in a world quite free from the gentility and snobbery of the Golden Age. But even more important than the existence of Hammett and Chandler as examples to learn from was the foundation in 1941 of *Ellery Queen's Mystery Magazine*. Here was a periodical which printed only short stories about crime and detection, and its influence upon the crime short story's development has been as great as that of the early *Strand*.

Ellery Queen, or at least half of him in the form of Frederic Dannay, exercised an active editorial interest from the beginning, and from the beginning he recognized that the form of the crime story was changing and that a successful magazine had to accommodate the old and encourage the new. The editors of *E.Q.M.M.* were prepared to welcome equally a new story by Carr or Allingham and the first short story of an unknown writer. They were ready to give the first prize in the yearly contest they inaugurated to stories which, as it seemed to some of their readers, were not detective stories at all, like H. F. Heard's "The President of the United States, Detective," or to a realistic story by an Italian-born writer. They gave special prizes for foreign stories, a gesture which produced in one year tales from Australia, Argentina (from Jorge Luis Borges), Portugal, the Philippines, and South Africa. They have given at different times awards for the best first story, the best tour de force, the best piece of Sherlockiana, the best short short story, the best riddle story, and the best story by a college student. A full list of the prize stories in the yearly *The Queen's Awards*, together with the new stories that have appeared in *E.Q.M.M.*, is a roll of honor of the crime short story in recent years. It is also, as Queen claims, a compendium of every possible kind of crime story. Some of the kinds are more important than others, not all of the stories are masterpieces, and some will madden anybody who has a fixed idea of what the crime short story should be like. The permanently excited editorial style will not be to everybody's taste. Yet the value of the magazine far transcends any criticisms that may be made of it. No doubt short stories would have been written if *E.Q.M.M.* had never existed, but they would have been much less various in style and interest, and almost certainly much poorer in quality. The editors have been directly responsible for encouraging the two most talented crime short-story writers of the past thirty years.

In November, 1946, the managing editor of the magazine told

Ellery Queen—in this case presumably Dannay—on the telephone that a remarkable new story had come in to the office. This was "The Specialty of the House," the first story published by Stanley Ellin. The story is now so famous that there can be no harm in revealing that it is about the delicious lamb Amirstan which is the specialty of an inconspicuous New York restaurant named Sbirro's, that the meat in the dish is human flesh, and that it is unwise for any diner to accept Sbirro's invitation to enter his kitchen. Stanley Ellin (1916–   ) was a steelworker before he became a full-time writer, and although he has said that his idea of an ideal workroom is Proust's cork-lined chamber plus a typewriter, he is in most respects a strikingly unliterary character, interested in baseball, boxing, and—surprisingly for an American —cricket. This earthy New Yorker from Brooklyn is, however, an exceptionally careful and easily dissatisfied writer, who revises each page several times and often tries out an opening sentence again and again until he "hits one that *feels* right." It was ten years before his first collection, *Mystery Stories* (1956), was published, and another eight before ten more stories were gathered between covers under the title *The Blessington Method*. His stories have been produced at an average rate of one a year.

Ellin has written several excellent novels, of which *The Eighth Circle* (1958) is the most notable, but his talent shows at its finest in his short stories. The great quality he has brought back to the crime short story is that of imagination. That concern with tricking the reader is all very well, but in the best crime stories it is subsidiary to the exercise of the imagination by which the writer becomes one with his subject. This is what makes us shiver a little when we read the Holmes stories. Ellin can be quite as ingenious as any Golden Age practitioner, but his ingenuity is turned to ends which produce the authentic shiver. The little final twist is a turn of the knife in the reader's sensibility. It is because he can imagine what might persuade a little man defeated by life to commit murder ("The Cat's-Paw"), or the existence of a society to ease a way out of life for old people who are a nuisance to the young or middle-aged ("The Blessington Method"), or what it is like to be a public executioner, that his work is a landmark in the history of the crime short story. His finest pieces go beyond the usual limits of the genre and turn into fables, occasionally tender but more often sharp, about the grotesque shapes of urban society and the dreams of the human beings who live in it.

The talent of Roy Vickers (1889–1965) was less remarkable than that of Stanley Ellin and was manifested late in his writing career, but it was wholly distinctive and operated particularly in the medium of the short story. Vickers wrote many crime novels from the twenties onward, but these books bear no mark of being produced by the same man who wrote the short stories which began with the invention of the Department of Dead Ends, an imaginary branch of Scotland Yard in which the details of all unsolved murder mysteries are kept. Vickers began to write the Dead End stories in the thirties, but found it hard to sell them, because their realistic tone was utterly incompatible with the requirements of magazines at the time. It was not until Ellery Queen discovered "The Rubber Trumpet" and one or two other stories in the dusty pages of *Pearson*'s, and asked if there was a series of these tales, that Vickers was moved to revive his highly original idea. "The Department does not grope for points missed in the investigation but] keeps an eye open for any unusual occurrence to any of the persons who were once in the orbit of an unsolved murder," as Vickers himself put it. When at last a collection of stories appeared in hard covers, as *The Department of Dead Ends* (1946), the brilliance of the conception was at once appreciated. A rubber trumpet thrown out of a railway train provides a link with seventy-seven other rubber trumpets, apparently sold over the counter of a chemist's shop, to bring George Muncey to justice; a begging letter which turns up in the Department two years after the apparently motiveless murder of Gerald Raffen leads directly to the murderer; and so on.

Vickers's method is generally to provide the setting for the crime, show it being carried out, and then go on to the accidental discovery that lays a trail to the criminal. He follows in this the pattern of the inverted story, but uses it with more flexibility and sophistication than its inventor. He also improves on the originals by giving almost every story a deadly probability. Many of the

cases have a suburban setting, and the murderers are often respectable people, people like us. To quote Vickers again: "Together we must reach a moment in which we agree that a particular
pressure of circumstance might well prove too much, not indeed
for ourselves but perhaps for our neighbours." This might be a
little dull but in fact it is not, because Vickers has his own, far
from mechanical ingenuity, exemplified in a story like "The Man
Who Murdered in Public," where George Macartney is acquitted
of forcibly drowning his wife because the two earlier "accidents"
in which women have been drowned cannot be put in as evidence
in relation to the third. George is eventually caught by one of those
felicitous oddities that are the hallmark of the Dead End cases.
The story obviously had its origin in the career of George Joseph
Smith, the "Brides in the Bath" murderer, and a number of the
other tales looked glancingly at real English murder cases.

Between the near-fables of Ellin and the near-documentaries of
Vickers, the modern crime story offers a great deal of entertainment and some serious writing. The six stories in *Knight's Gambit*
(1949), for instance, weigh lightly in the whole balance of
William Faulkner's achievement, but they are undoubtedly more
deeply conceived than most crime stories. One of them, "An
Error in Chemistry," was submitted for the first Ellery Queen
Detective Short Story contest, and won second prize. The stories
deal with the detective exploits of Gavin Stevens, county attorney
who is in these tales rather like Uncle Abner, although in the
whole Faulkner saga (he appears in several novels) he is developed as a very different figure. Some of the stories were published long before they were gathered up in book form, and they
show Faulkner's interest in the mystery story as a form. The
detective stories about Johnson and Boswell of Lillian Bueno
McCue (1902–   ), who used the name of Lillian de la
Torre, collected in *Dr. Sam: Johnson, Detector* (1946), are perhaps the most successful pastiches in detective fiction. *E.Q.M.M.*,
again, was responsible for their first publication. Miss de la Torre
caught most happily the tone and weight of Johnson's conversation and rightly made the puzzles almost incidental to the relationship between biographer and subject. One may dislike pastich-

of any kind, but here it is certainly done on a high level. No other collections of stories by individual writers come up to those already mentioned, but there are a great many which push the crime story into territory that had not been explored for a long time, like some of Jorge Luis Borge's extraordinary pieces, or one or two of the horrific tales in Roald Dahl's collections, *Someone Like You* (1953) and *Kiss Kiss* (1960), and some of Patricia Highsmith's intensely imagined pieces. Dahl's story "Lamb to the Slaughter" is about the literally perfect disposition of a murder weapon.

It is, again, important not to give a wrong impression. A great many crime short stories continue to be written with nothing but entertainment in mind. Among the best of them are Edmund Crispin's *Beware of the Trains* (1953), with its particularly tricky title story, and Michael Innes's two collections, *Appleby Talking* (1954)* and *Appleby Talks Agaii* (1956). At the same time, some of these stories, and many others written by talented British and American authors, suffer from the fact that they were commissioned by newspapers and magazines who confined their writers within a very short space. The short story has triumphantly revived, and it is time that a publisher brought out a selection of the best work published since the end of World War II, on the scale of Sayers's collections. Such a book would be a revelation of the treasures that have piled up. The achievement, really, is a kind of miracle. A continual flow of good crime stories presupposes magazines prepared to print them, and in Britain such magazines hardly exist. It is not too much to say that the continuation of the crime short story as we know it, like its development during the past twenty years, seems largely dependent upon *Ellery Queen's Mystery Magazine.*

---

* In America, *Deadman's Shoes.*

XIV

Crime Novel and Police Novel

THE CRIME NOVEL

The Detective story has changed into the Crime novel. Such a statement needs not so much justification as definition. A comparison of the main features in the two kinds of book may help in showing that they are really not the same article with a different label.

DETECTIVE STORY	CRIME NOVEL
Plot	*Plot*
Based on a deception which may be mechanical (locked room), verbal (misleading remarks), concerned with forensic medicine (poisons, blood groups, fake prints) or ballistics. Book is constructed backward from this deception, revelation of which is the climactic point to which everything else leads.	Based on psychology of characters—what stresses would make A want to kill B?—or on intolerable situation that must end in violence. No deception of locked-room or faked-print kind, no obscure poisons. Most often the problem is something like: "Has A really killed B and if he has what will happen to him?" Book is constructed forward from such a problem.

Detective

May be professional or amateur, and if amateur may run detective or inquiry agency, or get involved by chance in criminal cases. Always at the center of story's action, most often the hero, and generally a keen observer who notices things missed by others.

Method

If the crime is murder (it almost always is), method may be bizarre or misleading; i.e., the victim appears to have been shot but was in fact poisoned. Sometimes the method may be highly ingenious, as in locked-room mystery, or itself puzzling as in a poisoning case where everybody ate and drank exactly the same things.

Clues

An essential element. There will be perhaps a dozen of them in the story. The detective may explain their meaning at the time, or deductions may be left to the reader.

Characters

Only the detective is characterized in detail. Otherwise characterization is perfunctory, particularly after the crime,

Detective

Often no detective. Occasionally a detective runs through a series of stories, but rarely shown as a brilliant reasoning machine. Most often the central character is just somebody to whom things happen.

Method

Usually straightforward, rarely important. Sometimes ballistics play an important part, but mechanical devices are almost never used.

Clues

Quite often no clues in the detective-story sense.

Characters

The basis of the story. The lives of characters are shown continuing after the crime, and often their subsequent behav-

when people become wholly subsidiary to plot.

Setting
Mostly confined to what
happens *before* the crime. Later,
plot and clue requirements take
over, and setting (school, newspaper office, etc.) fades.

Social Attitude
Conservative.

Puzzle Value
Often high. The detective
and the puzzle are the only
things that stay in the memory.

ior is important to the story's
effect.

Setting
Often important to the tone
and style of the story, and frequently an integral part of the
crime itself; i.e., the pressures
involved in a particular way of
life lead to this particular crime.

Social Attitude
Varying, but often radical
in the sense of questioning some
aspect of law, justice, or the way
society is run.

Puzzle Value
Sometimes high, sometimes
almost nonexistent. But characters and situation are often remembered for a long time.

The distinctions are real, the articles are different. The distinctions are exaggerated a little here, perhaps, because the lines
of differentiation are frequently crossed. There are crime novels
which contain surprises as stunning as those of the best detective
stories, although they are obtained by different means, like Ira
Levin's *A Kiss Before Dying*. There are detective stories, like some
of those written by Michael Gilbert, which offer characterization
that is far from perfunctory. The categories are useful, though, because the aims of the detective-story writer and the crime novelist
are basically different. The detective story is concerned first with
setting a puzzle for the reader, and as Chandler put it in a letter,
"to get the complication you fake the clues, the timing, the play of
coincidence . . . to get the surprise murderer you fake the character, which hits me hardest of all, because I have a sense of character." The crime novelist is most often a fictionally split personality.

Half of him wants to write a novel about people affected by crime, but the other half yearns to produce a baffling mystery. This split almost down the middle is very evident in Chandler's own work. He might say that "those who say the problem overrides everything are merely trying to cover up their own inability to create character and atmosphere," but often in his early books the atmospheric brilliance that came to him as naturally as breathing is used to cover up his inability to devise a plot. The crime novelist tends to make the story secondary to the characters; the detective-story writer concentrates on the puzzle to the exclusion of reasonable behavior. Chandler thought that this was inevitable, that "something must always be sacrificed," but this is not true. When the fusion of puzzle and characterization is perfect, as in *The Glass Key,* you have books produced in the form of crime novels that have a claim to be considered as works of art.

The range of talent working within the crime novel is very wide. This form of sensational literature is so flexible, and in its recrudescence so comparatively fresh, that writers are trying to use it in very different ways. There are crime novelists who aim more or less consciously at blending the elements already mentioned into a story that has many of the values of a novel, and a few who work with a fairly distinct moral or social purpose. There are many who have given up most of the detective story's apparatus and offer a lively setting and credible characterization, but still write with a lightness of attitude that marks their books "For Entertainment Only." There are writers who attempt a realistic view of police work and procedure, writers whose books are basically psychological studies, and a few who have brought into the crime story the unusual element of wit. And although spy stories are dealt with separately, it would be wrong not to mention here the remarkable transformation of the spy story in the hands of John Le Carré, Len Deighton, and other writers into a kind of literature that gives room for the sharpest kind of comment on the realities of power and violence.

The divisions that follow are again to a certain extent artificial, and may be thought objectionable, but they do seem to me real. They are meant to define intention, rather than achievement. Seri-

ous writers can be boring and pretentious, and along with most
people I would prefer to them entertainers who by definition entertain. Yet there are differences. The best books of Emma Lathen
seem to me as wholly enjoyable as anything in modern crime
writing, but the kind of pleasure they give is different not in degree
but in kind from that given by the work of Patricia Highsmith.
Emma Lathen may be regarded as a descendant of the Golden
Age writers, although she writes much better than most of her
forebears. Patricia Highsmith owes nothing at all to them. Other
examples could be given, but I hope the point is made that some
distinctions are unavoidable in this account of the growth of the
crime novel in its various forms.

SERIOUS CRIME NOVELISTS

The writer who fuses characters and plot most successfully is
Patricia Highsmith (1921–   ), the most important crime novelist at present in practice. This statement will not receive general
assent in her native America, and it is curious that American
critics, who are so generous to British writers, have been slow
to recognize outstanding home-grown talents. For more than a
decade, Hammett was regarded as just another writer of pulp
stories, and Chandler when he came to England discovered with
delight that "over here I am not regarded as a mystery writer but
as an American novelist of some importance . . . there is none
of that snobbism which makes a fourth-rate serious novelist,
without style or any real talent, superior by definition to a mystery writer." Highsmith has observed that in France and England
(she could have added Scandinavia) "I fare much better as to
prestige, quality of reviewing and—proportionately speaking—
sales than in America." Crime stories have always been the Cin-
derellas of literature so far as reviewing is concerned, but in
Europe the best of them receive serious treatment.

Perhaps it should be added that Highsmith is an acquired taste,
which means a taste that some never acquire. When I was reviewing crime fiction regularly, Victor Gollancz used to write to me
before going on holiday, asking me to recommend the best books
of the year published by other firms than his own. (Many of

them, thanks to his critical susceptibility and intelligence, appeared in his own yellow covers.) He then bought these books and took them away with him. At my insistence, he bought one year *The Two Faces of January,* which he disliked intensely. To his letter in the following year he added a postscript: "Please—no Patricia Highsmith."

Most of Highsmith's books have their origin in some sensational idea. In her first novel, *Strangers on a Train* (1949), a young man who meets another on a train proposes that each of them shall murder a person whom the other wishes to see dead. Since neither killer will have any connection with his victim, there is no reason why these should not be "perfect murders." In *The Blunderer* (1954), a clumsy amateur killer sets out to copy a crime committed by a more professional one and finds himself being pursued by the murderer. Such tricky plot devices are often used by very inferior writers—Baroness Orczy used the *Strangers on a Train* plot for one of her *Old Man in the Corner* stories—but in Highsmith's hands they are starting points for profound and subtle character studies. She recurs often to the attraction exerted on the weak by the idea of violence. In *The Two Faces of January* (1964), when the emotionally footloose Rydal Keener sees the petty crook Chester MacFarland kill a man, his immediate reaction is to attach himself to Chester and his wife rather than to report the affair to the police. In the opening scene of *Those Who Walk Away* (1967), Ray Garrett is shot at and wounded by Coleman, but again his reaction is to link himself more closely to the would-be murderer rather than to attempt to escape from him. It may be said that this is not true to "life," but this means only that it is not the way most people would behave. It is true and convincing in the life of Highsmith characters, who find themselves linked to each other by the idea of crime. There are no more genuine agonies in modern literature than those endured by the couples in her books who are locked together in a dislike and even hatred that often strangely contains love.

Behind such relationships there are ideas about the relations of people within society that strike a distant echo of those views held by Godwin. Without being directly concerned with politics, Highsmith implicitly suggests that in a society where most people are imprisoned within the mechanisms of organizations, social groups or families, criminals are potentially free. Her heroes are there fore often criminals, heroic in the sense that they are the mos likable people in the story. Her personal expressions of her idea are often naive, but in this case unequivocal:

Criminals are dramatically interesting, because for a time at leas they are active, free in spirit, and they do not knuckle down to any one. . . . I find the public passion for justice quite boring and artifi cial, for neither life nor nature cares if justice is ever done or not

She realizes that the general public wants to see the law tri umph, and does not object to brutality so long as it is on the official side. "Sleuth-heroes can be brutal, sexually unscrupulous kickers of women, and still be popular heroes, because they are chasing something worse than themselves, presumably." Such comments help to explain why the book of hers that many people like best, *The Talented Mr. Ripley* (1955), is about a criminal who, after some narrow escapes, ends up going free.

But it is not the ideas behind her books so much as the intensity and skill with which they are presented that make her such a rewarding novelist. The original ideas on which her plots are based are sometimes far-fetched and in her early work much marked by coincidence, but she treats them with an imaginative power that gives the problems of the criminal hero a terrifying reality. Her settings—Venice, Crete, Tunis—are chosen with care. In strange surroundings her characters become uncertain of their personalities and begin to question the reasons for their own conduct. She has a professional ability to order a plot and create a significant environment, but what takes her books beyond the run of intelligent crime stories is the intensity of feeling brought to the central figures. Violence is necessary to her, because the threat or actuality of it produces her best writing, and the problem she faces in relation to its use is a way of coordinating sensationalism of theme with subtlety of treatment as she has not always been able to do in the past. The deadly games of pursuit played in her best novels are as subtle and interesting as anything being done in the novel today.

Highsmith has been discussed first because her approach makes her an exemplar of talented novelists whose spur to writing comes evidently from an interest in crime, but nothing in the way of a ranking order is being suggested, and the writers presented below are given in an order roughly chronological. The first two books of Margot Bennett (1912–   ) were published just after the end of World War II, and few books in the genre have a stronger period flavor. Within the detective story's framework she worked, as Graham Greene observed, with wit and a sense of character, in writing with the desperate high spirits of the time about short-ages and the black market and the problems of people at home in wartime but lost in the large acres of peace. *Time to Change Hats* (1945) contained, Greene said, "the finest evacuee family I have encountered since Evelyn Waugh's *Put Out More Flags.*" In the four novels she wrote after the war, the high spirits have changed to a kind of sorrowful wit, most evident in *The Widow of Bath* (1952) and the cunningly devised *The Man Who Didn't Fly* (1955). Here are two people, once in love with each other, meet-ing again after a long time:

They sat and looked at each other, thinking of the shared past, but they were like painters of different schools working on the same scene, and their separate pictures were almost unrelated.

Sometimes the dialogue sounds a little like that of an English Chandler, as when her doom-laden hero in *The Widow of Bath* meets a beautiful woman whose activities once landed him in prison. " 'Are you as luxurious, greedy, mercenary, unscrupulous, selfish, faithless, ambitious, and lax as ever?' " he asks, and she replies: " 'I'm a civilized woman.' " Often she is both observant and funny, as in her comment about the seaside home of a retired judge who has spent some time in the Colonies, that "it was a Folly, a merino millionaire's folly; perhaps there were some carved sheep on the lawns," or in her view of the judge himself, "an obsolete battleship, who believed that his guns could still roar." Turn to almost any page in her books and you will find an un-expected and right turn of phrase.

These talents are put at the service of a skill in plot construction that is never mechanical, although it is sometimes too intricate. She uses as mere incidents tricks that would serve another writer as material for a book. In *The Widow of Bath,* a girl is presumed to have left her clothes in a shed and then drowned while swimming. In fact she has been murdered, but what makes the Inspector say: " 'Why don't you think about the clothes in the swimming shed? What was missing from the picture?' " There is a dress, underclothes, handbag with lipstick, and other things, purse. . . . What *is* missing? " 'Wouldn't she take a towel if she went swimming?' " There are a dozen clever deceptions in the book, twice as many as most writers would have given us, and certainly more than are needed. *The Man Who Didn't Fly* has a plot just as ingenious, but simpler. Four men arrange to fly to Dublin but only three board the plane, which crashes over the Irish Sea. Which of the four men didn't fly? The puzzle and the solution are as good as could be wished, and they run perfectly with Bennett's sense of character and the constant flame of her wit. It is a sad thing that her last crime story appeared fourteen years ago.

That the sympathies of both Highsmith and Bennett are radical is evident from their books. John (Michael Ward) Bingham, the writing name and the family name of Lord Clanmorris (1911–), is by temperament a conservative, a man likely to deprecate Highsmith's sympathetic feeling for criminals and the idea that they are "free in spirit." His first book, *My Name Is Michael Sibley* (1952), however, is about an innocent man who tells lies to the police and is then pounced on, played with, endlessly interrogated, with each fresh questioning tightening the ropes around him. The book is a classic example of the crime story's new direction. The murder in it remains unofficially unsolved, and we know from the beginning that Michael Sibley is innocent. The question that holds our attention from the first chapter until the result of the trial at the end is what will happen to this innocent man? Unlike the earlier followers of Francis Iles, Bingham is able to dispense with the element of surprise and still tell a wholly fascinating story.

A large part of this fascination rests in his accurate account of police interrogation, something which had never been attempted before in the British crime story. We never learn anything about his Chief Detective-Inspector and Sergeant outside the limits of the case. They are the embodiment of potentially hostile officialdom, polite English versions of Chandler's policemen, but equally conscious of their power:

> The Chief Detective-Inspector was a broad-shouldered man well above average height. I should say he was in his late forties. He had a round head, with closely cropped fair hair, receding slightly at the temples, and a brick-red face so keenly shaven that it seemed to radiate hygiene and good health. His features were regular, the nose and jaw clean-cut, but the lips were thin and the general impression you had was of a hard character in which sympathy, or indeed any of the more human emotions, had long since died. . . . He did not impress me as the sort of man who would have a single one of those endearing little habits or whimsical sayings which are so often attributed to police officers.

The Sergeant is on the surface a little different, more relaxed and even slightly sporty, but basically equally anonymous and cold. These two policemen, at first polite and casual, play the wretched Sibley, giving him line and then slowly reeling him in with each fresh interrogation as he makes a statement, and then a revised statement, and at last a third admission of all his previous deceptions and untruths, after which they triumphantly land him gasping in a prison cell. In its time, the book was wholly original, and although Bingham has been flattered by a good many imitators, it remains supreme in its kind.

Bingham is a very variable writer. He always shows a respect for his material which is rare (several modern crime writers have a regrettable condescension toward the literary form in which they work), but at his weakest he can be clumsy in plotting and in style. At his best, though, he communicates as well as anybody writing today that uneasy feeling of violence moving under the surface of everyday life. *Five Roundabouts to Heaven* (1953)* and *The Paton Street Case* (1955)† are admired by some readers

* In America, *The Tender Poisoner*.
† In America, *Inspector Morgan's Dilemma*.

more than his first novel. He goes in very little for the usual deceptive tricks of the trade, but the sequence of small surprises in *A Fragment of Fear* (1965) shows that he can manage them as well as anybody when he chooses.

Nicholas Freeling (1927–   ) and Kenneth Millar (1915–   ), who writes under the name of Ross Macdonald, are among the few writers of crime novels today who have placed a single character at the center of a series of books. These characters are far from wholly original. Freeling's Dutch Inspector Van der Valk and Macdonald's Lew Archer began as something near to carbon copies of Maigret and Marlowe, and although they have become more distinctly individual with the years, it is doubtful whether they strengthen the novels of these writers, although undoubtedly they help to make them popular. However, Van der Valk is a figure inconspicuous enough to be fitted into Freeling's credo that

murder, and any other crime, is not a part of entertainment, but an integral part of life. We are all murderers, we are all spies, we are all criminals, and to choose a crime as the mainspring of a book's action is only to find one of the simplest methods of focusing eyes on our life and our world.

Basing himself on these ideas, which would probably receive assent from all the writers mentioned in this section, Freeling has moved almost continuously toward the creation of character studies which are also crime stories since his first book, *Love in Amsterdam* (1962). He looks with a sympathetic eye—or Van der Valk does, which is much the same thing—at the springs of criminal activity, which he sees almost always as some kind of obsession. The combination of a tragic love story with a smuggling investigation in *Gun Before Butter** (1963) shows his talent almost at full stretch, but probably the best of his books, and the one most clearly expressing what he is trying to do, is *Criminal Conversation* (1965). The anonymous letter sent to the police, with which it begins, turns out to be the work of a banker, "one of the half-dozen most important men in Holland," who is accusing a fashionable neurologist of murder. The incident leads

* American title: *Question of Loyalty*.

into a series of discussions and arguments between Van der Valk and the doctor which present a fascinating contrast, not of cat and mouse, nor even of accuser and accused, but of two different styles and temperaments, the policeman's coarse but subtle, the doctor's refined, charming, calm. The breaking down of this calmness to the point when, as Van der Valk says, the doctor realizes that " 'I'm the only friend he's got' " is the real subject.

Ross Macdonald's early books, written under his own name of Kenneth Millar, are uneven, but they show that vividness in the use of metaphor and simile which from the beginning pulled his work out of the ruck of reasonably well-written hardboiled stories. *Blue City* (1947), the best of these early books, is about the son of a murdered man coming back to a Midwestern town to find his father's killer. The development owes something to Hammett, but the turns of phrase are striking ("His face had thinned and died, so that his smile was like carefully folded paper") and so is the quality of observation that sees

Mr. Dundee's wig-brown hair, carefully parted in the exact centre of his egg-shaped skull . . . his fat, laundered little face and his dark little eyes, his very hard white collar and his pale-blue tie which was held in place by a gold-plated initialled clasp.

In the first half-dozen Lew Archer stories, written under the name of John Ross Macdonald, the setting is always California, sometimes its rich face and often its dirty backside; the plots are densely complicated; there is a great deal of gun play. The books are written with the exuberance and zest of a man intoxicated by his own skill with epithets. Chandler criticized Macdonald harshly, much too harshly, for saying that a car was "acned with rust" and for calling the words and drawings on lavatory walls "graffiti." There doesn't seem anything wrong with these expressions (Chandler's own suggested "spotted" and "scrawlings" are simply weaker), except that in the books as a whole there are rather too many of them. If you turn to almost any page, you are likely to be jerked to attention rather than lulled into repose, and that must be a good thing. A random opening of pages in three different books, all of them early Archer, gave "He had a bulldog face whose

only expression was a frozen ferocity intended to scare off tres-
passers." . . . "I caught glimpses of glass-and-aluminum living machines gleaming like surgical equipment in the clinical
moonlight." . . . "Geoff had lived too long among actors. He was
a citizen of the unreal city, a false front leaning on scantlings."
There is occasionally a sense of strain about such writing, but more
often it seems finely appropriate to the frenetic world that is
being described. If all this talent and energy could be more
closely harnessed, if there were a little less violence and a little
more detachment, it seemed that Macdonald might be not merely the
lineal successor to Hammett and Chandler but even their superior.

The development that one hoped for has not quite taken place.
Macdonald's later books are in many ways better than the early
ones. They are composed with less violence, more subtlety, more
satisfactory plots. The quality of the observation gives pleasure;
the view of California as a place of immense beauty made ugly
by man is expressed with passion; there is a lot of sympathetic
and discerning characterization, particularly of the young. All
these later books are good, and it is only naming personal preferences to mention particularly *The Zebra-Striped Hearse* (1962)
and *The Far Side of the Dollar* (1964). Yet an impression that
Macdonald has repeated too often the quest for personal identity
and the investigation of the past that marks these books, that he
has been too easily content with the things he can do well, remains. Perhaps it is a pity that he has retained Archer in every
story; perhaps his talent would have flowered more finely and
more variously if he had sometimes looked for a setting and a
theme outside California. But of course a writer must be judged
by what he has actually done, and such conjecture is more or less
idle. At his best, Macdonald is as good a writer as Chandler, and
that should not be taken for light praise.

"Among the crime writers who have come into prominence
since the war she has few peers, and no superior, in the art of
bamboozlement. She presents us with a plausible criminal situation, builds it up to a climax of excitement, and then in the last
few pages shakes the kaleidoscope and shows us an entirely different pattern from the one we have been so busily interpreting."

I wrote these words about Margaret Millar more than a decade ago. They seem still perfectly true and yet to do her less than full justice, for Margaret (Sturm) Millar (1915–   ), the wife of Ross Macdonald, is also a most accomplished novelist, and it is this that should be mentioned first in any account of her writing. She is one of those novelists whose imagination is sparked off by the element of mystery, and the four "straight" novels which she published in the forties and early fifties are much less impressive as novels than her best mystery stories. As a mystery writer, too, her early books, which centered around a psychiatrist investigator called with infelicitous symbolism Dr. Paul Prye, were comparatively commonplace. It is the half-dozen books beginning with *Beast in View* (1955) that show the full scope of her skill as a novelist whose chosen theme is almost always a mystery with roots deeply hidden in the past.

This skill is shown at its finest in *How Like an Angel* (1962), which begins when Joe Quinn, a former casino cop at Reno who has lost his money gambling, lands up at the home of the True Believers in California, out in the bleak mountainous country forty-five miles from the nearest large town. The True Believers is a religious cult whose members believe that they are preparing for the ascension of a Tower which has five levels, of the earth, trees, mountains, sky, and at the top "the Tower of Heaven where the Master lives." A dotty cult, you might say, but nothing could better show the difference between the Golden Age story and the crime novel than the treatment given to similar groups by Allingham and Marsh. For them the cult serves merely as a background, ridiculous and slightly distasteful. Millar treats it seriously, describing its beliefs, physical situation, and adherents in detail. The practical good sense of Sister Blessing, the silence of Brother Tongue of Prophets, the excitement when a new convert arrives to join the slowly disintegrating group are conveyed with a powerful sense of pathos and absurdity joined to a respect for a way of life. The tension of the novel is partly created by the contrast between the simplicities of the group and the complexity of the investigation which Quinn undertakes on behalf of Sister Blessing into the background of Patrick O'Gorman, who apparently died five years earlier in a car accident. The puzzle is there all right, and its solution on the last page lives up to those phrases used about Millar's work, but by that time many readers will have become so much concerned with the fate of the characters that the problem itself is a secondary matter.

The best of the other Millar books show her ability to create an atmosphere of uneasiness and terror, which in other hands might have descended to the absurdities of the Gothic novel, but in her case is always used to create a situation based on the conflict of character. *Beast in View*, with its perfectly fair bit of conjuring on which the whole story depends, *The Soft Talkers* (1957),* *The Listening Walls* (1959), with its apparent double bluff and brilliant trick ending, and *A Stranger in My Grave* (1960) are all very good indeed.

Shelley Smith, the pseudonym used by Nancy Hermione Bodington, began by writing conventional stories about slightly simple women in danger, more sophisticated versions of the essential Rinehart story. In the thirties, such books were one of the chief variants to the orthodox puzzle, and in Britain Ethel Lina White wrote several stories of this kind, of which *The Wheel Spins* (1936) was probably the best. Smith's *Come and Be Killed* (1946) showed a development of this plucky-little-lady-in-trouble theme. Florence, dim, dullish, and highly neurotic, makes a half-hearted attempt to commit suicide, and then runs away from the nursing home to which her busy sister sends her. When she meets the weather-beaten and apparently kindly Mrs. Jolly, we know that Florence is in trouble, and prepare ourselves for her hairbreadth escape from death. Not so. Florence is murdered by jolly Mrs. Jolly, and the book is a portrait of a murderess rather than of a woman in trouble. Mrs. Jolly is too tender-hearted actually to watch her victim die when the poison acts less quickly than she had expected, and after the affair has been successfully concluded, the author investigates in a long flashback the basic reasons that turned Mrs. Jolly into a murderess. Mary Roberts Rinehart, one might say, has been transformed into Francis Iles.

Good though *Come and Be Killed* was, it hardly prepared one

* In America, *An Air That Kills*.

for the skill shown in *The Lord Have Mercy* (1956). Here Shelley Smith used the conventional background of middle-class English village life, the Conservative dance, the Dr. Barnardo's fête, little dinner parties, to show in half a dozen excellent portraits the worms of hatred and frustration working away under the surface. The butch lesbian about to leave her clinging partner and the local doctor's frigid bitchy wife are particularly good. After the wife's death from an overdose of barbiturates, everybody goes on behaving as they might do in real life. The final crime, by which the situation is resolved, has in retrospect a fine inevitableness. *The Ballad of the Running Man* (1961), although marred by some improbabilities, gave us another full-length portrait of somebody pushed to murder by personal weakness and the need for money rather than by inherent viciousness.

Roy (Broadbent) Fuller (1912) has written three crime stories, interspersed between orthodox novels and poems. (He is the present Oxford Professor of Poetry.) All are marked by the exactness and elegance of his poetry, but perhaps the most successful of them is *With My Little Eye* (1948). The subtitle calls the book "a mystery story for teen-agers," but this is deceptive, for it means only that the murder and other crimes are seen through the eyes of an intelligent adolescent narrator, conscious of the pain and loneliness of growing up. And to say this is still slightly deceptive, for the light sophistication of the tone is conveyed in the first paragraph with its apology for kicking off with "a boring explanation":

It would be pleasant to start with the astonishing thud of the pistol shot, but then the explanation would have to come in the middle of the excitement, which would be even more boring.

With My Little Eye is a little-known book, yet it is in its small way a perfect example of a modern crime story, finely constructed and balanced, with the solution to the various problems that baffle Frederick French (what could make a man move from one bookmaker to another on a racecourse, putting five pounds on every one of the nine horses in a race?) dropping perfectly into place. *The Second Curtain* (1953) finds George Garner, a timid publisher's reader, nursing the hope that through the box files in which he keeps carefully the whole of his correspondence he will one day be acknowledged as "a sort of Horace Walpole." Garner becomes immersed in the problem posed by the disappearance of his constant correspondent and old friend Widgery, and his quest for the truth about Widgery (for that is what it proves to be) leads him up to an abyss of violence into which he looks for a moment before flinching away. The book, again beautifully composed, might serve as a model of how little rather than how much violence is needed to make a successful crime story. *Fantasy and Fugue* (1954) looks back to Godwin in its central character who is both hunter and hunted. It is less successful than the other books chiefly because the theme is treated with a too insistent Freudianism. Since then Fuller has given up crime as a theme in his novels, and one can only hope, without great expectation, that he will return to it.

Perhaps the crime stories of Julian Symons (1912–   ) should be mentioned here. Symons began with some moderately successful stories rather in the Innes or Crispin style, and then moved on to books in which he attempted to explore the springs of crime. The most interesting of them are *The 31st of February* (1950), *The Progress of a Crime* (1960), and *The End of Solomon Grundy* (1964). His writing is at its best powerfully horrific, at its least successful uneven and ragged. He has said himself:

The thing that most absorbs me in our age is the violence behind respectable faces, the civil servant planning how to kill Jews more efficiently, the Judge speaking with passion about the need for capital punishment, the quiet obedient boy who kills for fun. . . . If you want to show the violence that lives behind the bland faces most of us present to the world, what better vehicle can you have than the crime novel?

But the intentions implied here are often rather inadequately fulfilled in his books.*

* This diffident paragraph scarcely does justice to Symons's importance in the postwar crime-fiction scene, and several further points call for mention.
First, Symons's earlier work, mostly using the framework of orthodox

There are not many recent European writers who can be considered seriously in the context of the crime novel, but their contribution is particularly interesting because it is so unlike anything from Britain or America. Friedrich Dürrenmatt (1921–   ), the Swiss playwright and novelist, is unquestionably the most notable of them. Dürrenmatt writes in German, and has obviously been much influenced by Expressionism. His work is relentlessly moralistic, and every social point is driven home with the insistent irony of an Emil Jannings film. The most important of his short novels is *Der Richter und Sein Henker* (1952), translated as *The Judge and His Hangman* (1954), a book masterly in its control of the crime-story medium for the author's symbolic and moral purposes. Inspector Barlach, an old detective who knows that he is dying, uses criminal means to trap the master criminal he has been hunting over a period of forty years. Barlach's behavior often seems unintelligible or stupid, but in fact has its own logic. In this book, Dürrenmatt uses much of the apparatus of the detective story. Why did young Lieutenant Schmied wear evening dress on days which he marked with a "G" in his diary? What happened

---

detective fiction, culminates (1954) in an outstandingly fine example of the genre, *The Narrowing Circle*. Second, a recurrent, highly agreeable factor in many of his stories—from *The Immaterial Murder Case* (1945) right up to *The Man Who Lost His Wife* (1970)—has been a mordantly effective sense of satire. Thirdly, his accomplishment has been much more varied than his own brief account of it implies. In particular, he has in him a marked talent for "mere ingenuity"; this can be seen at its fullest stretch in *The Man Who Killed Himself* (1967), where psychological interest is underpinned by a dazzlingly clever plot.

Few critics would consider raggedness a fault in Symons's work. Most would be likely to remark, instead, on its equability of tone, which, while seldom allowing interest to flag, on occasion militates against suspense. Incidentally, it is noticeable that while Symons excels in describing the antecedents and consequences of sex and of violence, *acts* of sex and violence, considered as topics in themselves, interest him very little. For this reason, his political thriller *The Broken Penny* (1952) is a relatively unsuccessful book.

As a reviewer and critic, Symons has wielded considerable influence; the reputations of Highsmith and Bingham, to name only those, owe much to his advocacy. In addition, his standing as a "serious" writer (of poetry and of social history) has helped to gain him a respectful hearing for a large number of shrewd, well-argued articles on crime fiction in general.

—EDMUND CRISPIN

to the body of the dog killed by Barlach's assistant Chanz when the dog attacked the Inspector? The apparatus is used as part of a fantastic game which Barlach is playing with the other characters, and which Dürrenmatt is playing with the reader. The revelation of the murderer comes as a surprise, but it is subservient to the points the author is making about the nature of justice and the need to extirpate evil by violence.

Dürrenmatt's other crime stories do not fuse the investigatory and symbolic elements quite so successfully, but they are all remarkable for their originality. *Der Verdacht* (1953), translated as *The Quarry* (1962), finds Barlach in hospital, slowly recovering from what had been thought a fatal illness. The doctor treating him thinks he identifies in an old picture from *Life* a German concentration-camp doctor who took pleasure in operating on inmates without anesthetics. Has this man committed suicide, or is he in fact still alive and the head of a clinic which takes in only wealthy patients? There follows a struggle of wits and wills between Barlach and this man, which is also a struggle between freedom and nihilism. "Freedom is the courage to commit crime, for freedom itself is a crime," the doctor says, adding: "I devote myself to that which made me free—murder and torture." Again his destruction is achieved only by the use of a force greater than his own.

Das Versprechen, translated as *The Pledge* (1958), is about the transformation of Inspector Matthäi from an emotionless machine into a man with a passion for justice, intent to discover the murderer of three young girls. In pursuit of the man, Matthäi becomes for years a petrol station attendant, and with the utmost ruthlessness uses another young girl as bait for the killer. The bait is not accepted; the girl becomes a sluttish prostitute; the defeated Matthäi sinks into a sodden wreck. At the end of the story, it is revealed that he was "a genius, more so than any of your fictional detectives," and that all of his deductions were correct. Again, what might have been a mere clatter of ironies is kept finely under control.

Dürrenmatt's use of coincidence and fantasy is justified by his moral force. This cannot be said of the two French writers,

Pierre Boileau (1906–   ) and Thomas Narcejac (1908–   ), who collaborate as Boileau-Narcejac, or of Jean Baptiste Rossi, who uses the pseudonym of Sébastien Japrisot. Boileau-Narcejac and Japrisot are rather like a blend of Gaboriau and Leroux, combining the realistic detail of the one with the implausible or outrageous surprise endings of the other. Boileau-Narcejac usually presents us with a sexual tangle which looks straightforward, and then reveals a previously laid plan which is always ingenious but often strains credulity. A good example is *D'Entre les Morts,* in English *The Living and the Dead* (1956). Here a detective down on his luck is hired by his old friend Gévigne, who is now a rich man. Gévigne wants his wife, Madeleine, watched, not because he suspects adultery but because her behavior is strange and apparently suicidal. The detective follows Madeleine, falls in love with her, saves her from an attempt at drowning, is present when she kills herself by jumping off a tower. In fact, he is being used as a dupe. Madeleine is indeed dead, killed and disfigured by her husband who threw her off the tower, and the "Madeleine" known to the detective is Gévigne's mistress, whose behavior was designed to provide a witness who would say that the dead woman was suicidal. The idea is ingenious, but the plan when seriously considered has as many holes as a watering can. *A Cœur Perdu* (*Heart to Heart,* 1959) similarly sacrifices probability for immediate trick effects, and so does Japrisot's *Piège pour Cendrillon* (*Trap for Cinderella,* 1962), in which we are confronted with the problem of whether a girl badly burned in a fire and then equipped with a plastic face is really who and what she seems to be. Yet although there is something strained and artificial about these writers, it has to be said that their often outrageous deceptions certainly do deceive, much more dramatically than those of most contemporary British and American crime novelists.

The work of the Swedish writer Peter Wahloo (1926–   ) is of two different kinds. He has written at least two novels which combine the moral symbolism of Dürrenmatt with a flavor of Orwellian fantasy. *Murder on the Thirty-First Floor* (1966) and *The Steel Spring* (1970) make their points about dictator-

ship and paternalism through the medium of crime, and Chief
Inspector Jensen, who appears in both books, is trying to discover
the nature of society in terms of what is called criminal activity.
The books that Wahloo (now Per and not Peter) has written in
collaboration with Maj Sjöwall are less ambitious and more successful. They are police investigations carried out by Inspector
Beck, a gloomy version of Freeling's Van der Valk, and they
might come under the heading of "Police Novels" except that the
authors are still more interested in the philosophic implications of
crime than in straightforward police routine. *The Man on the
Balcony* (1968), *The Man Who Went Up in Smoke* (1969), and
The Laughing Policeman (1970) are markedly individual and very
good.

Looking at the work of these writers, it is possible to make a
rough division between those who have abandoned altogether the
puzzle element (Highsmith, Bingham, Freeling, Smith) and those
who retain it although in a changed form, or between those who
use the crime story primarily to investigate human personality and
those chiefly concerned with expressing an attitude towards society,
like Bennett, Macdonald, Dürrenmatt, and Wahloo. But although
such divisions cast some illuminations, the important thing is that
these variously talented novelists have chosen deliberately to use
the crime novel as a way of expressing their insights. One negative
quality they have in common, with the partial exception of
Sjöwall/Wahloo, is a deliberate avoidance of detailed routine
police work. There is some office background in Freeling's books, a
good deal of police interrogation in Bingham's, but these are used
in one case to show Van der Valk's relationships with other policemen, in the other to demonstrate the technique of breaking down
a suspect. None of these writers uses the examination by the
detective in charge of one suspect after another that often filled
a third of an orthodox detective story; few go into scientific or
forensic detail. In part this is a recognition of the limitations in
their knowledge, but in part it springs also from a feeling that this
kind of detailed investigation is not relevant to their own basic
interests. In this they differ noticeably from Simenon, who often
occupies several pages with questions and answers that may well

be verisimilitudinous but have no material effect on the course of
the story. Detailed accounts of police investigation have become
the province of the police novel. Such selection of the material
needed by the writer to advance his story, and the omission of what
seems otiose, is an indication of the puzzle story's development into
the crime novel.

ENTERTAINERS

The essential distinction between serious writers and entertainers
is one of attitude. The writers mentioned previously in this chapter
do have in common the fact that they are all to some degree emotionally involved in their work. Their books offer some personal
feelings about the world and society. The entertainer thinks
instead of what will amuse his audience, and if an idea or a subject
seems disturbing it is put aside. Often the entertainer shares
the preconceptions of the audience so completely that no adjust-
ment is necessary. This is obviously true of Christie and the early
Queen, less true of Sayers and the later Allingham—to take
examples almost at random—but even the less orthodox entertainer tries not to injure the susceptibilities of the reader. In our
time, there are many skillful writers who put into their books
little or nothing of their own personalities. The name of such
writers is not legion, but it is certainly many, and now that the
old rules no longer apply they are able to treat lightly and
amusingly many subjects that would not have been touched thirty
years ago. Eight out of a hundred of them are mentioned here.
The faithful reader of crime fiction will be able to fill in the other
ninety-two names.

Emma Lathen in America, Michael Gilbert in Britain are two
outstandingly skillful writers of this kind. Emma Lathen is the
pseudonym of Mary J. Latis and Martha Hennisart. Her detective
stories, produced at the rate of one or two a year since *Banking on
Death* (1961), offer mysteries which are solved by John Putnam
Thatcher, the silver-haired senior vice-president of the Sloan Guar-
anty Trust in New York's Wall Street. One reads Lathen primarily
for the always shrewd and often funny descriptions of Thatcher's

relationships with other people connected with Sloan who are drawn into cases—the tetchy president Bradford Withers; the pessimistic Everett Gabler, who is the most trusted of Thatcher's section chiefs; the emotionally erratic Tom Robichaux—and for the settings, which often play an important part in the story and are always done with a convincing show of knowledge. They range from the problems involved in developing a new car (*Murder Makes the Wheels Go Round*, 1966) to racial problems on Wall Street (*Death Shall Overcome*, 1966).

It is apparent that Lathen has a thorough grasp of banking procedure, and the best of the stories are firmly centered on Wall Street dealings. It is difficult to recommend any book in particular where all are conspicuously lively and none is really notable as a mystery, but *Murder Against the Grain* (1967) and *Accounting for Murder* (1964) are among the best. In the first of these, Sloan finds itself threatened with the loss of a million dollars when a shipment of grain for the Soviet Union proves to have been loaded on the strength of forged documents, and in the second an implacable little man named Clarence Fortinbras (author of "Fortinbras on Accounts Receivable") presses an investigation into the affairs of a firm called National Calculating and is murdered for his pains. Lathen always knows exactly what she is doing, and does it with supreme confidence and a humor that is never overemphasized.

The first novel of Michael (Francis) Gilbert (1912–   ) was *Close Quarters* (1947), an orthodox detective story of what might have been pre-1939 vintage. It even included a map of the Cathedral Close as ornamentation for an ecclesiastical murder case. Gilbert quickly moved away from this classical pattern, and in *Smallbone Deceased* (1950) made splendid use of his own professional legal knowledge to construct a puzzle that also offered a nicely comic view of life in the office of Horniman, Birley and Craine, solicitors. Since that time, Gilbert has wavered between a wish to be fairly realistic in depicting people and a feeling that one shouldn't be too serious in a crime story.

He is not tied to a series character—his first investigator, Chief Inspector Hazlerigg, was replaced by the insomniac Bohun, who disappeared in favor of Sergeant Petrella and others. And he is not afraid to experiment with settings—one of his best books, *Death in Captivity* (1952) is set in a prisoner-of-war camp, and in *The Crack in the Teacup* (1966) he concentrates very successfully upon some apparently petty crookedness in the affairs of a local Council. He has written skillful and enjoyable thrillers and short stories. Yet there remains an impression that he is not quite content to be appreciated just as an entertainer, but that some restraint (legal caution, perhaps) checks him from writing in a way that fully expresses his personality. *The Crack in the Teacup* was his best book for a long time, and it is possible that future stories may offer some development of the implicit social comedy in that book.

Successful comic crime stories, short or long, are rare. One turns away with a shudder from the many Holmes parodies and from such collections as Sir Basil Thomson's stories about Mr. Pepper, and with not much more cheerfulness from the conscientiously crazy detective stories of the English Pamela Branch and the Americans Craig Rice and Elliot Paul, but the postwar period has produced at least two successful writers of crime comedy. The first book by Joyce Porter (1924–   ), *Dover One* (1964), introduced one of the most successful inefficient detectives in crime fiction. Chief Inspector Dover is a fat, lazy beer-swilling boor who leaves all the actual work to his assistant Sergeant MacGregor, and either stumbles across the solutions to crimes by accident or takes credit for MacGregor's legwork. The climax of *Dover One* is both gruesome and extremely funny. Unfortunately the law of diminishing returns operates most forcibly in relation to comic detectives, and having established Dover's characteristics in her first book, Porter has not found it possible to do much more than repeat them less effectively in later ones, or to create another comic figure of similar caliber.

The work of Colin Watson (1920–   ), however, has triumphantly survived similar problems through the delicacy and intelligence with which he handles those fireworks of comedy which in his hands go up, as they are intended, in a dazzling show of stars instead of spluttering miserably into silence. All his books

are genuine mysteries, and all gain something from being placed
in the firmly realized country town of Flaxborough with its once
popular Moorish Electric Theatre which is now the Alhambra
Billiards Club, and its slyly lecherous respectable citizens. Watson
also deals tactfully with his comic characters. Harcourt Chubb
Flaxborough's Chief Constable, is pompous and sometime
obtuse, but he is not merely silly. *Hopjoy Was Here* (1962), hi
most notable performance, contains some brilliant comedy about
a James Bond-like secret agent who is investigating the disappear
ance of Hopjoy, one of his agents. Here again the portrait of "the
man known as Ross" never slips over from engaging comedy into
unbelievable farce. The most recent Watson stories, in which the
important figure is a demurely crooked spinster named Miss Tea
time, are not quite so convincing as the earlier ones, but he
remains a comic writer with the gift of originality.

It may have been noticed that the entertainers tend to use a
series detective (the inconspicuous Inspector Purbright runs like a
vein of common sense through Watson's stories), but that hi
detectival skills are often deprecated rather than emphasized
This is certainly true of H. R. F. (Henry Reymond Fitzwalter)
Keating's Inspector Ghote of the Bombay police, who often teeters
on the edge of a totally disastrous mistake without ever actually
committing it. The development of Keating (1926–   ) has been
interesting. He began with three elliptically written books, at times
semi-Surrealist in style. *A Rush on the Ultimate* (1961) was
perhaps the best of them, but they are all interestingly odd. *The
Perfect Murder* (1964) introduced the often naive, sometimes
shrewd Ghote, who has been the central character of all his sub
sequent books, except one which was written before the invention
of Ghote but published after his arrival on the scene. These later
stories have a good deal of charm, although they tend to be
devised rather too much as demonstrations of Ghote's reactions
to a particular place. *Inspector Ghote Hunts the Peacock* (1968)
for instance, shows him on a first visit to London, where he is
standing in for his Superintendent at a drugs-smuggling conference
Ghote is prepared to be delighted by everything English, from
policemen to the Tower of London, is distressed when he discovers

color prejudice and is treated brusquely, and makes a disastrous mess of delivering the speech written out for him by the Superintendent. His face and reputation are saved, however, when he unwittingly finds a clue that leads to the discovery of an opium cache, and almost as unwittingly solves a crime relating to an Indian girl. The picture of Ghote let loose in London is delightful, but as a crime story the book is less than satisfactory. Only in *The Perfect Murder* has Keating managed fully to integrate the detective with his criminal problem.

Andrew Garve is the pseudonym under which Paul Winterton (1911–) has produced his best books—he once used, but has now abandoned, the names of Roger Bax and Paul Somers. Garve began with some straight detective stories which did not really fit his talent. His most successful stories lie somewhere between the crime story and the thriller, like *The Megstone Plot* (1956), with its clever fake-blackmail plan, and *The House of Soldiers* (1961), which makes intelligent use of an Irish setting to show the development of violence. Before Paul Winterton became Andrew Garve, he was a talented and respected liberal journalist, and one feels about him, as about Michael Gilbert, that he has not let much of himself get into his books.

Many of the stories written by John (Dann) MacDonald (1916–) and by William P. (Peter) McGivern are almost indistinguishable from the production-line efficient fast-moving American thriller, but MacDonald particularly has at times done better than this. His recent books about the salvage expert Travis McGee have a different flavor. The style is still too often reach-me-down Chandler, but behind the machined efficiency of the plotting in books like *A Key to the Suite* (1962) and *The Deep Blue Goodbye* (1964) there are interesting ideas about the nature of corruption and the increasingly mechanical form of life in America. At the end of *A Key to the Suite,* the central figure, Floyd Hubbard, after being betrayed for a time into human warmth and emotion, turns back into the mechanical man of American big business. McGivern's work is less individual, but he has produced some interesting books on what might be called the cops-and-robbers theme, notably *The Big Heat* (1953) and *Rogue Cop* (1954).

THE POLICE NOVEL

The police novel, or the police-procedural, as it has recently been called, concentrates upon the detailed investigation of a crime from the point of view of the police, and in the best examples of the kind does so with considerable realism.

This is a recent development, not to be confused with the work of the Humdrums, which sometimes traced the course of a police investigation but did so rather superficially and often from the lofty viewpoint of a Superintendent. It is not often that any form of crime fiction has taken anything from cinema or TV, but the American TV series "Dragnet" and the British "Z Cars" and "Softly Softly" showed that the routine of police investigation could be fascinating as a thing in itself. Perhaps because the British series were more firmly centered upon the day-to-day activities of a police station or department, leaving (as writers may have felt) little for them to add, the police novel has been developed principally by Americans. Considerable variety is offered within it. One possibility, soon seen and used, was that of showing half a dozen cases going on at the same time, all of them handled by a single officer. This has become a specialty of J. J. Marric in Britain and Elizabeth Linington under four different names in America. The early Ed McBain stories developed in considerable detail the links between detectives and forensic laboratories, with reproductions of important clues in the text. Later McBain turned to characterization of the various detectives, giving each a distinct personality and the lion's share in a particular book. Hillary Waugh has exploited successfully the operations of a small local police force and its relationship to other forces in dealing with cases outside its own boundaries.

The early police novels had great zest and freshness (McBain's first books appeared in 1956, Marric's first Gideon book a year earlier), but their limitations soon became apparent. A fair degree of realism is possible, but it cannot be pushed too far for fear that the book might be as dull as the actual days of a policeman. The division of interest between several unlinked cases means that some are more interesting than others, so that one hurries through the pages dealing with the attempt to identify a crook practicing a long firm fraud, to get back to the more absorbing hunt for a child killer. Laboratory details can be fascinating, but they have to be informed by some human interest that often strains credulity. Details of the lives and loves of the detectives are sometimes brought in so that they may be, again improbably, personally involved in the cases they set out to solve. Of course there are similar improbabilities in other kinds of crime story, but they are particularly damaging to the police novel because its effects depend so much upon surface realism. This is, in fact, another branch of crime fiction and not a separate tree.

The most consistently skillful writer of police novels is undoubtedly Ed McBain. Under his real name of Evan Hunter (1926–) he has written some highly successful novels, and he has used other pseudonyms, but the formula of the police novel suits his talent particularly well. He began with Steve Carella, a detective working for an unnamed big-city police force, and equipped him with a wife named Teddy, who is beautiful but both deaf and dumb. As the series developed, Carella's fellow detectives—like Cotton Hawes, who was named after Cotton Mather, and Meyer Meyer, whose father thought it would be an excellent joke to duplicate surname and first name—were introduced. Sometimes half a dozen detectives appear in a book, sometimes only one or two. The cases vary from the macabre to the comic, and the stories are told largely in crisp believable dialogue between detectives and suspects, or between the detectives themselves. Often the dialogue has a nice note of deadpan comedy. Here is Cotton Hawes in *Till Death* (1959), thinking he may find a suspect in the bathroom:

The door to the bathroom opened. A slender man wearing eyeglasses stepped out, zipping his fly.

"Anybody else in there?" Hawes asked him.

"What?"

"In the bathroom."

"No," the bespectacled man said. "Of course not. Who else would be in there with me?" He paused. Indignantly he said, "Who are you?"

"Water Commission," Hawes said. "Just checking."

This is the characteristic McBain tone. *Till Death* is actually not one of his better books, involving as it does the wedding of Carella's sister and bringing in the family complications that lend themselves to his characteristic weakness of sentimentality, but the brisk dialogue carries it along. The sum of the books so far has given us an informative and never boring account of police procedure, some good puzzles, some excellent chases, occasional psychological insights, much variety of plot and incident. A good view of McBain's varied skills can be got from *Cop Hater* (1956), *The Mugger* (1956), *Like Love* (1962), *Shotgun* (1968).

J. J. Marric is one of the many pseudonyms used by John Creasey, a name in this case derived from his own and his wife's initials, and the Christian names of his sons Martin and Richard. The early books about Commander George Gideon of Scotland Yard's C.I.D. are the best things in Creasey's large output. A C.I.D. Inspector who once lived next door to Creasey asked, "Why don't you show us as we are? You don't have to put in the dull part." The portrait of Gideon is an attempt to show a fully rounded character—excellent up to a point but marred in the end by excessive hero worship, and lack of humor. Apart from Gideon, the strengths of the books are those of other Creasey work, an apparently inexhaustible flow of ideas and the ability to generate excitement in describing action. The weaknesses are again characteristic, lack of the imagination necessary to vary a formula once it has been established, as McBain has done so skillfully, and a level of writing that at its best is no more than flatly realistic. The first Gideon books were pioneering works in the form of the police novel, and they promised more than Marric has been able to perform.

Once the idea of telling three or four stories between one set of covers had been devised (and the credit for this seems to belong to Creasey/Marric), it quickly became rather too easy a way of writing stories that were fairly effective when counterpointed, although none would have stood up on its own. This applies strongly to the work of Elizabeth Linington (1921–   ), who under her own name writes books about a Los Angeles (Hollywood) detective named Ivor Maddox, and under the names of Dell Shannon and Lesley Egan about other Los Angeles detectives named Lieutenant Luis Mendoza and Sergeant Andrew Clock, as well as about Vic Varallo of the Glendale police. The Linington stories are efficient and readable, but the essential quality of the police novel at its best is that it shall be closely based on the operations of an actual force, and Linington clearly has much less direct knowledge of the Los Angeles force than McBain has of the New York police or Creasey has of Scotland Yard.

If a single book had to be chosen to show the possibilities in the police novel which are outside most crime fiction, no better example could be found than *Last Seen Wearing*— (1952), by Hillary (Baldwin) Waugh (1920–   ). This brilliant, realistic novel opens with the disappearance of Marilyn Lowell Mitchell, a pretty eighteen-year-old freshman at Parker College, Bristol, Massachusetts. We see the wheels move slowly as her friends become alarmed, the housemother rings the girl's father in Philadelphia, her address book is examined, a telephone call is reluctantly made to the Bristol police. Thereafter we follow the investigation as Chief Frank W. Ford and Detective Sergeant Burton K. Cameron conduct it, with all its false trails, fending off of newsmen, consultation with parents, teachers, friends. Perhaps Creasey should have ignored that advice not to put in the dull part of police work, for it is "the dull part," the painstaking checking and the following of every thread until it breaks in the hand, that Waugh makes most interesting. By treating seriously the anguish of the parents and their certainty that their daughter would never have done anything they did not approve of, he produces some fine character studies. And the ending has the neatest possible twist, with one of the chief characters never appearing on stage at all.

Like other writers of the police novel—and he preceded both McBain and Marric—Waugh was confronted with the problem of writing similar books sufficiently varied to keep the reader's interest. He solved it by replacing Ford and Cameron with Fred C. Fellows, Chief of a small-town police force, and his right-hand man, Detective Sergeant Sidney Wilks. Fellows and Wilks have more humanity than the earlier detectives—indeed, Fellows is a little too folksy for some tastes—and the small-town atmosphere gives their activities a personal flavor. *Last Seen Wearing*— remains Waugh's best book, but almost all the later ones manage to be reasonably realistic without dullness. *That Night It Rained* (1961) and *Pure Poison* (1967) are particularly good.

Should the books of Chester Himes (1909–   ) be classed as

police novels? It is certainly hard to know what else to call them, and his black detectives, Coffin Ed Johnson and Grave Digger Jones, make an exhilarating black comic comment on the activities of all other policemen. From *Cotton Comes to Harlem* (1964) onward, Himes has recorded the activities of these fierce thugs in a world more thuggish still, in rattlingly vigorous prose, and with equal feeling for violence and for comedy. Coffin Ed has been quick on the trigger ever since a glass of acid was thrown into his face by a hoodlum, and when we first meet Grave Digger he has been off duty for six months after being shot up, although, "other than for the bullet scars hidden beneath his clothes and the finger-size scar obliterating the hairline at the base of his skull where the first bullet had burned off the hair, he looked much the same." The humans among whom the detectives move are credulous, lecherous, treacherous, greedy, and savage. Coffin Ed and Grave Digger are savage, too, although they are not monsters masquerading as heroes like Mickey Spillane's Mike Hammer.

There are several other more orthodox practitioners of the police novel, but none who equals McBain in variety of treatment or Marric in handling several stories at once or Waugh in originality. One can imagine further developments, like the treatment of a case wholly from the point of view of a forensic laboratory expert, but they do not seem likely to extend the range of this kind of crime story much further.

XV

Big Producers and Big Sellers, Curiosities and Singletons

There are several crime and thriller writers who, although they have not influenced the development of the form and although few of their books are of much individual interest, must still be noticed in a study of this kind. They are authors who have written a great many books, or who were and in some cases are still immensely popular, the Big Producers and the Big Sellers. Of course many big producers and big sellers have been discussed already, from Agatha Christie to Raymond Chandler. Their work, however, has some specific literary quality, while the prime interest of the authors listed below is their character as suppliers of a public demand for sensational fiction upon a low level of literacy, intelligence, and particularly imagination.

It is the machine-like nature of almost all this work that removes it from the sphere of literary into that of sociological consideration. A popular character is devised, the formula for treating him established, and it is then just a matter of producing stories to feed the demand. If there are too many stories about one character, a new series must be started with another. Much, perhaps most, of

crime fiction is of this kind, a ready-made product like cornflake(
or puffed wheat. The Big Producers are among those who hav(
filled that need most efficiently. They are alphabetically listed here(

LESLIE CHARTERIS is the pen name of Leslie Charles Bowye(
Yin (1907–   ), who has been writing stories about the Saint
"the Robin Hood of Modern Crime," for over forty years. Th(
Saint is a compound of all the most obvious features of a romanti(
hero, put down in terms of cliché. He is "always immaculatel(
dressed," has "luxurious tastes," and is a "connoisseur of food an(
wine," although he does not go much further along these line(
than knowing where you can get a succulent steak or "the bes(
omelette in North America." He bears some relationship to th(
Four Just Men—he is a self-appointed agent for terrorizin(
criminals against whom no evidence justifying arrest can be secure(
—or he might be called an unsadistic Bulldog Drummond wit(
the looks of a prewar matinée idol. The stories about him occasion(
ally have a pleasant double twist of ingenuity, as in *The Saint i(
New York* (1935), in which he disposes of a number of th(
city's nastier gangsters only to find that he has been doing so wit(
the help of the biggest gangster of all. They are too often writte(
with the sort of rodomontade that makes Charteris say that some(
body has "a weakness for the stuff that maketh glad the heart o(
man" when he means that he is slightly tight. For those, however(
who can endure the Saint's total invincibility and self-satisfaction(
his adventures are lively and marked by some touches of humo(
His immense popularity was enhanced through "Saint" clubs, an(
in recent years by a successful and long-running TV series.

The output of René Raymond (1906–   ), who becam(
famous as JAMES HADLEY CHASE, is the comparatively modes(
one of some sixty books. Raymond was a traveler for the larg(
firm of book wholesalers Simpkin, Marshall when he wrote *N(
Orchids for Miss Blandish* (1939), which has already bee(
mentioned. Five years after its publication, it was said that th(
book had sold 500,000 copies, and probably no other book b(
Chase has had anything like the same sale.

In France, Chase has been compared with Dostoevsky and éline, but such critical absurdities can spring only from the amour given by translation or by cinema adaptations. Some of e films made in France from Chase's work show subtleties that e books themselves do not possess. At worst the writing in his ooks is shoddy, at best competent but unimaginative. In his oc- isionally misdirected but often perceptive attack on *No Orchids*, eorge Orwell acutely remarked that the prime motive at work is e pursuit of power. This remains true of almost all the books, hether they are about gangs who hate everybody or individuals ho hate each other. Love, where it occurs, is often used as a eans of obtaining dominance over another individual. It is be- use such power fantasies reflect the frustrations of many people at Chase is a popular writer.

REGINALD SOUTHOUSE CHEYNEY (1896–1951), who added eter Evelyn to these names, had had a varied career as book- aker, hack journalist, and unsuccessful songwriter before, in 936, he published his first full-length piece of fiction, *This Man Dangerous*. The man was Lemmy Caution (i.e., "let me cau- on"), and thanks to Caution and another detective named Slim allaghan, Cheyney was able in 1944 to publish audited sales gures for the year of more than 1½ million copies. Two years ter, he had added another million. At his peak, he sold 300,000 opies a year in the U.S. (astonishingly, since much of his dialogue as in ludicrous pidgin American) and 900,000 in France.

Cheyney was a precursor of Mickey Spillane in his zest for olence, and in exploiting the public taste for cruelty. (He had een an early, and active, supporter of Oswald Mosley.) Lemmy aution is the first "good" man in crime fiction to torture for easure, while giving an assurance to the reader that he can enjoy too, because Caution is on the "right" side. Direct violence is the ing, and these unlovely books contain little sex in spite of the romise in such pseudo-American titles as *Dames Don't Care* and ll Say She Does. There are one or two less objectionable and etter-written books in the "Dark" series that began with *Dark uet*.

One can safely say that JOHN CREASEY (1908–   ) h
produced more books than any other living writer. The numb
is well over five hundred, and there seems no reason why, giv
his inexhaustible energy, the thousand mark should not be reache
The books have been appearing since 1932 at rates varying f
the most part from seven to fourteen a year, and they are writt
under at least ten different names, each representing a separa
kind of story. The reader of a book by "Michael Halliday" kno
that it will have some psychological flavor, while an Inspect
West story is a mixture of police work and thrillerish detectio
and a book with "the Baron" (said by Jean Cocteau to be l
favorite character in crime fiction) at its center will be an adve
ture story.

Creasey's Gideon books, written as J. J. Marric, are his be
work, and they have already been mentioned. His stories a
notable for the ingenuity of the ideas with which he overflows, ar
also for his very slight attention to sex and his total avoidance
cruelty. Unfortunately the writing of the books is never equal
their often clever conception, and his people think and behave wi
a schoolboyish naiveté. The best of his series after the Marric titl
are some of the Inspector West books, which began in 1942 and,
the time of writing, number 38, and one or two of those writt
as Michael Halliday.

ERLE STANLEY GARDNER (1889–1969) had 135 million copies
his books in print in America alone in the year of his death. H
complete output is said to have totaled 120 books, but it wou
not be surprising if this were an underestimate. He was in his forti
when he began to have really considerable success with the Per
Mason stories that began in 1932 with *The Case of the Velv
Claws*. Later he added the D.A. series dealing with a count
district attorney, the Bertha Cool and Donald Lam books writt
as A. A. Fair, and others.

Gardner never pretended to be anything but a commerci
writer, but he took great trouble to make sure that every detail
his intricate plots was right. When he wrote about ballistics
medical matters, he always had authority for what he said, but l

)ecialty was the law. He had spent more than twenty years racticing law in California, and the knowledge he gained was put) good use in the Perry Mason stories, which hinge on points of w, forensic medicine, or science as clever as a watch mechanism. 'he TV series faithfully reflects the cunning legal tricks, and also ie total lack of characterization. Upon the whole, the early lason stories are the best, although Gardner achieved a pleasant :xibility in the lively, often funny A. A. Fair books. By all ac->unts a modest and likable man, Gardner was, within the limits of 'hat he attempted, a highly competent writer.

The world created by E. (Edward) PHILLIPS OPPENHEIM 1866–1946) in his 115 novels and 39 books of short stories had ie virtue of resembling in some degree his own life, unlike that f those fictioneers who spin out violent stories from suburban :udies. Or at least it resembled the life Oppenheim led after the ge of forty, when he disposed of the family leather business. His hief success came after World War I, with books like *The Amaz-ig Quest of Mr. Ernest Bliss* (1919)* and *The Great Impersona-on* (1920). During the years between 1923 and the Depression, early thirty of his novels, stories, and articles were sold in .merica to magazines like the *Saturday Evening Post, Collier's* nd the *Cosmopolitan*, as well as to the *Chicago Tribune*. These ales alone brought in more than $350,000 during the period, and .merica was his principal source of income. For example, *Nicholas ʻoade, Detective* (1927) brought in nearly $22,000 from the U.S., nd less than £1,500 from other rights, including only £300 :om British book sales, and a novel called *The Glenlitten Murder* 1929) earned nearly $25,000 in the U.S. and just over £1,500 lsewhere, including £600 from the British publisher. Later on, iese figures dropped, but they remained high enough to keep im in luxury on the Riviera and elsewhere for the rest of his life.

The Riviera was Oppenheim's favorite stamping ground, and ie best of his books are set there. In an interesting recent article bout him, Reg Gadney quotes from a newspaper interview in 919 when he said: "I am a maker of stories while you wait. Sex

* In America, *The Curious Quest.*

is dropping a little. Crime is coming in. A good, sound, romanti
story is what they want." This seems fair enough, if one adds th
large lacing of snobbery given to all the stories. Oppenheim wome
are frighteningly elegant rather than sexy; his heroes still remembe
Eton and the Guards; his plotting is crude. He provided the edg
of snobbery as he dictated the stories in the intervals of yachting
visiting casinos, fishing, and making love, and left the editing c
them to his series of young girl secretaries. There were few poin
at which his books touched life as most people live it. In his time
he was called the Prince of Storytellers, but a better name woul
have been the Great Escapist.

MICKEY (Frank Morrison) SPILLANE (1918–   ) makes hi
appeal to the human desire for power, like Chase and Cheyney
He is a more efficient writer than his English colleagues, and mor
explicit in linking violence with sex. Power is the law of the worl
to Spillane's Mike Hammer, who says, "The cops can't break
guy's arm to make him talk, and they can't shove his teeth in wit
the muzzle of a .45 to remind him that you aren't fooling." Ham
mer, however, can and often does do these things, and they ar
described with relish. When he breaks a man's fingers and the
smashes an elbow into his mouth, the "shattered teeth tore my arr
and his mouth became a great hole welling blood" while "hi
fingers were broken stubs sticking back at odd angles."

The treatment of sex is of some clinical interest. Women ar
seen as sexually desirable objects, and there are a good man
descriptions of their bodies, but intercourse is often replaced b
death or torture. In I, the Jury (1947), Charlotte the beautifu
psychiatrist makes several unsuccessful attempts to get Hamme
to bed. At the end, when she turns out to be a multiple murderess
he shoots her in the stomach with pleasure. " 'How could you?' " sh
asks incredulously, and he replies: " 'It was easy.' " At the end o
Kiss Me, Deadly (1952), the apparently lovely Lily reveals herse
as "a horrible caricature of a human" whose body has been burne
so that it is "a disgusting mass of twisted, puckered flesh from he
knees to her neck." Hammer goes on to burn her to death, so tha
she becomes "a mass of flame tumbling on the floor with the blu

flames of alcohol turning the white of her hair into black char and her body convulsing under the agony of it."

The most nauseating, and clinically disquieting, thing about these books is that Mike Hammer is the hero.

Of all the Big Producers, (Richard Horatio) EDGAR WALLACE 1857–1932) was the only one who possessed genuine imaginative talent, shown most clearly in his crime plays *The Ringer* and *On the Spot*, but present also in some of his 173 books, of which roughly half were crime stories. Wallace was a totally slapdash writer with a genuine gift for dialogue. His biographer Margaret Lane has said that he made no notes beyond a list of the characters' names, and that when writing serials he rarely knew what was going to happen in the next installment. "Inside the frame of the principal mystery, minor mysteries, slightly overlapping, were started like hares and pursued for a short distance, each new problem being set immediately before the solution of its predecessor." His characters, apart from the detective, hardly exist, although Wallace had a wide knowledge of crooks and their language which he used to good effect.

Wallace came to real success late in life, after a career in which he had been a war correspondent, a racing journalist, and a crime reporter. His first crime story, *The Four Just Men* (1905), published at his own expense, gave no solution to the problem of how the Just Men had killed the Foreign Secretary. Wallace offered a prize of £500 for the correct solution, with disastrous results. Several correct solutions were sent in, and the costs of production, advertising, and prize money were not covered by the sales profits. Failure had been his companion too long for him to use his talents with any care when, in the last decade of his life, he wrote successful plays, and books that sold in millions. The best of his crime stories are *The Crimson Circle* (1922), in which the "amazing psychometrical detective" Derrick Yale is pitted against Scotland Yard; the ingenious *The Clue of the New Pin* (1923); and perhaps the preposterous but enjoyable *The Fellowship of the Frog* (1925). The most clearly realized of his detectives is the absent-minded spinsterish Mr. J. G. Reeder, and *The Mind of Mr. J. G. Reeder*

(1925)* is probably his best collection of crime short storie
Konrad Adenauer was a great admirer of Wallace's work.

The enormous sales of the crime and adventure stories writte
by DENNIS (Yates) WHEATLEY (1897–   ) indicate how low
one literary level of popular success. A characteristic Wheatle
book contains great chunks of predigested history served up in
form which may appeal to readers with a mental age of twelv
plus dialogue and adventures described in a manner so outdate
that they are reminiscent of a boys' adventure paper in the perio
before World War I. *Come Into My Parlour* (1946), whic
Wheatley thought "one of my better stories," begins with th
invasion of Russia in 1941 while people in Berlin regret that "thos
arrogant and accursed islanders remain[ed] unsubdued," b
reflect that "their glorious Führer" has "added that Saar, Austri
and Czechoslovakia to the Reich without firing a shot; eliminate
Poland in one short month of war; forced Denmark and Norwa
. . ." and so on through half a page. When the satanic-lookin
Gregory Sallust meets his chief, Sir Pellinore Gwaine-Cust, he
told that "whether we like the Bolshies or not, Winston was on
hundred per cent right to declare that any enemy of Hitler's is
friend of ours," although "They haven't shown up any too well—s
far." Sallust's reply is, "If the main German armies had not gon
into Russia this summer, they wouldn't be sitting on their bo
toms"—and we are off on another piece of potted history for th
semiliterate. Much of the dialogue is on the level of Sir Pellinore
jovial " 'Drat the boy,' " and a typical piece of third-person nai
ration begins: "Having partaken of Sir Pellinore's Luculla
hospitality . . ." Wheatley's works would provide valuable materi
for a sociologist writing a history of modern public taste.

CURIOSITIES AND SINGLETONS

Within this portmanteau, I have put books by writers well know
in other fields who have dipped pseudonymously into the waters c
crime fiction, or writers who have produced a single excellent, c

* In America, *The Murder Book of Mr. J. G. Reeder.*

t least unusually interesting, crime story among a commonplace
eneral output. I have added to these a few of the oddities of the
enre, and a few personal observations and discoveries. It seemed
etter to put them together in this rag-bag form rather than to
rrange them carefully into categories. The choice made is wholly
ersonal. Other readers will have worthy singletons of their own,
nd the fields of crime fiction abound in curiosities ready to be un-
arthed by devoted readers. I hope that some of my singletons will
e new even to those with a wide knowledge of the form. The
rrangement is alphabetical, like that of the Big Producers.

GEORGE ANTHEIL (1901–1959), who in the twenties was the
'bad boy" of avant-garde music (his *Ballet Mécanique* for sixteen
ianos, some typewriters, buzzers, an airplane propeller, and an
lectric drill, among other instruments, was much admired by Ezra
ound), wrote two crime stories under the name of Stacey Bishop.
have read only the first of these ventures into "glandular crimin-
logy" in which Antheil proclaimed himself an expert, and certainly
eath in the Dark (1930), with its several apparently impossible
murders solved by an investigator who talks often about Pound and
ehaves rather in the style of Philo Vance, is an extraordinary per-
ormance.

There are a good many ASSOCIATIONS of crime writers. The two
nost important are the M.W.A. (Mystery Writers of America)
nd the British C.W.A. (Crime Writers Association). M.W.A. was
ounded in 1945, has four "regional chapters," publishes a yearly
nthology, and is undoubtedly the most influential organization of
rime writers in the world. M.W.A. sponsors a whole series
f Edgar Allan Poe Awards, for first novels, short stories, and
ooks about real-life crime. There are several other less important
ategories, as well as the one most highly regarded, the award for
he "Best Mystery Novel" of the year. (The difficult "detective
tory" has been avoided.) These awards are celebrated at a yearly
linner. A monthly publication, *The Third Degree,* is sent to all
nembers.

C.W.A. was founded in 1953, at the initiative of John Creasey, who was largely responsible for nursing the association through its first shaky years. Like M.W.A., it publishes anthologies, and produces a monthly newssheet called *Red Herrings*. C.W.A. gives a yearly Golden Dagger Award for the best crime novel of the year, with a Silver Dagger for the runner-up. In addition, C.W.A. has published several pamphlets on subjects like poisons, revolvers, espionage work, written by anonymous experts, for the benefit of its members. Both M.W.A. and C.W.A. hold lively meetings regularly for drink and conversation.

There are no organized bodies of crime writers in France, Germany, Holland, or Italy—or if there are I have not discovered them. The Poe-Klubben, which has its headquarters in Copenhagen, draws its members from all over Scandinavia. Discussion of crime stories at their meetings is much better informed and on a higher critical level than those of any British—or perhaps even American —group. There was, at least a few years ago, a flourishing association of crime writers in Japan, although it is likely that their standards, like those of their crime stories, are far removed from those in Western countries.

The Detection Club has already been mentioned. Membership of it is by invitation only (unlike M.W.A. and C.W.A., for which anybody with professional qualifications is eligible), and its activities are now purely those of a dining club. There are Sherlock Holmes societies in a great many countries, with names which vary from the staid Sherlock Holmes Society of London to the American Baker Street Irregulars and Speckled Band of Boston.

Two American periodicals exist which are devoted entirely to crime fiction. The *Armchair Detective* is a quarterly edited by Allen J. Hubin. It contains well-informed articles about all kinds and levels of crime stories. Joan M. Mooney's valuable thesis "Best-Selling American Detective Fiction" has been published through several issues. Treatment of books and authors is critically uneven, and indeed information rather than criticism is the periodical's function. The *Armchair Detective* can be obtained from Allen J. Hubin, 3656 Midland, White Bear Lake, Minnesota 55110, for $4 a year. Much the same remarks apply to the slighter, but still often interesting and valuable *Mystery Reader's Newsletter,* published bimonthly and obtainable from Mrs. Lianne Carlin, P.O. Box 113, Melrose, Massachusetts 02176, for $3 a year to Americans, $3.50 for others.

In The Heat of the Night (1965), the first crime story of JOHN (Dudley) BALL (1911–   ), was an excellent detective story almost in the Golden Age style, which introduced the color problem by way of a colored detective named Virgil Tibbs, who is set to swim against the tide of feeling in a bigoted little Southern town. Ball's later work has been much less successful.

Among the several engaging but rather too hectic stories written by (Mary) CHRISTIANNA BRAND (1907–   ), *Cat and Mouse* (1950) stands out through the firmness of its setting in wildest Wales, and because the author seems here to take her characters just a little more seriously than usual.

VERA CASPARY (1904–   ) has written a number of crime stories, among which *Laura* (1943) is done with unusual wit and style, particularly in the sections written by the aesthetic criminologist Waldo Lydecker, a figure pretty evidently based on Alexander Woolcott. The book was made into a successful film, with Clifton Webb playing Lydecker.

CRITICISM of crime stories has always been bedeviled by the question of whether they should be corraled separately or reviewed with other novels. In theory the latter is preferable, but in practice crime stories which go out with other novels are hardly reviewed at all. So they are hived off, and in the process treated as necessarily inferior literature. In the years before World War II, the London *Sunday Times* and *Observer* gave considerable space to crime reviewing, sometimes nearly a column a week, and in America the *New York Times Book Review,* the New York *Herald Tribune* (since deceased), and the San Francisco *Chronicle* treated them at length. In Denmark, Germany, and Holland, the best crime stories were and are reviewed seriously.

In general, however, reviewing has been too kind, making little distinction between books well and badly written. It is disturbing to find, in English crime reviews of the thirties, quite notable books and evident rubbish being treated on the same level by reviewers as intelligent as Dorothy Sayers and Milward Kennedy. In recent years, the British situation has improved in some national newspapers. With the cooperation of literary editors, reviewers are allowed to give special treatment to what they regard as an exceptionally good book. On the other hand, weeklies like the *New Statesman* now do not review crime stories at all, and its present literary editor has gone on record that he cannot bring himself to prepare copy for such trivia. Edmund Crispin, Maurice Richardson, Dorothy Sayers, and Julian Symons in Britain, Anthony Boucher, Dorothy B. Hughes, and James Sandoe in America are among those who have most nearly succeeded in doing the crime reviewer's perpetual tightrope-walking act between the drop to one side of considering these books purely as literature and on the other of regarding them all as merely amusing trivia.

ANTHONY FIRTH appears here on the strength of his first, and so far only, book. *Tall, Balding, Thirty-five* (1966) is a spy thriller, always stylish and often witty, which manages to be an exciting story, a mild send-up of the form, and a slightly horrific study in psychology. The material is baroque, the manner cool, the whole unmistakably original.

Reputation for a Song (1952), the first crime novel by a North Country English solicitor, EDWARD GRIERSON (1914–   ), sprang from that realistic ironic tradition established by Francis Iles which lay more or less fallow for so long. The exposure of a family skeleton in the household of a country solicitor leads to murder, and then comes the account of a trial, done with great skill and assurance and with a nice awareness of the law's fallibility. Grierson's second crime story, *The Second Man* (1956), was marred by some improbabilities, but this first book remains an outstandingly interesting account of crime as it is committed and endured.

Of the detective stories written by FRANCES NOYES HART (1890–1943), only *The Bellamy Trial* (1927) has distinction. Based on a famous American murder case of the period, it is remarkable for the care with which it gets the feeling of a courtroom. Like an actual trial (the whole book takes place in court), it is slow, repetitive, at times obscure. These are hardly recommendations, yet the method is justified in this one case by the powerful climax and the semi-hypnotic effect of that courtroom buzz upon the reader.

A Taste for Honey (1941), by GERALD (Henry FitzGerald) HEARD (1889–   ), is about death caused by a strain of Italian bees that sting like hornets. They are used by an apiarist to kill a man who has already used the bees to commit his own undetectable murder. This short but still long-windedly philosophical book ranks as a curiosity.

Two detective stories appeared under the professional name of striptease artist GYPSY ROSE LEE, whose real name was Rose Louise Hovick (1914–1970). Much the better of them is *The G-String Murders* (1941),* a cheerfully ribald book about the murder of stripper La Verne in the lavatory with its newly acquired throne. The tone of the book is set by the backstage notice: "Full Net Pants. No Bumps. No Grinds. Keep Your Navel Covered." Her second book, *Mother Finds a Body* (1942), contained the splendid malapropism spoken by a woman on leaving a party: "I'm going. I find the company very uncongenital," but was upon the whole much inferior.

A Kiss Before Dying (1953), the first crime story by IRA LEVIN (1929–   ), was a most brilliant performance, one which showed clearly that if there are no brand new tricks to be played on the reader, the old ones can be made to seem new in sufficiently

* In Britain called *The Striptease Murders* (1943). The only connotation of G-strings in Britain at that time was with violins.

cunning hands. Rex Stout called the book "a masterpiece of the genre," and if that seems to be overstating the case it is only because the story changes style and becomes thrillerish after the surprise has been sprung halfway through. Some would remove Levin from the singleton class on the strength of his second crime book, *Rosemary's Baby* (1967), but in comparison with the earlier novel this seems forced and unconvincing. On the screen, strangely, it seemed much more plausible.

MEYER LEVIN (1905–   ) has written only one crime story. *Compulsion* (1956) is very closely based on the Leopold and Loeb case. Its originality lies in the psychoanalytical interpretation of the murderers' actions, which is both relentless and persuasive. There have been many documentary case histories that read like fiction, among them Truman Capote's *In Cold Blood*. Meyer Levin is the only writer who has reversed the process, by making fiction convincingly enlarge and illuminate the facts.

LOCKED ROOMS. The first locked-room mystery was "The Murders in the Rue Morgue," but what was the first locked-room novel? Israel Zangwill claimed the palm for *The Big Bow Mystery* (1892), and Queen calls him the father of the modern locked-room mystery, but it is possible that the honor belongs to a writer named John Ratcliffe and a book called *Nena Sahib*. In 1881, the wife and five children of a German named Fritz Conrad were found dead behind a bolted door. Conrad had killed them all, and then tried to make the deaths look like suicide. The police found that he had been reading a translation of *Nena Sahib,* a book about a "perfect murder" in which a locked-room effect had been created by drilling a hole in the door, using a wire to draw the bolt from the outside, and then filling the hole with putty.

Was this the first locked-room novel? Well, perhaps. The British Museum has no copy of *Nena Sahib* or any other novel by John Ratcliffe, and further research seems to indicate that it resembles one of Aldous Huxley's *Tales of Knockespotch*, which existed only as book covers. Does any copy of the book exist? And was it really a locked-room mystery? It would be interesting to know.

The detective story to end detective stories was published in 1937 by Ernest Julius Borneman, under the name of CAMERON MCCABE. *The Face on the Cutting-Room Floor* is at first sight a tautly told detective story about the murder of a film actress whose part in a film has been completely eliminated in the cutting room. McCabe, the narrator, is tried and acquitted. It is then revealed that he was in fact the murderer, and at the end of the story he kills the detective, Smith, who was on his track.

So far the apparent novel. But all this is really only a prelude, or demonstration of what the "detective story" is like. The heart of the book is in the epilogue, told by a minor character named A. B. C. Muller. In this epilogue, Muller first considers McCabe as a man who became a murderer "merely through a concurrence of certain typical present-day tendencies, each of which can be found in almost every contemporary big-city middle-class man." But was McCabe the murderer? Muller examines the case against other characters in the story, including Smith himself, to show that they would also fit the murderer's role. He then offers a critique of the detective story as a form by assuming that *The Face on the Cutting-Room Floor* has already been published, and fitting remarks made by critics about other detective stories to his own book. He observes that "the possibilities for alternative endings to *any* detective story are *infinite,*" and shows this by ending the epilogue with Muller himself murdering one of the characters in the novel. The whole thing is a dazzling, and perhaps fortunately unrepeatable, box of tricks.

If Ordean A. Hagen's valuable but erratic *Who Done It?* is correct, the book was not published in America. Hagen lists two later books by Borneman which I have not seen.

The single crime story written by JOHN MAIR (1913–1942), whose review of *No Orchids* has already been quoted, was *Never Come Back* (1941). Mair, who was killed in a flying accident during the war, rightly called the book "an intellectual thriller," and it is in the first class of its kind. Not too much characterization (the thriller can do without it), what was at the time a very modern cowardly hero who broods on poisoning his Fascist girl friend while knowing that he will never do it, the excitement of a man on the run—the book provides all these. It is a little like John Buchan brought up-to-date, and in everything essential it remains up-to-date today.

WADE MILLER is one of the several pseudonyms under which Bill Miller (1920–   ) and Bob Wade (1920–   ) produced a lot of books which show no more than average competence. *Deadly Weapon* (1946) stands out from them by the cleverness with which wool is pulled over the reader's eyes, blinding him to what is really a logical obvious conclusion.

Under the name of KENNETH O'HARA, the neglected, talented novelist Jean Morris (1924–   ) has written four tangled and extremely intelligent crime stories about power and corruption, of which *Underhandover* (1961) is the most successful.

The Ingenious Mr. Stone (1945) is a very surprising piece of work. In describing "the methods used by Lysander Stone in solving the Langdon-Miles problem," the author has used the several narrators and the leisurely manner of *The Moonstone*. Part of the story is told by Adam Muir, a dryish Writer to the Signet; part by the garrulous secretary and bursar of an expensive girls' school; part by an old lady of eighty; and, as Muir says, some of the gaps are filled by Lysander Stone himself. The book is raised above the level of pastiche by the evident enjoyment with which it is written, by its humor, and by the outrageous (in 1945) use of more than one successful disguise. The author, ROBERT PLAYER, has recently produced another, but less successful crime story. His psuedonym conceals the identity of Robert Furneaux Jordan.

The use of PSEUDONYMS by writers of crime fiction deserves a separate essay. Why do so many resort to them? On the surface it is a matter often of convenience, or of a publisher's insistence that too many titles under one name will flood the market (hence the development of John Dickson Carr's *alter ego* Carter Dickson), or in the past of a snobbish feeling that writing crime stories was a low pursuit. Yet there is surely something beyond or beneath all this. The essence of most crime stories is that they conceal something, and it is psychologically appropriate that the author's identity, too, should be hidden. Is it going too far to suggest that through use of a pseudonym some writers have been able to indulge secret thoughts, and write about subjects which they would otherwise have found it difficult to approach? Well, I do no more than make the suggestion. Certainly there is room for a thesis on "The Hidden Self: Personal Concealment and Revelation in the Crime Novel" by some industrious researcher.

Arthur Sarsfield Ward (1883–1959), better known as SAX ROHMER, was discovered in the early fifties living in the New York suburb of White Plains, a small gray nervous man who was able to report that Dr. Fu Manchu was not only still alive but had greatly changed in character. He remained a villain, but had now the redeeming feature that he was "flat out against the Communists and trying to help democracy," instead of trying to establish a personal domination over the world against which the dogged Nayland Smith, even though he was the Burmese Commissioner and was "empowered to control the movements" of the British C.I.D., struggled at times almost alone.

Rohmer remains a faintly enigmatic figure. According to Ellery Queen, his pseudonym sprang from the Anglo-Saxon for "a sharp blade" (*sax*) and "a wanderer" (*rohmer*). Put them together and you have, with a touch of imagination, a free lance. Rohmer had by his own account brief careers in the City and as a journalist before the appearance of *Dr. Fu Manchu* in 1913 made him famous and comparatively rich. In 1955, he sold the TV, film, and radio rights to the doctor for four million dollars.

The Fu Manchu stories are absolute rubbish, penny dreadfuls in hard covers, interesting chiefly in the way that they reflect popular feeling about the "yellow peril," which in these books, as a character remarks, is "incarnate in one man." The doctor's hands are like claws; he generally wears a little cap on his "amazing skull"; his green eyes are like "an emanation of Hell." The stories proceed with practically no regard for possibility, and several of the books include scenes in which Smith and his friend Petrie

face some kind of torture. One or two of Rohmer's other books
are a little better, and the short stories in *The Dream Detective*
(1920), about Morris Klaw, who has dreams which help him to
solve crimes with the assistance of his somnambulistic daughter
Isis, have a sort of ludicrous logic about them which is amusing
in small doses.

PETER SHAFFER (1926–   ), later a highly successful dramatist, wrote with his brother ANTHONY SHAFFER (1926–   ),
whose affectionate send-up of Golden Age stories in the play
Sleuth has been much acclaimed, three detective stories, two
under the pseudonym of Peter Anthony and the best, *Withered
Murder* (1955), under their own nominal colors.

B. C. (Britiffe Constable) SKOTTOWE'S *Sudden Death: Or, My
Lady the Wolf* (1886) is a curiosity among curiosities, the first
transvestite detective story. In the opening chapter, the narrator,
Buchanan, sees an unidentifiable woman push a man off a cliff.
The crime remains unsolved, and a little later Buchanan meets a
dashing, slender young man named Gordon Leigh, with whom he
becomes extremely friendly. Leigh has, as all his male friends
agree, "something peculiarly nice and attractive about him." Two
more murders are committed, one victim being a woman to whom
Buchanan had become engaged. Later suspicion falls on a woman
named Astarte, who has the reputation of being "the most reckless heartless cruel daredevil that ever walked the earth for man's
undoing," and in the final chapter, "Unmasked," Astarte and
Gordon Leigh are revealed as identical. Astarte/Leigh has lived
"sometimes as a man, sometimes as a woman, but more often as
the former because I liked it better." Undone by her love for
Buchanan, she confesses her crimes and takes poison. Skottowe
wrote one or two historical studies and textbooks, but no other
novels.

MONTAGUE SLATER, famous as the librettist of *Peter Grimes* and
a talented novelist, used the name of Richard Johns for his single
crime story, *Man with a Background of Flames* (1954).

The first book written by C. P. (Charles Percy) SNOW (1905–
), now Lord Snow, was a detective story, *Death Under Sail*
(1932), a work orthodox in the tradition of the period, but written
with what was already a very distinctive skill in characterization.

CHRISTOPHER ST. JOHN SPRIGG (1907–1937) reversed the usual
pseudonymous course by producing under the name of Christopher
Caudwell the poems, essays on politics and culture, and the philosophical work *Illusion and Reality* by which he is remembered as
the most interesting English Marxist theorist of his generation. His
detective stories were written without a protective mask. He
produced eight of these lively but orthodox (and unpolitical)
books between 1933 and 1937, when he was killed fighting on
the Republican side in the Spanish Civil War.

The accomplished historian and biographer FRANCIS STEEG-
MULLER (1906–   ) wrote three smoothly sophisticated crime
stories during the forties under the name of David Keith, and then
abandoned the form.

Among the readable books written by DARWIN L. TEILHET,
some in collaboration with his wife Hildegarde Tolman Teilhet, is
one work of considerable distinction. *The Talking Sparrow Murders*
(1934), which was written by Teilhet alone, is a mystery story
set in Germany just after the Nazi accession to power. It is well
worth reading both for its picture of the time and place and as an
unusual blend of spy story and mystery.

The Death of the King's Canary was a "fantastic thriller," as
he called it, written by DYLAN (Marlais) THOMAS (1914–1953) in
collaboration with John Davenport. It was completed in 1940,
and although Thomas was interested in crime stories and for a
short time reviewed them very intelligently, the book is, according
to his biographer, primarily a satire on the leading English poets
of the time (the King's Canary being the Poet Laureate), and as
such apparently remains unpublishable.

In 1945, the Scottish poet, novelist, and expert on Blake, RUTHVEN (Campbell) TODD (1914–   ), wrote ten detective stories in six months under the name of R. T. Campbell. One of them was written in three days. They were published in England by the small and soon defunct firm of John Westhouse, and are now distinctly rare. After this burst of more than Creaseyan activity, engaged in to pay off some debts, Todd/Campbell wrote no more detective novels.

All the books written by MILES TRIPP (1923–   ) under his own name (he has written some commonplace thrillers as Michael Brett) are about people whose nerve ends are showing, but *Kilo Forty* (1953) is outstanding among them, a psychological study of the emotional conflicts of four people on holiday by the Red Sea which explodes into savage violence. There is a touch of Simenon, some similarity to Highsmith, but a sort of tortured veracity runs through the story that is conspicuously Tripp's own.

Some may feel indignant at finding the Chinese detective stories of R. H. (Robert Hans) VAN GULIK (1910–1967) placed among curiosities. Yet what else, truly, can they be called? The traditional Chinese or Japanese "detective story" is really a tale of crime and punishment, in which it is part of the convention that the criminal shall be known from the start. The reader's pleasure (or the listener's, for most of the tales had an oral tradition) came from the magistrate's trapping of the villain. The Chinese tales were so far removed from Western feeling that in them animals and even objects might suddenly become vocal and give damning evidence.

Van Gulik, who was for some time the Dutch Ambassador in Malaysia, seems to have begun with the intention of translating some Chinese stories, going no further in the way of invention than was necessary to smooth out what would be obviously unacceptable to Western readers, and to devise a mystery which should not be solved until the end of the book. But even at the beginning, in his "translation" of the novel *Dee Kung An,* this was already an abrogation of the real Chinese tradition, and the later books are no more than well-informed pastiche. The best of them are clever, but they proceed from such fantastication of style and motive that they remain simply curiosities.

GORE VIDAL (1925–   ), who will hardly need introduction, wrote three detective stories in the early fifties under the name of Edgar Box. *Death in the Fifth Position* (1952), *Death Before Bedtime* (1953), and *Death Likes It Hot* (1954) are all lively books. Their sexual outspokenness, which caused some comment at the time, seems mild enough in the days of Myra Breckinridge.

Among the saccharine family chronicles of SIR HUGH WALPOLE (1884–1941) are a few books as tart as damsons. Like many sentimentalists, Walpole had a feeling for fear and cruelty, and both get into his neglected thriller, *Above the Dark Circus* (1931). As he conceived the book, it was to be "all Piccadilly, crowds and corpses, with a jolly villain and no sadism," but sadism comes in against his intention in the picture of the mean-faced Pengelly, with his love for the blackmail game, which, as he says, can't be touched for fun and excitement. A synthetic melodrama? Perhaps, but one touched by quite genuine fears and horrors.

XVI

A Short History of the Spy Story

It has been said already that crime fiction is a hybrid, and that too much categorization is confusing rather than helpful, but within the hybrid form detective stories and crime novels are of a different strain from spy stories and thrillers. The lines of demarcation are vague, but everybody recognizes their existence. It would be absurd to consider John Buchan and Eric Ambler together with R. Austin Freeman and Agatha Christie, but equally absurd to ignore than in a book of this kind. It seemed best to give them a separate chapter, a sort of appendix. The chapter is about spy stories, and about thrillers. But "thriller" is so loose a word that it should really be abandoned as a form of description. Some spy stories may be called thrillers; some adventure stories may be called thrillers. The label is very much a matter of taste.

The spy story owed its existence to awareness of the threat to national security implied in professionally organized spying, and also to the slow realization that the spy's activities may be both intricate and dangerous. In Elizabethan England Walsingham established a considerable spy network, and under Napoleon's reign, Fouché, the Chief of Police, became known as the spy master, but no books were written about an occupation that was regarded as unpleasant and unglamorous. In 1771, the first edition of the Encyclopædia

Britannica defined a spy as "a person hired to watch the actions, motions, &c. of another: particularly of what passes in a camp," adding that "when a spy is discovered, he is hanged immediately." The phrase finds an echo in the first spy novel known to me, James Fenimore Cooper's *The Spy* (1821). Harvey Birch, a peddler, known to be a spy for the British during the American War of Independence, is called a traitor by the American Major Dunwoodie, who says: "I should be justified in ordering your execution this night." Birch survives, and is in fact the hero of the story, a double agent whose real allegiance is given to his own country. The book's subtitle is "A Tale of the Neutral Ground," and although *The Spy* is not a very good novel, it anticipates in some respects the ambiguities of the modern spy story. Cooper, of course, thinks of the spy in exclusively military terms—there is a subsidiary plot about a young English officer who has gone behind the American lines to see his family, and who, although not a spy, is sentenced to death as one because he was not in uniform and was wearing a ridiculous disguise. Cooper's spy is conceived as an important but humble figure, and he was not used as a central character by any other novelist until late in the nineteenth century. The entertaining pamphlet *The Battle of Dorking* (1870), written by the military historian Sir George Chesney, dealt with an imaginary successful invasion of England, but was not concerned with the activities of spies.

The development of the spy story was directly linked to the inventions that came in the wake of the Industrial Revolution. As the breech-loading rifle replaced the muzzle-loader, and the quick-firing mitrailleuse, Gatling, and Maxim guns seemed to threaten the effectiveness of many other weapons, and naval power increased with the development of dreadnoughts and submarines, and airplanes turned from dream into possibility and then reality, a genuine threat was implied in the theft or copying of secret plans and documents. The highly developed industrial countries were those with most inventions to uncover, and this was the primary reason why the spy story had its origins in Europe, and particularly in Britain.

It was first exploited by William (Tufnell) Le Queux (1864–

1927). If Le Queux's biographer is to be believed (something that is by no means certain), Le Queux himself was a British Secret Service agent both before and during World War I. Such agents were not well paid and, again according to his biographer, his books were written chiefly to defray the heavy expenses of Secret Service activities. Le Queux was a journalist, and his first novel, *Guilty Bonds,* appeared in 1890, after he had visited Russia and written for the *Times* a series of articles on the Revolutionary movement and the condition of exiles in Siberia. *Guilty Bonds,* which dealt with a political conspiracy, was banned in Russia, and so was *A Secret Service* (1896), which had as its hero a Jewish Nihilist and treated in some detail the anti-Jewish pogroms after the assassination of Alexander III.

During the next thirty-odd years, Le Queux wrote more than a hundred books, of which perhaps a quarter were spy stories. His low opinion of his own work was not shared by Arthur Balfour, who when discovered reading Le Queux asked: "Are you criticizing my taste in literature?" The stories are atrociously written and full of padding, especially in the treatment of love affairs, but they are laced with a good deal of material obviously based on considerable knowledge of military and political affairs. Richard Usborne said in an article that between 1894 and 1910, Le Queux "mapped the guidlines for all subsequent British spy fiction," and this is certainly true up to the advent of Eric Ambler. He followed faithfully the current line of military thinking, by which France was regarded as the prime danger to British security until the end of the nineteenth century, and was then replaced by Germany. *England's Peril* (1899) begins with the murder of Lord Casterton, who has been protesting in Parliament about our inadequate military preparations, a constant theme in the press at that time. His face is shattered beyond recognition, and at the end of the book it turns out that he has been the victim of an explosive cigar given him by his wife. She is in love with Gaston la Touche, who under cover of being an explorer is also the chief of the French Secret Service, and is after the plans of Portsmouth Harbor. *The Great War in England in 1897* (1894) had the Russians joining the French in the invasion of England which was again a constant theme, particularly of military historians.

In *The Invasion of 1910* (1905) the enemy had changed to the Germans, and in the preface to *Spies of the Kaiser* (1909) Le Queux warned his readers that England was "in grave danger of invasion by Germany at a date not far distant," and suggested that 5,000 agents of Germany were active in Britain, being paid between £10 and £30 a month. These short stories, although full of absurd dialogue, contain interesting details like drawings of "the new British submarine" and "the new British Army aeroplane." When World War I began, Le Queux went about armed, with a hand on the revolver in his pocket ready for an attack which apparently never came. His fictional occupation, however, had been heavily damaged by the impact of reality, and the later books lack the zest which slightly redeems the early ones.

By the early years of the century, then, it had been established that the Germans were the enemy, although in the Sexton Blake penny dreadfuls the Kaiser was treated with respect until the outbreak of World War I. The first spy story with any literary pretensions, *The Riddle of the Sands* (1903), by Erskine Childers (1879–1922), is about two young Englishmen who stumble across some German exercises for the invasion of Britain which are taking place in the Frisian Islands. This is one of the best spy and adventure stories ever written, from the leisureliness of the opening, which describes the disillusionment suffered by young Carruthers of the Foreign Office when he joins his friend Davies on what he expects to be a lazy holiday on a luxury yacht, and finds that the *Dulcibella* is a little 7-tonner on which he is the only member of the crew. There is a lot of well-described detail about the business of managing a small boat in difficult waters, all of which is a necessary prelude to the very exciting fogbound journey in a dinghy through the narrow waters of the Memmert Balje that is really the climax of the story. The conversion of Carruthers from a peevish dandy to a resourceful amateur agent is excellently done through the contrast of his character with that of the verbally clumsy but practically skillful Davies, and the whole story has immense charm, vivacity, and an underlying idealism that takes for granted the way in which an honorable man must act.

In *The Riddle of the Sands,* it is accepted that such a man cannot be a spy. The Englishman acting for the Germans, who calls himself Dollmann is, Carruthers says, "the vilest creature on God's earth." But what about the young men themselves? " 'Mightn't we come to be spies ourselves?' " Carruthers asks, and Davies responds indignantly that they have a right to expose Dollmann. " 'If he's in with Germany he's a traitor to us. . . . If we can't do it without spying we've a right to spy.' " This is the first adumbration of the double standard by which They are viewed as spies pursuing evil ends, while We are agents countering their wicked designs with good ones of our own. For Buchan, Oppenheim, Sapper—in fact, for all spy writers before Ambler—the moral problem involved in spying was thus easily solved.

The tragedy of Childers's own life had some relationship to the morality of spying for or against your own country. During World War I, he worked as an Intelligence Officer, was several times mentioned in dispatches, and received the D.S.C. After it, he determined to devote his life to working for an independent Irish Republic. He was principal secretary to the delegation which negotiated an Irish Treaty with the British government, but opposed it in the interests of complete independence. He joined the Republican army fighting against the newly established Irish Free State, was captured by Free State soldiers, court-martialed, and shot. This undoubtedly gallant and honorable Anglo-Irishman was regarded by both British and Irish governments as a traitor and renegade at the time of his death.

The slipperiness of identifying books as "spy stories" is shown by consideration of the two novels by Joseph Conrad (1857–1924) about revolutionary agents, *The Secret Agent* (1907) and *Under Western Eyes* (1911). Clearly the material of these books is that of spy stories—in the first book an attempted anarchist outrage in London's Greenwich Park which follows fairly closely the details of an actual case, in the second the activities of the counter-agent Razumov. Yet Conrad's novels somehow do not seem to fall quite within the scope of this book, any more than does Henry James's distant vision of anarchist activities in *The Princess Casamassima*. Although one critic has said that Conrad "pioneered the political detective novel in English," these books seem distinct in spirit from both detective and spy stories. Dilys Powell has remarked acutely that in a thriller "too much character clutters up the plot," and Conrad is chiefly concerned with characterization. Verloc and Razumov are both double agents, the first to be seriously recorded in fiction, but it is not the nature of the double agent that interests their creator so much as the desire to capture "the very soul of things Russian" in these self-destructive figures. Is all this merely saying that Conrad is too good a writer to be considered as a teller of "spy stories"? Not quite. Certainly both stories have a dimension of seriousness that is not present in Childers or John Buchan, but the real thing is that for Conrad spying is not an end but a means. The end is the (in Conrad's view) wholly evil nature of revolution, in which spies play naturally their loathsome part. An earlier version of *Under Western Eyes,* called *Razumov,* was much more concerned with the personal problems of the central character. In the published book, the conspiracy seems at times to have been grafted onto the original manuscript for the sake of excitement. In spite of their subject matter, Conrad's books do not seem to me to be spy stories.

After World War I began, spy stories became unequivocally nationalist in tone and Right-Wing in political sympathy. Sometimes these feelings were expressed with the moderation of John Buchan, sometimes with the crudeness of Sapper, but the underlying assumptions were always there. The enemy in spy stories written up to 1920 was almost always Germany, later joined and superseded by Soviet Russia. Sometimes there is treachery at home, inspired from abroad. So Buchan's Richard Hannay, in *The Thirty-Nine Steps* (1915), finds somebody impersonating the First Sea Lord at a meeting of the Defence Council and walking out with all their plans. In *Mr. Standfast* (1919), the treatment of the conscientious objector Launcelot Wake is tolerant but condescending. He is allowed to retain his feelings and dies heroically in carrying a vital message across a river (" 'That's too damnably dangerous,' " Hannay says. " 'I won't send any man to certain death.' "), but of course Buchan would not have found it tolerable if Wake had adhered more firmly to his principles by refusing to be involved. At the end of *Bulldog Drummond* (1920), the first of his four rounds with Carl Peterson, Drummond discovers that a gigantic conspiracy to overthrow the government by means of a General Strike is being backed with Moscow gold, and that people whose names are household words secretly support it. How can this be? The American Jerome K. Green explains things in simple terms: " 'They're out for Number One, and when they've talked the boys into bloody murder, and your existing social system is down-and-out, they'll be the leaders in the new one.' " Drummond is horrified. " 'Why can't they be made to understand, Mr. Green?' " he asks. " 'The working-man—the decent fellow—' "

Buchan and Sapper are compared here only because they used similar material. Buchan was a talented writer, Sapper a producer of blood and thunder. John Buchan (1875–1940) regarded himself as a serious politician and an amateur novelist. During World War I, he was Director of Information and then Director of Intelligence. Later he was for eight years M.P. for the Scottish Universities, was created Baron Tweedsmuir of Enfield, and became Governor General of Canada. He had a busy official life, but along with his determination to be one of the men who counted (the phrase was Arnold Bennett's) went a high romanticism expressed particularly in the stories about Hannay, a character founded upon one of his military heroes, "Tiny" Ironside, who later became a Field Marshal. Buchan blended invention with material drawn from his own knowledge in these tales, which are notable for their sense of scenery and weather rather than for the plots. Perhaps the best of the Hannay books is *Greenmantle* (1916), in which the hero, helped by his friends and by the American agent Blenkiron, acts as a spy—the word is never used —trying to stop the Germans from raising the Islamic prophet Greenmantle for military ends. The books, like those Buchan wrote about Edward Leithen, are tales of adventure as much as they are spy stories. The author's own word for them was "shockers," and in their unsophisticated kind they are very good.

The real name of Sapper was Herman Cyril McNeile (1888–1937). The Bulldog Drummond stories that made him famous are markedly xenophobic, and full of clichés of phrase and situation. A girl has "a skin like the bloom of a sun-kissed peach"; Drummond himself is "a sportsman and a gentleman. And the combina-

tion of the two is an unbeatable production"; Europeans are
rarely referred to except as wogs and dagos. The plots are absurd,
but undeniably have their ration of excitement.

The essay by W. (William) Somerset Maugham (1874–1965)
on "The Decline and Fall of the Detective Story" (1952) is upon
the whole not very original, with its observations that there is
little room for humor and none for love interest, and its insistence
that "fine writing is out of place." All this had been said before,
notably by Wright. The stories in *Ashenden* (1928), however,
which sprang from Maugham's own experience in the Secret
Service, were something new in spy fiction. After the easy, absurd
assumptions made by Buchan, Sapper, and Oppenheim, the
Ashenden stories have the reality of a cold bath. The coldness
of "R," Ashenden's chief; the rejection by Ashenden, as absolutely
useless for fiction, of stories like one told him by R about the
beautiful blonde who drugged a Minister's drink and took the
secret papers (it would have seemed a highly original story to
Sapper) set the scene for an attempt to treat the affair of spying
with much more realism than had before been considered possible. The characterization has no particular subtlety, but is
marked by this downbeat leveling tone which insists that spies
and their masters are in many ways ordinary people—the ruth-
less, powerful R cannot face tipping a waiter without fearing that
he will make a fool of himself. Spies may have to use the services
of a killer like the Hairless Mexican, and they can make mistakes,
as in the assignment when the Mexican kills the wrong man. An
Englishman in the pay of the Germans is not regarded as the
vilest creature on God's earth, but simply as a man who may be
bribed to act as a double agent. The double agent turns out to be an
amiable character, but when it has been decided that he is not
to be trusted, a trap is laid for his destruction. The Ashenden
stories are among Maugham's best work as a short-story writer,
and they had as great an influence on the development of the
spy novel as Iles's books had on the crime story. Their morally
neutral attitude provided the ground on which Ambler and, much
later, John Le Carré, worked, and R's coolness about killing was
to be adopted and adapted by Ian Fleming.

A neutrality that is not only moral but also political and personal weakens Ashenden himself, so that he comes through less as a character than as a piece of litmus paper on which events produce a reaction. In the six novels he wrote before the outbreak of World War II, Eric Ambler (1909–   ) infused warmth and political color into the spy story by using it to express a Left Wing point of view. In a sense, what Ambler did in these books was to turn Sapper and Buchan upside down. The central character is an innocent figure mixed up in violent events who slowly comes to realize that the agents and spies working on both sides are for the most part unpleasant but not important men. They murder casually and without passion on behalf of some immense corporation or firm of armaments manufacturers whose interests are threatened. These, rather than any national group, are the enemy. *The Dark Frontier* (1936) is the least important of his books, but it contains one prophetic note in the detonation of the first atomic bomb, and also reflects Ambler's own feelings at the time, put into the mouth of the atomic physicist Professor Bairstow:

> It looked too as if there would always be wars. . . . What else could you expect from a balance of power adjusted in terms of lands, of arms, of man-power and of materials: in terms, in other words, of Money? . . . Wars were made by those who had the power to upset the balance, to tamper with international money and money's worth; those who, in satisfying their private ends, created the social and economic conditions that bred war.

The conclusion is emphasized in the conversion of Schimmler from social democracy to Communism in *Epitaph for a Spy* (1938), in the friendly portrait of the Greek Communist Marukakis in *The Mask of Dimitrios* (1939),* and particularly in the activities of the Soviet agent Zaleshoff, a broad-shouldered pleasantly ugly man who is always helping innocent Englishmen out of trouble, incidentally for his own ends. A nice Soviet spy? It seemed a contradiction in terms, but such unorthodoxy helped

* In America, *A Coffin for Dimitrios*.

Ambler to keep what was occasionally shopworn material looking bright and fresh.

The political side of the books lies under the surface. Almost
all the best thrillers are concerned, in one form or another, with
the theme of the hunted man. Ambler was fascinated by European
cities, and his hunts take place against a convincing background
of places like Istanbul, Sofia, Belgrade, and Milan. He was interested also in the problems of frontiers and passports, so that
the difficulty of moving from place to place plays a large part
in the stories. And he showed from the beginning a high skill,
which became mastery, in the construction of plot. His finest book
of this period, a masterpiece of its kind, is *The Mask of Dimitrios,*
in which flashback follows flashback in the attempt of the crime
novelist Latimer to trace the career of the dead Dimitrios, and
there is little direct action until three-quarters of the way through
the book. To develop interest through a book composed in such
a way is a mark of the highest technical skill. The story sparkles
with incidents, like the interview with the retired spy, or the account of the white-slave traffic, that could be extracted as separate
stories and yet continue to advance the plot.

The attitude that inspired the early novels did not survive
in a postwar world where shadowy cartels and puckish Soviet
agents were evidently a long way from reality. Ambler's later
books are more like plain thrillers than spy stories. The best of
them, *The Night Comers* (1956),* *The Light of Day* (1962), and
Dirty Story (1967) are less sensational than some of the prewar
novels, and they show the same mastery of construction. Something
has been lost, however; a certain world-weariness has replaced enthusiasm and hope. They are detached from events rather than
involved in them. There is much to admire and enjoy, but nothing
to equal *The Mask of Dimitrios.*

Once the convention of the agent as hero had been questioned
by Maugham, it collapsed, and from the mid-thirties onward
the spy story and thriller became for British writers a vehicle
through which to ask the questions about society which still
could not easily be expressed in the detective story. The novels

* In America, *A State of Siege.*

that Graham Greene (1904–   ) wrote in the thirties and called "entertainments" are mostly thrillers, with an attitude toward the corruption of international politics which is not very different from Ambler's. The theme of hunter and hunted is strong in these stories. Often the two figures are interchangeable, and sometimes the villain is seen as a kind of pathetic hero. Typical figures of this kind are Anthony in *England Made Me* (1935), who is in love with his sister but unable to do anything about it; the paid assassin Raven in *A Gun for Sale* (1936);* the boy gangster Pinkie in *Brighton Rock* (1938); and D, the agent of a government strongly resembling the Spanish Republican government, in *The Confidential Agent* (1939). And the figure of the hunted man is often, although not so plainly, seen in Greene's later work, in books like *The Power and the Glory* (1940) and *The Quiet American* (1955).

Greene himself has defended the thriller as a form, suggesting that it should not be regarded patronizingly, yet there is something defensive about his own labeling of some books as "entertainments." Does he mean that these books are not serious, or that his other work may not entertain? In any case, the distinction helps to perpetuate the snobbishness which he has deprecated, although the effects of the entertainments are often as serious as those of his other books. They are not upon the whole achieved through deeply perceptive characterization, but by the vision of places and objects seen both in themselves and as symbols, in a way that has made several of them the basis of successful films. The entertainments resemble his other books more than they differ from them, and it cannot truly be said that he is, like Conrad, a novelist who has occasionally used the thriller's apparatus, but rather one who begins with the material of a thriller and then loads it with a weight of meaning that is occasionally too great for the form to bear. His books are exciting, dramatic, and visually extraordinarily vivid, but although they have enlarged the range of the thriller they suggest also that, as a means of dealing with the subtleties of politics and religion, it has some limitations.

* In America, *This Gun for Hire.*

THE MODERN SPY NOVEL: PIPE DREAM, REALITY, FARCE

During World War II, Anthony Boucher remarked on the wave of British national patriotism which "led almost every top-flight mystery writer to save the Empire from Fascism by the intervention of his star detective," adding that their work "brought to international espionage a literacy and dexterity hitherto lavished on purely private murder." One can see that it may have looked like that at the time, but what is most noticeable now is the weakening of the tendency toward realism engendered by Maugham and developed by Ambler.

For the most part, these writers simply grafted the spy theme onto their usual detective-story pattern, sometimes with engaging results, as in Allingham's *Traitor's Purse* (1941), but still producing work closer to the detective than to the spy story. A book like *Rogue Male* (1939), by Geoffrey Household (1900–   ), which begins when the narrator is caught by the police watching the terrace of an unnamed dictator's house through the telescopic sights of his rifle, and develops into an exciting story of pursuit, is closer in spirit to the spy story than the books of the detective-story writers who fitted the spy theme into their usual setting and characters. The work of Michael Innes offers the only real exception to this generalization. His spy stories, which began with the highly literary *The Secret Vanguard* (1940), in which directions are conveyed in an invented stanza added to Swinburne's "Forsaken Garden," are secondary to his detective stories, but the important thing is that they are entirely different from them. A great deal of romantic excitement is generated in *The Journeying Boy* (1949),* *Operation Pax* (1951),† and *The Man from the Sea* (1955). These books, closer to Buchan than to Ambler, are too fantastic to be quite convincing, but the spy theme gives Innes's work a fine romantic freedom that is rarely present in his later detective stories. But in spite of Innes and Household (who has never equaled his early performance) the renaissance of the

* In America, *The Case of the Journeying Boy.*
† In America, *The Paper Thunderbolt.*

spy story clearly dates from 1953 and the publication of *Casino Royale,* the first novel of Ian (Lancaster) Fleming (1908–1964). For a period that can be put roughly at fifteen years, the spy story as developed by Fleming, Le Carré, and Len Deighton became the most exciting form of sensational fiction.

Fleming is the heir of Buchan and Sapper, and James Bond was a more sophisticated version of Bulldog Drummond. The ethos which orders his actions is very much the same. As Kingsley Amis has pointed out, "Throughout all Bond's adventures nobody English does anything evil," and Amis found this quite acceptable, just as he thought that to use foreigners as villains was merely "a convention older than our literature." In essence, the Bond pipe dream was the Sapper pipe dream tuned to a mood of the fifties. So although Bond is a patriot prepared to suffer torture for his country, he is also a killer who works for pay, and his brand-name code of behavior does not prevent him from laying all the girls. All this, in the fifties, was acceptable, and readers responded to Bond because he provided in a peculiarly modern way an excitement lacking in their lives. Into the British postwar atmosphere of virtuous puritanism he brought a celebration of physical pleasures including those of sadism and masochism. He was a perfect pipe-dream figure for organization man because he was an organization man, too, but unlike the standard model he was individually powerful. He could act, he could destroy, he appeared to be free. In America, the books had at first very little success, and that was at least partly because there was no welfare state to which Bond could provide the antithesis. As Fleming's biographer has pointed out, the growth of Bond as a mythical figure, with its accompaniment of brand-name shirts, shoes, drinks, cigarettes, games, came after the immense success of the first Bond film, made in 1962, two years before his death.

But it would be wrong to see the Bond books chiefly in sociological terms. In cruelty he had already been exceeded by Chase, and in brutality by Spillane. Fleming's insistence that Bond was satisfied only by the very best, and his desire to put a brand name to everything, seems in retrospect harmless vulgarity. The books are blood-and-thunder thrillers, done at first in a strongly personal style and with a convincing appearance of expert knowledge. If it is true, as his biographer says, that he relied for technical details on other people, and that "it is hard to think of a single subject on which he was a genuine expert," then he was a very skillful assimilator. The first half-dozen Bond stories are extremely lively sensational entertainments. They are very much on a level, and to pick out *Casino Royale* and *From Russia with Love* (1957) is to state a personal preference. Later, Fleming became bored with Bond, and the books lost the freshness that was their chief charm.

Fleming represented *a* mood rather than *the* mood of the period in Britain. David John Moore Cornwell (1931–   ), who used the name of John Le Carré for his first book, *Call for the Dead* (1961), was a member of the Foreign Service at the time of its publication. This spy novel was followed by a straightforward and very good detective story, *A Murder of Quality* (1962). Neither book had more than moderate success, but *The Spy Who Came in from the Cold* (1963) found a response almost equal to that roused by the Bond books, although of a different kind. The Bond stories were enjoyed as pipe dreams, Le Carré's for their approach to reality.

It is right, I think, to see two traditions in the spy story as in the crime novel. The first is conservative, supporting authority, making the assertion that agents are fighting to protect something valuable. The second is radical, critical of authority, claiming that agents perpetuate, and even create, false barriers between "us" and "them." Fleming belongs to the first tradition, Le Carré to the second. The actual texture of Le Carré's writing owes something to Maugham and Green, but his material is most firmly rooted in the revelations about Soviet agents that shook Britain in the fifties. The messages of the unjustly neglected *Call for the Dead*, of the *Spy*, and of Le Carré's later books are that authority is not benevolent but often destroys those who serve it, that espionage and counterespionage work is often fumblingly uncertain in its aims and effects, that "our" men may be personally vicious and "their" men decent human beings—and, most of all, that an agent is generally a weak and not a strong character, powerless once he has been caught in the spy net.

The special qualities of Le Carré's books are their sense of place, their sense of doom, their irony. The irony is most powerful in the *Spy,* because there it is most closely associated with the fates of individuals. As layer after layer of deceit is lifted in the story, and the way in which "London" has cynically used its own agent is revealed, the effect is to show the two apparently opposed organizations on one side and helpless human beings like Leamas and Elizabeth on the other. Le Carré shows a strong sense, both here and in *The Looking Glass War* (1965), that spying is a sort of game in which, without wearing comic noses or any kind of disguise, people pretend to be what they are not. The whole apparatus of the trial in the *Spy* is a game, and so of course are the ridiculous, out-of-date operations in the later novel. And the purpose of such party games is betrayal; this is what is required of human beings by the players "sitting round a fire in one of their smart bloody clubs." If none of Le Carré's other admirably written novels comes up to the *Spy,* it is because here the story is most bitterly and clearly told, the lesson of human degradation involved in spying most faithfully read.

Through Fleming and Le Carré, pipe dream and reality, the spy story in Britain flowered remarkably until the late sixties. The prime cause of British supremacy in this field is probably the prevailing air of sophisticated coolness about ends and means. Certainly the Americans, perhaps because of their direct involvement in various wars, have never been able to treat the existence of spies threatening or betraying their security with anything but the most narrowly nationalistic seriousness. Bond has had a number of efficient disciples, and of the several writers halfway between pipe dream and reality William Haggard, the pseudonym used by Richard Henry Michael Clayton (1907–   ), is the most interesting. Perhaps he is nearer to pipe dream. The operations of Colonel Russell of the Security Executive, from his first appearance in *Slow Burner* (1958), are marked by a feeling for aristocratic attitudes, linked less with birth than with behavior, that is unique in the modern spy story. Haggard is a Right Wing romantic of the Buchan kind (Colonel Russell would surely find Drummond much too violent, and Bond distressingly vulgar) who has an agreeable streak of realism. Russell is capable of getting on perfectly well, on a basis of *Realpolitik,* with his Soviet opposite number, but cannot bear the pettifogging liberal equivocation of his own country's politicians. *The Arena* (1961) and *The Unquiet Sleep* (1962) are among the best of his books, which are all cunningly plotted, although the motivations of his characters seem at times to be of Jamesian complexity.

In the years following *Casino Royale*'s publication, almost all the possibilities in the spy story were exploited in books, films, and TV, often with damaging results. The Bond films almost parodied the books, but the character was so amorphous that the standard man of action shown on the screen was immediately accepted all over the world just as, much earlier, William Powell had been acceptable as Philo Vance and Nick Charles in turn. TV series like "The Man From UNCLE" and "Danger Man" expanded the absurdities of the films to a point that destroyed the requisite minimum of belief. Yet in *The Ipcress File* (1963) and his subsequent books, Len Deighton (1929–   ) gave a new twist to the form. His anonymous central character (called Harry Palmer in the films) is a working-class boy from Burnley, opposed to all authority, who dislikes or distrusts anybody outside his own class. He is set down in a world of terrifying complexity, in which nobody is ever what he seems. The Deighton stories are elliptically—sometimes too elliptically—told, but their sudden shifts of tone and scene are extremely effective, and the technological expertise is impressive because it is not just there for show. Deighton's fascination with what in another writer would be gimmicks comes through, like Kipling's feeling for machinery, and there is something almost lyrical about his re-creation of the dangerous and transitory lives of agents, as well as something sharp and knowing. From his most brilliant performance, *Billion-Dollar Brain* (1966), one carries away admiration for a plot as intricate as the lock of a good safe and for the characterization of the clownish double agent Harvey Newbigin, but even more for the evocation of General Midwinter's dotty neo-Fascist organization in Texas and the wonderfully vivid picture of the shooting of Harvey in the snow outside the Russian train. Writing of this quality, combined or contrasted with the constant crackle of the dialogue, makes Deighton a kind of poet of the spy novel.

One seems already to be writing of a period that is past. Fleming is dead, and his fame greatly in decline. Haggard's Colonel Russell is said to have retired. Le Carré is moving with each book further away from the spy story. Deighton has put Harry Palmer at least temporarily on the shelf. Recent writers of talent like Gavin Lyall and Dick Francis are more interested in adventure stories than in any kind of mystery.

Spy stories continue to be written, but the renaissance that began with a pipe dream and approached both reality and poetry has dropped to deliberate farce in the adventures of John Gardner's Boysie Oakes, the cowardly spy who hires Soho gangsters to do his killing, or to various kinds of unconvincing nastiness in books among which Noel Behn's *The Kremlin Letter* is most notably unpleasant. The early Boysie Oakes stories are very funny, but the balance of the spy story is permanently precarious, and many books of this kind would distort it for good.

After the varied talents of Fleming, Le Carré, and Deighton, it is difficult to see how the spy story can go much further at present, although perhaps it can be absorbed into a novel or be used as the basis for a new kind of documentary approach. Readers may demand more ingenious variants on the triple-cross, more unusual methods of murder and escape, but writers are not likely to be able to feed such appetites for long while retaining self-respect. At present, several of the best writers of spy stories give the impression of having exhausted, or of being exhausted by, the medium. It would be in everybody's long-term interest if a moratorium could be declared on the writing of spy stories for the next ten years.

XVII

In the Crystal Ball

THE PAST

The most spirited controversion of the ideas about crime stories advanced in this book was made by Professor Jacques Barzun in 1958.* In a lively article, Barzun deplored the loss of the detective stories, chiefly represented by those here called the Humdrums, that embodied not only "the entrancing facts about *rigor mortis* or the onset of arsenic poisoning . . . but also certain abstractions—Intellect, Knowledge, and the workings of Reason itself." What were we offered instead? he asked. Why, the swampy ground of psychology, "just what the older *genre* was created to avoid." At that time, Barzun had to wade through psychology knee high, and probably he now finds himself in it up to the neck. Modern crime stories, he said, made him feel not only old but sold, for the whole point of the detective story was its specialized character. Delight in it accompanied "the belief in greatness, intelligence and integrity . . . the recognition of law, and the directed curiosity of science." In new and for the most part unspecified hands (although Hammett and Chandler were rebuked by name), it had "lost its aim and possibly its place in

* This book was written before I had the chance of reading Barzun's interesting and valuable, but extremely eccentric, *A Catalogue of Crime* (1971).

literature," had "ceased to give entertainment and proffered nothing in exchange."

Obviously my point of view is so much opposed to that of Barzun (what he finds entrancing I think dull) that we really have no common ground on which to argue. But it is interesting that his diagnosis of what has happened is similar to mine, except that what he regards as a flight from Intellect and Reason I should call an escape from self-deception and a move toward realism. It is interesting, too, that he makes no attempt at an artistic defense of the detective stories he most admires, beyond saying that they were "dependable as entertainment and respectable as literature." But what are *dependable* and *respectable?* Many of the Humdrums he calls dependable are not writers I should care to rely on for entertainment in a snowbound hotel or a desert island, and "respectable" is in this context an ambiguous word, for it is politicians and not literary critics who have respected such books. The claim made for modern works is that the best of them are good novels, and also interesting crime stories. There is not such a difference between past and present as Barzun and others pretend—the gap only appears so great from a point of view that considers Collins, Le Fanu, and Doyle important chiefly as the precursors of "the detective story," something that was truly authentic only from the early twenties up to the beginning of World War II.

The progression indicated here seems to me a more reasonable one. The crime story as a literary form has developed alongside other fiction, in a way shaped largely by social events, and its course has been roughly like this:

1. Stories about crime as a form of radical social protest, in Godwin, Lytton, Balzac. The criminal is seen as a hero, or as a victim of social injustice.

2. Stories about detectives as protectors of society, or as intellectual Supermen. These began with Poe and were developed by Collins and Gaboriau.

3. The idea that the Superman detective alone might operate above or outside the processes of law, which began with Sherlock Holmes.

4. The commercially dictated change from short story to novel, and the emergence of women writers whose detectives followed the Holmes pattern, and whose work emphasized the importance of preserving the existing state of society. (It would be interesting to relate the invention of the "rules" to this overriding social need.)

5. The attempts to break the "rules," partly on the ground that their literary products were so boring (by Francis Iles), partly because they were so silly (Hammett and Chandler).

6. The development of crime novels, a bag of literary all-sorts, ranging from comedy to tragedy, from realistic portraits of a society to psychological investigation of an individual, together with the astonishing flowering of the spy story as a literary form.

This seems to be just about where we are at present. What does the crystal ball show for tomorrow; that is, for the next ten years?

THE FUTURE

What it seems to indicate, rather undramatically, is more of the same. If we extrapolate from present tendencies, the result may look something like this:

1. The Detective Story

A declining market. Some detective stories will continue to be written, but as the old masters and mistresses fade away, fewer and fewer of them will be pleasing to lovers of the Golden Age. The revival of "entrancing facts about *rigor mortis*," or even about the unique nature of hairs and carpet threads, as the most important features of a crime story, seems very improbable. Clues of this kind are now, and will remain, the affair of the forensic scientist and not of the amateur detective. There will be no plans of the house and grounds; locked rooms will be passed over to writers of science fiction. If there are mysterious murder methods, they will be up-to-date, being concerned with laser beams, poisons in frozen food or smeared on the elements of electric fires, and so on.

2. Spy Stories

Also probably showing a temporary decline, in quality if not in number. Fewer stories about European spying; more about comparatively unexplored areas, particularly the Far East and South America. An upbeat tone seems likely after the Le Carré depression. Why have the French written so few good spy stories? The form should appeal to them, and it would not be surprising to see some strongly nationalistic spy stories from France, Israel, Argentina.

3. Adventure Stories

A steadily rising market. Much of the talent that went into the detective story, with its nice uncomplicated view of character and scene, has now entered the adventure story. It is likely that more writers who don't want to take themselves or their readers seriously will move over to some kind of adventure story (men authors) or to Gothic novels with a mild mystery element (women). Considerable expertise is employed already here, as in Dick Francis's adventure thrillers based on his expert knowledge of horse racing. Why not similar books based on motor racing, on athletics?

4. Police Novels

Likely to provide more of the same, although in another decade that idea of running three or four cases side by side in one volume will surely be worn out. TV will continue to provide a visual rival to this kind of semi-documentary fiction, although there is no reason why the two shouldn't exist side by side. Possible variations are more emphasis on laboratory work, as already suggested, exploitation of a small-town or country police force, and stories about police in countries apart from Britain and America. What are the cops of Tokyo's 87th Precinct like? It would be interesting to know.

5. Crime Novels

Capable of any sort of development, according to the talents they attract. If "the novel" continues to become even less concerned with realistic narrative, and still more with linguistic or science-fictional experiments or with states of mind symbolically seen (a tendency noticeable from Burroughs to Mailer to Murdoch), then "the crime novel" may partly fill its place. It could attract writers who twenty years ago would have written novels, readers who would have read them. If this happens, we can expect the links with the detective story (what were six cat hairs doing on a saucer in the refrigerator?) to become more tenuous, storytelling to be more direct. But a lot of crime novelists will still be blending psychology, clues, and social comment in the way that infuriates Barzun.

6. Who Will Write Them?

There are some signs that British-American supremacy in crime writing, based partly on the social stability of those countries and partly on the fact that English is for readers a world language (in Scandinavia and Holland many people read crime stories in English for preference), may be challenged. There are some new Scandinavian writers, one or two French, at least one Italian, and their work is interesting particularly because it has a flavor quite unlike that of the Anglo-American product. The Wahloo/Sjöwall and Dürrenmatt novels, for instance, have no counterparts elsewhere. In ten years' time, there may well be a lot of new writers, not all of them Anglo-Americans, widening the field of crime fiction still further.

Those who look in the crystal ball often see what they wish. I would not expect these predictions to be more accurate than weather forecasts, which in Britain are right about three-quarters of the time, and they could easily be falsified still further.

How? Crime fiction, more than any other form of literature, is the product of a society and a way of life. If, by some unlikely stroke, the whole of Europe became Communist-controlled, novels would continue to be published, films to be made, but there would be no crime stories of the kind discussed in this book. There might be a few patriotic thrillers (we have had one or two already, from the Soviet Union and elsewhere), that is all. Another Depression on the scale of the thirties would also be likely to falsify most of the predictions above, and might even lead to a revival of the detective story, traditionally a solace in hard times. The emergence to power of extreme Left or Right Wing movements in any country would affect its production of crime fiction. It is not accidental that the Nazis condemned crime stories, and that the Russians dismiss them as decadent. They flourish only in a liberal air.

Some predictions may be falsified for reasons unconnected with social change. It is possible, although most unlikely, that a new writer of immense talent may use or adapt the form of the Golden Age detective story. In the spy story, a really strong new talent could easily provide a new impulse and a new direction. A talented writer, possibly one with as close a knowledge of police work as Hammett had of detection, could do the same for the police novel. And the course of the crime novel would be affected if "straight" novelists chose to write books more clearly dependent upon plot and character. Again, this doesn't seem at all likely. In the course of five years of steady fiction reviewing, which succeeded a decade of reviewing crime stories, one of the things that has most depressed me is the fact that novelists often have something to say but very rarely a story to tell, in the sense that Balzac or Zola or George Eliot or Stevenson told a story. Partly because of this gap in storytelling, partly because of the material used in it, the crime novel has a symbolic value and interest for our age. The moral attitudes involved in crimes of violence have today a quite special significance, whether they are on a large or a small scale, and whether they are private like the Moors Murders or public like the slaughter at My Lai. The crime novel is a much better medium for asking questions or making statements about such events than the semi-science fiction of William Burroughs.

At the same time, one shouldn't expect too much. Crime fiction has always been, and will remain, primarily an entertainment created by popular demand, whether its form is that of detective story, spy story, or crime novel. Most of it has little to do with literature, but is designed to give pleasure—to Professor Barzun, to me, to nice old ladies using country libraries, and young men buying Spillane in paperback. The medium has limitations, and its writers have them, too. There is something in all crime novelists and detective-story writers that demands the puzzle element in a book, or at least the element of uncertainty and suspense, as a diabetic demands insulin. In the highest reaches of the crime novel, it is possible to create works of art, but because of their sensationalism they will always be works of a slightly flawed kind. *The Moonstone* is not a great novel; *The Glass Key* is not a great novel: the attitudes from which they are written preclude greatness. Yet they are fine books of the second order, masterpieces in their kind. The double standard mentioned at the beginning comes into play for the writer of crime stories, as well as for the critic. Chandler put this very well:

It is no easy trick to keep your characters and your story operating on a level which is understandable to the semi-literate public and at the same time give them some intellectual and artistic overtones which that public does not seem to demand or, in effect, recognize, but which somehow subconsciously it accepts and likes.

This is the game that the best crime novelists are always playing, and that gives their work its flavor and its style. To use a popular literary form and understand that you are a craftsman working to please the groundlings, but at the same time to treat what you are doing seriously and without condescension, to "accept a mediocre form and make something like literature out of it"—these are the achievements of the best crime novelists. Not many novelists at any time or in any period get so far.

Index